Elvira

A Mexican Immigrant Woman
1909-2012

Elvira is the poignant life story of a girl whose family immigrated to the U.S. to escape the violence of the Mexican Revolution of 1910.

It is a heartrending memoir of hardship and survival and of a woman who fights for a meaningful life in a land once alien, now native.

Her narrative projects a strong sense of personal courage and determination, qualities that she displays from a very early age.

Elvira describes simply – though often with wry humor – arduous labor as a way of life, the hardships of poverty, racism and cultural clashes, and control by domineering men.

Her narration is spoken in the down-to-earth language of an unpretentious farmworker, and her natural integration of key Spanish phrases into her English vernacular infuses it with a powerful authenticity.

Elvira's memoir will appeal to readers attracted to stories of strong women, Mexican immigrant farmworkers, and the resolution of cultural differences.

It will also be of strong interest in women's studies, language a studies, history, anthropology, anc

D1157480

*At her kitchen table, Elvira relates her stories to her son
Eduardo, compiler and editor of her memoir.*

Elvira C. Hernandez emigrated from Chalchihuites,
Zacatecas to the United States in 1916 at the age of six. Her
family worked on the railroad and the meat packing industry
before settling in Scottsbluff, Nebraska where Elvira labored
in the sugar-beet fields for nearly fifty years.

She attended primary school in Mexico and elementary
school in Nebraska. Despite such a meager education, she
became highly proficient in two languages.

After the death of her husband, she dedicated herself to
service in the Mexican immigrant community.

Eduardo Hernández Chávez also worked in the sugar-
beet fields as a youth. After college, he taught languages
and went on to earn a Ph.D. He then taught linguistics at
Stanford and the University of New Mexico. He has many
publications in linguistics and has compiled a number of
literary works.

Since the 1960's, Eduardo has been deeply involved in
Chicano community issues and in supporting Chicana/o
students.

Elvira

(Pronounced *el-VEER-ah*)

"You know, Cuca, my son here is recording my life story and he's makin' a book out of it. It's gonna be so my grandchildren and all the rest of the people can read about our history – how we came from Mexico and what we suffered here in the United States. It's my book, and it's got all my life in there. I'm so proud of what he's doing."

Elvira C. Hernandez

COVER ART
SUGAR BEET WORKERS/TRABAJANDO EN LA REMOLACHA

The art work on the cover is a reproduction of a mural by Carlos Hernández Chávez, painter and muralist who was born in León, Guanajuato, México and is currently a resident of Hartford, CT. The imagery represents a significant chapter in the saga of Mexican immigration to the United States. The focus is on the historical settlement of farmworkers in the area around Scottsbluff, Nebraska during the early part of the Twentieth Century.

Fleeing the Mexican Revolution of 1910-1921 and drawn by the need of the railroads, farming, and the meatpacking industry for cheap and hardworking laborers, many of them – including Elvira, the author of this book, and other family members of the artist who settled in the Scottsbluff area – emigrated from the Mexican states of Zacatecas, Guanajuato and Durango. They crossed through El Paso, Texas long before border restrictions were enacted.

The images of crouching field workers are based on the artist's actual family members of the era. Elvira is shown fourth in the line of workers in the center of the painting. The artist's mother, Elvira's sister Teresa, instilled in him an existential desire to learn more about his early farmworker roots. The mural is the latest product and expression of his insights.

The salient themes symbolized are migration, stoop labor, poverty, and racism. The immigrants are depicted in myriad ways. First is the peaceful and purposeful stride of a multitude of people seeking to offer their only resource – their labor – both for their own survival and for the benefit of the people they worked for. The rich valleys at the foot of the bluffs in western Nebraska represent the promise of a better life. But, bent over a short hoe for twelve or more hours a day for low pay, scarcely tolerable working conditions, and deplorable living accommodations, their reality was a dismal and exhausting life.

The presence of poor brown-skinned Spanish speakers – foreigners in their once-native land – soon aroused racism, and Mexicans were placed third on the list of undesirables, below dogs and Negroes! Yet their overriding role remained – to set, upon their stooped backs, the abundant table for the American palate.

Using powerful impressionistic imagery, the artist links the hardships of these early farmworkers to the current generation of brave and intrepid workers. Now persecuted and rendered illegal by exclusionary laws, Mexican immigrants today continue to fulfill the need for labor, not only in agriculture but in construction, service, and other industries.

MILESTONES IN THE LIFE OF ELVIRA C. HERNÁNDEZ

June 27, 1909	Born in Sombrerete, Zacatecas, Mexico.
April, 1916	Emigrates from Chalchihuites, Zacatecas to the United States with other members of her extended family. They live for a time in El Paso, Texas.
Summer, 1917	Extended family arrives in Kansas City, Kansas.
Spring, 1918	Elvira begins her responsibility as the family tortilla maker at age nine.
May, 1920	Elvira and her family arrive in Scottsbluff, Nebraska.
August 3, 1928	Elvira meets her future husband, Maique, in a mudhole in Gering, Nebraska.
January 10, 1929	Elvira and Maique are married at Our Lady of Guadalupe church in Scottsbluff, Nebraska.
Spring, 1935	Elvira and Maique leave his parents' house to make their own lives.
1935 and 1936	Elvira's and Maique's parents are repatriated to Mexico.
November, 1936	Elvira and Maique obtain work on the Neil Barbour farm and move into "*el chante*".
February, 1945	Maique's father dies in Mexico; he and Elvira, Jr. travel to the memorial.
May, 1945	Elvira's family moves to the "big house" on Neil Barbour's farm.
Spring, 1952	Maique and Elvira rent the Summerville property and become farmers.
June, 1958	Elvira and Maique's son, Bobby, dies in San Francisco.
August 13, 1965	Maique dies; Elvira later finds work as a kitchen helper in the public schools.
Summer, 1971	Elvira begins work with the Community Action Program in Scottsbluff.
January, 1974	Elvira and Maique's son Leonard dies; later that year she starts a Senior Center for women in her church.
Fall, 1992	Elvira closes the Senior Center; she takes a job with a day-care center.
May, 1998	Elvira retires at age 89, both from her job and from her life-long responsibility as the family tortilla maker.
April 24, 2012	Elvira dies at age 102.

Academic and Community Accomplishments of
Eduardo Hernández Chávez, Compiler and Editor of *Elvira*

Ph. D. in Linguistics, University of California, Berkeley, 1977

Key Positions Held:
Assoc. Prof. of Linguistics and Director of Chicano/a Studies, Univ. of NM.
Founder, Academia de Lengua y Cultura Charter School, Albuquerque.
Director, Cross Cultural Resource Center, CSU Sacramento, CA.
Director, Migrant Farmworker Rights Project, Sacramento, CA.
Assistant Professor of Linguistics, Stanford University.
Coordinator, Chicano Studies Program, University of California, Berkeley.
Teacher of Latin and Spanish, California public schools.
Farmworker in the sugar-beet fields, Scottsbluff, Nebraska.

Community Participation:
Recuerda a César Chávez Committee, Albuquerque NM, organizer.
Southwest Organizing Project (SWOP), Albuquerque NM, member.
MEChA, University of New México, advisor.
Movimiento de Liberación Nacional Mexicano, Tierra Amarilla NM, associate.
Land Grant Forum of New Mexico, Albuquerque NM, associate.
Coalition against English Only, Albuquerque NM, organizer.
Chale con English Only, Albuquerque NM, founder and organizer.
New Mexicans Against California Prop. 187, Albuquerque NM, organizer.
Curriculum Advisory Committee on Migrant Education, Davis CA Schools.
Royal Chicano Air Force (RCAF), Sacramento, CA, associate.

Publications and Other Works
El Lenguaje de los Chicanos (ed.), Center for Applied Linguistics, 1975.
Numerous academic articles and monographs on language maintenance and loss, language policy, bilingual education, sociolinguistics, Spanish linguistics, phonetics, acquisition of language and literacy.
Bilingual Syntax Measure I and II. Spanish and English versions, (Member of the development team), NY: Harcourt Brace, 1973, 1978.
One Day I Lost My Head, stories written and illustrated by 1st grade children, (Compiler and production editor), Elmira, CA: *Instituto de Lengua y Cultura*, 1984.
Casindio: Chicano Music All Day, LP music album. (Producer and author of the libretto), Elmira CA: *Instituto de Lengua y Cultura*, 1985.
Prueba de Español para Maestros de Educación Bilingüe. (Member of the development team), New Mexico State Dept. of Education, 2006.
Ysidoro Castillo Pérez: Castillo family genealogy. (Author), 2006.

Elvira

A Mexican Immigrant Woman
1909-2012

**A memoir compiled by her son
Eduardo Hernández Chávez**

ISBN: 978-0-9989740-1-9

BISAC CODES
Biography and Autobiography (Women, Cultural Heritage, Personal Memoirs)

KEY WORDS
Mexican Americans: Immigration, 20th Century ; Mexican Revolution, 1910-1921; Farmworkers; Sugar Beet Workers; Tenant Farmers; Life; Culture; Families; Mexican Emigration; Discrimination; Racism; Gender roles; Courtship practices; Bilingualism; Celebrations; Self help.
Women: Strong Women; Immigrants; Farmworkers; Community action; Chicano Studies; Women Studies; Languages.
Locations: El Paso, Texas; Kansas City, Kansas; Chicago, Illinois; Scottsbluff, Nebraska.

Cover image by Carlos Hernández Chávez, Hartford, CT
Graphic design by Kimmer Sue, Vision Graphix, Modesto, CA
Printing by IngramSpark/Lightning Source

DEDICATION

On behalf of my mother, Elvira C. Hernández, the author of this book – and for my own part as compiler and editor of her life history – I dedicate this book, first of all to *Jacobo Chávez Rodarte,* or *Jake,* Elvira's father. She modeled her thinking and her actions after him, in particular his strong work ethic, his fierce sense of independence, and his intolerance for injustice. All of this was in spite of her continual struggles to help him control his anger and his mistreatment of her mother and her siblings.

We further dedicate this story of her life – by no means in any secondary way – to her beloved husband, Mike or *Maique,* who fought back against his father's heavy-handedness to become his own man and a significantly better person. His faith in God, his firm yet civil hand with their children, and his struggles for a better life for their family matched Elvira's own. They had a deep and enduring devotion for each other that was founded on their shared religious, cultural, and personal values.

Both of these men – *Jacobo* and *Maique* – more than anyone or anything else, shaped Elvira's world view and her way of life, a reality so clearly reflected in her narrative.

Elvira personally also dedicated this book to her children, grandchildren, other family members, and future progeny for whom this work was initially undertaken. In the beginning, Elvira did not want her life story tape-recorded. She relented only when she realized that it would be an important record of her family history that would be of value to her descendants.

ACKNOWLEDGEMENTS

First of all, I wish to express my gratitude to my dear wife, Ysaura Bernal, for her unfaltering support and encouragement throughout the challenging process of organizing Elvira's myriad family stories. Indeed, it was Ysaura who first proposed that I record my mother's conversations as a way to document her important history. Ysaura made many valuable recommendations about the structure and content of the emerging narrative. She also proofread the entire text for both the English and Spanish versions, providing extremely helpful checks on accuracy and style. Ysaura endured with wonderful patience the long days and weeks that I spent closed up in my study, leaving precious little time for the normal activities of everyday life.

I am also greatly indebted to several family, friends, and colleagues who read and commented critically on developing versions of the book. They are:

My colleague and friend, Garland D. Bills, Professor Emeritus of Linguistics at the University of New Mexico, read drafts of both language versions of this book. He made some particularly incisive comments about the handling of code-switching as well as techniques to facilitate the comprehensibility of the bilingual texts, especially in the English version. His suggestions to include a family genealogy as well as biographical information about Elvira were extremely well taken and have been incorporated into the final versions of the book.

My good friend Anne Fairbrother, Assistant Professor of Education at New York State University, Oswego, felt that, in addition to general readers, a professional audience, especially educators and sociolinguists, would find this book highly rewarding. This will affect my promotion of the book. She also made a number of important observations about the structure of the book that were crucial for improvements in the clarity and coherence of a complex narrative.

My son-in-law, George Galaza, Retired Deputy Director of the California State Department of Corrections, offered some extremely relevant and useful ideas about the organization of the book. He also noted that Elvira's story has a broad cultural and historical appeal and encouraged me to direct the book to a wider readership than that of my extended family, which initially had been my intended audience.

My son, Michael F. Hernandez, provided me invaluable assistance in understanding and manipulating the computer programs necessary for the proper compilation, editing and formatting of the book. His help was crucial in the design and development of the maps and the cover art of the book, and he furnished me with a wealth of ideas about materials for its eventual promotion.

My daughter, Michelle Medina, read an early draft of the manuscript and guided me toward a much more open narrative, especially in segments that described Elvira's extended family. She also helped me make sections of the text much more comprehensible to general readers.

Several others of my children listened patiently and often to my animated explanations of progress on the book. Thanks to Mary Galaza, Barbara Vittitow, Veronica Quiris, Robert and Ramona Hernandez, all of whom offered much-needed supportive feedback.

I acknowledge with much gratitude the great support given me by my children in contributing funds – without my knowledge – for the publication and promotion of their grandmother's book.

My brother César Hernández Chávez and my sisters Marah Shai, Therese Chavez, and Mary Lou Hernandez-Kelley all read drafts of the manuscript for historical accuracy. Each of them offered corrections and other changes, most of which are incorporated into the final document.

Hernán Chávez, a cousin and troubador from Colima, Mexico, read the Spanish version and made some extremely useful comments about the code switching to English in that version.

Carlos Hernández Chávez, very generously permitted me to use the image for the cover which is a reproduction of one of his murals. Its subject is sugar beet workers of Nebraska, a most fitting theme for the content of this book. Carlos also undertook the draft of the design for the cover.

A million thank-you's also to my cousin Joy Gonzales, eldest daughter of Johnny Mack and Ramona Hernandez. Joy received from her mother several letters that her parents wrote to each other that led to their courtship and marriage and which Elvira spoke about. It is with a great deal of pleasure that I reproduce here Ramona's answer to Johnny's first letter and his response in which he proposes matrimony.

A special thank you to my sister-in-law, Jan Hernandez, a retired administrator and English teacher with the San Francisco Unified School District. Jan carefully pored over both the Spanish and English manuscripts, not only pointing out spelling and punctuation errors but discussing with me at length many questions of grammar, style, and substance.

Finally, a word of appreciation for David and Nancy Zimmerer of Lingle, Wyoming who were so kind as to allow me the use of their photos of sugar-beet workers. Such photos are extremely difficult to find since most farm workers, then and now, are too busy working to take pictures, or else very rarely have access to a camera.

LIST OF FIGURES

CONTENTS

PREFACE

COMPILATION OF ELVIRA'S LIFE STORY.

The Tape Recordings. The narratives in this book were extracted from a large number of conversations between my mother Elvira and me that I tape recorded over a many years during my visits to her home in Scottsbluff, Nebraska. In the course of my visits, our conversations invariably turned to her personal history that included a wide range of anecdotes about her parents, her grandparents, and other family.

In listening to Elvira's anecdotes, I realized that these genealogical accounts represented an important record for Elvira's descendants and for her extended family. So, in nineteen eighty-eight, at the urging of my wife Ysaura Bernal, I began to tape record our conversations, continuing with this endeavor until 2010, two years before her death.

An Emerging Life History. As I listened to her narrations in light of the taping project, it became increasingly clear that, over and above the genealogical information, embedded within the diverse recordings was a rich series of interconnected descriptions of her experiences that could – and should – be compiled into a single coherent and intriguing life history.

Elvira told her stories as short vignettes or longer anecdotes, usually around the kitchen table, woven into her stream-of-consciousness conversations and scattered throughout the many hours of recordings. Also, for many of her experiences, the tapes contain several similar, though slightly different, retellings over the

i

years. Therefore, many of the individual episodes in the book represent a synthesis of these diverse accounts told by Elvira.

So, in order to unravel her story and to construct the desired unified narrative, the emerging life history needed to be transcribed from the tapes and would require much organization and editing of the individual accounts.

I liken this entire undertaking to that of assembling a giant jigsaw puzzle, made up of hundreds of little pieces of her oral history, one that has no completed picture on the outside to use as a guide.

Translation to English. Even though Elvira was fluently bilingual, the greater part of my own conversations with her were in Spanish because for most of our lives, this had been the normal language of communication between the two of us. So, Elvira's original narrative is written almost entirely in Spanish,

Because of this, her life history would be largely inaccessible to many members of Elvira's own extended family, some of whom, although they may be bilingual, are not necessarily fluent readers of Spanish. For the most part, this is true because all their schooling has been in English.

Moreover, I expect that this memoir will attract a more general English readership that includes persons interested in immigration history, Mexican-American life and culture, and the roles of women within that social milieu. It will also be very relevant in academia to scholars and students of Chican@ studies, women studies, family studies, and bilingualism.

For these reasons, I have translated the entire Spanish text into English, and the two language versions are published as separate volumes.

Elvira's Voice. It was my intention, throughout each language version, to represent as genuinely as possible Elvira's own way of talking, i.e. her 'voice'. In her original Spanish narrations, the familiar content and her conversational manner of story-telling both lent themselves directly to an informal, colloquial manner of speaking.

Whenever Elvira conversed in English, her language was equally informal. So, I have written the translated version in the closest approximation as possible to her own English vernacular which she very often spoke in her home and in her community – that is to say, in her own English voice.

Elvira acquired English as a young school child in Kansas and Nebraska. As a result she was, for all intents and purposes, a native speaker of each of her languages. Her English usage consisted largely of a colloquial midwestern variety of the language. In addition, it was occasionally interspersed with constructions and expressions that are remnants of her early experience as a second-language learner.

Colloquial pronunciations and structures are, of course, not comparable across languages. Thus, the forms I used to represent her casual speech in the translation involve pronunciations and sentence structures specific to the English that Elvira herself used.

Some readers may look askance, or even with outright disapproval, at the use throughout the narratives of nonstandard spellings and constructions such as gonna, could'a, she told 'em, or they was. It is important to note, however, that all native speakers – *of whatever language, in any part of the world and of whatever social class* – vary their speech, using words and constructions that range from the most casual and informal to the very formal. So, in one situation in English, we might hear I don't wanna talk to 'im, but in a different context, that same speaker might say I do not want to talk to him, or even I prefer not to speak with him. Such stylistic variation is completely normal in all languages and has been shown to correspond, in intricate ways, to the social and psychological conditions of speaking.

So, maintaining the authenticity of Elvira's voice requires the faithful use of her own informal, vernacular in all the contexts in which it is called for. A critical aspect of this *linguistic realism* is the use not only of colloquial forms of expression, but also – within a bilingual conversational context – the rapid and unconscious insertion into the English stream of speech of words, expressions, and longer segments taken directly from Spanish. These segments retain completely their Spanish pronunciation and structure and are referred to as "code switches".

Elvira engages in this form of language switching mostly when she speaks in Spanish although in English, too, she occasionally switches to individual words or short phrases in Spanish. Thus, this limited use of code switching is also reflected in the English translation. For a somewhat more extensive discussion of this phenomenon, the reader is directed to *"Appendix I. Code Switching by Elvira"* on p.401.

FORMAT AND LAYOUT OF THE BOOK

Footnotes. Given the imperative to represent Elvira's natural uninhibited speech, it was important to include at least some code switches in the English version. These are found in places where they would be very likely to occur within a bilingual discourse because of the cultural content. Yet, such switches may be problematic for readers who are monolingual or nearly so, even though they are kept to a minimum. Most of them, precisely because of their cultural content, may not be understood without a knowledge of Spanish.

Of the several techniques considered to address this issue, the one that seemed least intrusive and most reasonable was to translate code switches in footnotes. These will provide a relatively straightforward way for monolingual readers to understand explicitly the meanings of such switches.

On the other hand, many words and expressions that appear as switches are very similar in form and meaning in English and Spanish. It is expected that readers will understand these directly, perhaps with a little bit of effort, so these will not be footnoted.

Footnotes will also prove useful in clarifying familial and personal relationships referred to in the English text. In addition, they are used to provide brief explanations for terms and actions that are specific to Elvira's life experiences and which may not be part of general knowledge.

Cultural and Linguistic Explanations. Some such expressions and activities call for fuller descriptions or explanations in order to provide a more complete understanding of the narrative. Presenting these longer commentaries in footnotes would be much too cumbersome and, perhaps, of limited interest for many readers. Moreover, some of these descriptions and explanations are somewhat technical, especially those dealing with linguistic processes.

For these reasons, such in-depth explanations are provided for interested persons, but they are placed at the end of each chapter in a section labeled *Comments on Language and Culture,* where they may be examined at the reader's leisure. These cultural and linguistic observations are indicated in the text through special endnotes written in small roman numerals, for example *desahije*(iii), which references an endnote comment on how thinning the sugar beets takes place.

Glossary. Certain terms that Elvira uses in code switches to Spanish are used more than once, some fairly frequently. Similarly, there are terms that are specific to the farmworker experience and that are not generally known, even in English. These various terms are footnoted the first time they appear only. It is expected that the reader will recall their meanings when they are encountered in subsequent uses.

Of course, it is entirely possible that a reader will forget the meaning of a previously footnoted term. For the reader's convenience in such cases (also not to tire with an overabundance of footnotes), I provide a glossary of terms as an appendix. The glossary includes all footnoted individual words that are used more than once, as well as a few commonly used expressions.

Family Trees and List of Names. Because of Elvira's strong focus on family stories, she mentions various persons' names at different points in the narrative. Where the relationship is not clear in the text, a footnote explains the relationship the first time it appears. For subsequent mentions, which are not footnoted, the reader may wish to review the "Family Trees" for particular branches of the family which are provided at the end of relevant chapters (see *List of Figures* preceding the *Table of Contents*).

Italicization and Punctuation of Text. Throughout the book, in both the Spanish and English versions, all instances of text that represent pronunciations in the other language are written in italics. This includes proper names and code switches. So, italicized text in this English version is an explicit visual indication either that a switch to Spanish is taking place or that a Spanish pronunciation is intended for a proper name.

In translated quotations, the Spanish-specific punctuation marks '¿' and '¡' at the beginnings of sentences are retained as indications that the original dialogue was spoken in Spanish.

Photos and Illustrations. At the end of many of the chapters, I incude a small album of pictures and illustrations. Most of these were taken from the collection that Elvira saved over the years throughout her family's numerous moves. Some are digital renderings of objects provided by other members of the family. The selection of images to include was based primarily on their relevance to the narrative of the particular chapter in which they're found. In addition, an important criterion was the historical and cultural value of each image.

INTRODUCTION

Elvira: A Mexican American Woman is the story of a woman who struggles to find a meaningful life in a land once alien, now native. It is a narrative of hardship and survival, of enduring love and family cohesion, and of grief and healing.

The author, Elvira C. Hernandez, speaks in a natural, humble language, describing both her tribulations and her achievements in an unpretentious way that lends power to her narration.

In this story of her life, she relates the intriguing personal history of a girl whose family fled Chalchihuites, Zacatecas, leaving behind the violence of the Mexican Revolution (1910-1921) to seek a livelihood in the United States.

On crossing the border, Elvira's father and uncles immediately found jobs working on the railroad. Traveling long distances laying track for the expansion of the rail lines, they left their families behind in El Paso, Texas, where the women were obliged to live in cramped boxcars with their children and to work as domestics.

Her restless father, Jacobo, took them from state to state and town to town seeking better opportunities. From the itinerant life of railroad workers, the men were recruited into the dank meat-packing plants of Kansas City. There, they encountered a stable and thriving Mexican immigrant community where Elvira and her future husband, unknown to each other, attended the same school. It was also in Kansas City that, for the first time, she became conscious of racism against Mexicans.

Ever intent on finding a more gainful life, Elvira's father once more uprooted his family, moving them to Scottsbluff, Nebraska where Elvira was to live for the rest of her life

She provides heartrending accounts of this fateful move to what would be an onerous existence as laborers in the sugar-beet fields. There, even the children would work alongside the adults. As a result, Elvira herself labored in the fields during all of her youth and for most of her adult life. She describes ruefully her family's continual efforts to scrape out a living and to become full members of the alien society they encountered there.

In telling her story, Elvira reveals many of the social and cultural norms of her Mexican community of origin. Some of these involve the effects of an earlier migration by one family on later immigration patterns of other members of the family. And she describes the severe constraints on girls' dress and on boy-girl interactions, in addition to providing illuminating and thoroughly entertaining views of courtship practices and cultural celebrations in their new community.

Tortillas were an indispensable food in the diet of the Mexican immigrant family of the period, who normally consumed several dozens of tortillas per day. From the time she was nine yers old, Elvira was called upon by her mother to make the tortillas for the family. Thus, alongside her other household duties and her long hours working in the fields, tortilla-making became an integral part of her daily reality – with but brief hiatuses – until she could no longer perform that task at age 89. Along with being a farmworker, a Mexican, a woman, and a Catholic, her identity was inextricably bound up with her role in the family as the maker of tortillas.[1]

Out of these varied experiences, Elvira's narrative is told with the honest authenticity of an unassuming farmworker. In her down-to-earth way of speaking, she freely uses the modest vernaculars of her community, drawing matter-of-fact portrayals of back-breaking labor, deprivation, death and disease, and abuse by domineering men. She speaks, with undisguised contempt, of her and her new husband's strained relationship with *don Juan,* her malicious father-in-law. In her interactions with him, Elvira draws on her inner strength to challenge his otherwise undisputed authority.

Throughout the book, Elvira's standpoint is her family. She relates many poignant anecdotes about the life experienced by her parents' families – the *Chávezes* and the *Castillos* – both in

---

[1] In the final chapter of her history, Elvira traces her tortilla-making career through all the important stages of her life.

Mexico and in the United States. Her father, *Jacobo*, for all his faults, is her hero and role model as well as her nemesis. She talks about her many efforts to temper his temper. And she remembers affectionately her mother's soft, often futile, persistence and recalls her own somewhat detached relationship with her many siblings.

As her narrative unfolds, she focuses on her life with her own growing family, her relationship with her devoted husband, *Maique*, and the events surrounding his death. After his death, she grapples with her grief and struggles with the need to provide for her two youngest sons.

When her sons leave home, she dedicates herself to community service, first working with a community-action program that advocated for migrant farmworkers, then creating a center for elderly Mexican- and German-American women, and eventually serving as a 'foster grandparent' in a daycare center for small children until her retirement at age 89.

Evident throughout her narration is Elvira's staunch and unabashed religiosity. God, religious practices, and the church form the backdrop of her life, and they focus the lens through which she views, either explicitly or implicitly, her varied experiences.

Yet, despite her firm belief that worldly events are controlled by God, Elvira reveals a remarkable determination to shape their impact, whether by direct confrontation of wrongdoing, disdain for misguided authority, or questioning the denial of her aspirations. In recounting this story of her life, she consistently projects a firm sense of personal courage, determination and dignity, qualities that she displays from a very early age.

I have tried to compile her stories into an integrated narrative that I hope provides a fascinating and moving reading experience.

Enjoy!

–Eduardo Hernández Chavez

ix

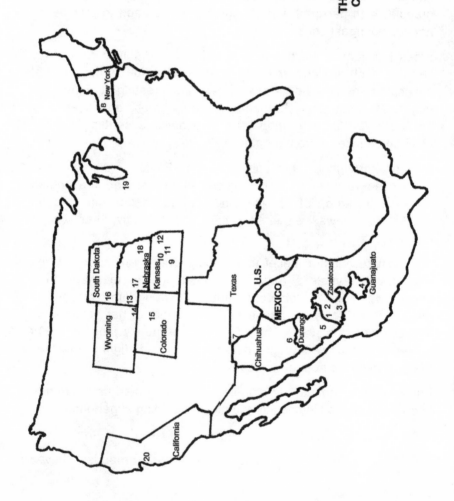

Map 1.

THE MIGRATION ROUTES OF THE
CHÁVEZ Y CASTILLO FAMILIES

x

1. Chalchihuites, Zacatecas. The Chávez and Castillo homeland.
2. Sombrerete, Zacatecas. Elvira's birthplace.
3. Zacatecas, Zacatecas. Jacobo Chávez' birthplace.
4. León, Guanajuato. Hometown of the Hernández family. Birthplace of Maique Hernández.
5. Durango, Durango. Where the Chávez family settled many years later.
6. Parral, Chihuahua.
7. El Paso, Texas. Where the Chávezes and Castillos entered the U.S.
8. Buffalo, New York. Terminus of the first railroad job of Jacobo Chávez and his brothers.
9. Wichita, Kansas. The first stop in the U.S. by the Juan Hernández family.
10. Topeka, Kansas. doña Eleuteria cures Jacinta Chávez when she was dying of influenza.
11. Lawrence, Kansas. The final railroad stop for the Chavezes. Elvira enters school here and learns English.
12. Kansas City ("Quianses"). The Chavezes worked here in the meat packing houses.
13. Scottsbluff, Nebraska. Final *enganche* of the Chavezes to work in the sugarbeet and potato fields. Elvira and Maique are buried here.
14. Pine Bluffs, Wyoming. Where Maique suffered his stroke.
15. Denver, Colorado.
16. Mt Rushmore ("The Faces").
17. North Platte, Nebraska.
18. Lincoln, Nebraska.
19. Chicago, Illinois.
20. San Francisco, California.

Chapter One

FROM CHALCHIHUITES TO EL PASO DEL NORTE

My dad said, "Vámonos. We gotta get outta here right now.
We're leaving 'cause the Revolution is coming."
Dice, "With the little bit I have, they'll come and burn everything
and kill all of us."

Let's Get Outta Here!

My dad brought us to the United States in nineteen sixteen when they still had the Revolution in Mexico. In those years, when a lotta people came to the United States, it was mainly because of that. They couldn't do any business over there 'cause the Revolution soldiers came, and they took everything away and gave it to the people.

At that time, there was a lotta work here in the United States. I think it was in the First World War, that they call it. Over here, the government was takin' a lotta men to the army, and there wasn't enough people for the jobs. They were building railroad lines – tracks over here and tracks over there. And the people who came, we were the ones they needed. They even had women working on hard jobs.

My dad was a hard worker. He became an orphan when he was little, and him and his brothers had to work real hard to support themselves. My dad was always goin' over here and goin' over there, lookin' for better work. If it finished in one, there he goes again to find what he could. If they gave 'im some wood to chop it with an axe, he did what they gave 'im. 'Cause he never went to school. He didn't know how to read nothing. *Nada.*

He was born in *Zacatecas, Zacatecas.* Later on he moved to *Chalchihuites, Zacatecas* to find work because there was a lotta the *Chávez* family there. I think he was already grown up when he moved because he went to work with an aunt and uncle who had a little farm.

And over there is where he met my mom, in *Chalchihuites,* because there was a lotta *Castillos* there, too. That's where they got married in nineteen oh-six. He was twenty-eight years old, and my mom was eighteen.

But after Miguel died – their first little baby – they moved to *Sombrerete,* which is a town not too far from *Chalchihuites.* That's why I was born in *Sombrerete, Zacatecas.* My dad was always goin' to one place and then to another place to see what was over there – to see the other one, to see what it was like. I think maybe he didn't like any place, or maybe it didn't go too good for him. I don't know.

From *Sombrerete* they went to *Durango* to look for better work, and that's where Jobita was born. But they didn't like it there, either, so they went back to *Chalchihuites* where they had their families. He built a little house there, and that's why Alta and Ruth were born there.

I think that was when my dad started to sell *provisiones* to make a better living. We lived better than other families because he had a little room there full of merchandise. He had everything – dry food like sugar and corn and *piloncillo,*[1] and he brought a lotta clothes and *tablones* – cloth that he sold by the yard, *o por metro.* He was a traveler, like a merchant. His brothers worked with him. They came to *Chalchihuites* from *Zacatecas* when my dad started his little business.

They all got their *mulas,* their *burros,* their horses – whatever they could – and they went to other towns to buy things that they

---

[1] 'a form of brown sugar', usually sold in small solid cones or blocks.

didn't have in *Chalchihuites*, and then they came back to sell 'em again. So, here they come, with their horses all loaded up with I don't know how much sacks of food. That was the only way they was living. They even crossed to the other side of the *Sierra* to bring things from over there. Sometimes they stayed two or three weeks on those trips.

I don't remember too much about those times. But all us kids loved to be outside playing in the yard. We had like a big *pila*[2] there full of water. I think I was climbing on top of it, and I fell in the water. I thought I was gonna drown. I don't know how they got me out.

But I can remember that I was four years old when I started Catholic school. That's when I learned to read and write. I think that's why I still know how to write a little bit in Spanish. I didn't forget it. Because here in the United States we didn't have school in Spanish. *¿Dónde?* Nowhere.

That's when I made my first communion just before we came to the United States. I was six years old. I was gonna be seven in June. Oh, I was so excited. All of us were so excited because we were gonna receive Our Lord God for the first time! I have a picture of me in my first communion dress, and someplace in here I still have the crown I was wearing. It was about in April because it was during Lent.

So that's where we lived, in *Chalchihuites*, before my dad brought us to the United States. That's when that terrible war started in Mexico, *y dijo mi papá*,[3] "*Vámonos*. We gotta get outta here now. As soon as she makes her first communion, we're leaving 'cause the Revolution is coming." One side started to fight with the other one. Catholics against the government. They were burning churches. Knockin' 'em down.

---

[2] 'cistern'.

[3] 'and my dad said.' **Note to the reader:** The verb *decir*, 'say' or 'tell', has several forms meaning 'I said' (dije), 'he said' (dijo), 'he says' (dice), etc. which will generally introduce dialogue originally spoken in Spanish.

3

And here in the United States, the great big war started in nineteen sixteen. But they really never had a war here. They go someplace else to kill the other people. They don't make war here. So when we came from Mexico, it was on account of the Revolution, and not because my dad couldn't support us.

Nos dijo, "I didn't come because we was starving." *Dice,* "With the little bit I have, they'll come and burn everything and kill all of us. They'll take everything. I seen 'em come and kill whole families so they can steal from 'em."

That's why we came. They say that everybody comes because they don't have enough to eat, but not us. I guess a lotta people did the same thing. I think if the Revolution didn't come, we probably would'a stayed.

He said, *"Vámonos."* He sold the little house and all the things, and we came.

When we left, my dad's brothers and their families came with us, all of them except my *tía Adela.* She was already married with *José Valdez,* and they lived in *Zacatecas.* They came over later.

My *tía Adela* and my uncles were all *Chávez.* But some of them were my dad's half-brothers because my grandma, *Mariquita Rodarte,* was married to another *Chávez* first. And then when that one died, that's when she married the second *Chávez,* the one that's my grandpa on my dad's side. His name was *José Chávez* – *José Ventura Chávez.* Maybe those two *Chávezes* were cousins. I don't know.

So, my grandma's children were all *Chávez.*[4] From the first husband, there was my *tío Carlos,* my *tío Daniel,* and I don't remember the other one. They all had eyes that were *zarcos,* kind'a like greenish, because *Mamá Mariquita's* father had a lotta Spanish. Then after she got married the second time, she had my *tío Santos* who was the oldest, then my dad, and my *tía Adela* who was the youngest one. My dad's eyes were also light in color, real light brown.

---

[4] See *Figure 1. The Family of María Rodarte de Chávez (Mamá Mariquita)* on p. 12.

4

Crossing the Border

We all came together on the train from *Durango* – *en uno de esos trenes viejos* full of chickens, pigs, and who knows what else. It had a lotta people. We never saw my grandma *Mariquita* no more because Mexico seemed like it was way on the other side of the world.

Well, when we got to the border, I wasn't seven years old yet, but I was almost seven. We came in *por la garita*, because my dad said that we had to register instead of just crossing at the bridge.

Dijo, "No. Let's put ourselves down right away that we're comin' over here to live. That way, everything is done right."

That was a good thing. Because afterwards they knew if we crossed as *contrabando* – illegals, I guess. Then they couldn't say, 'We don't find no record. You can't become a citizen.'

My dad had to sign for all of us, but because he didn't know how to read or write, they told him to just put his initials. I remember that he didn't even know how to hold the pencil, so they had to help him. I don't know how long we stayed in *Juárez* to see if Dad could at least get his "J" and "C". That's all he had to do, but he couldn't. He didn't learn and he didn't learn. Finally, they let 'im write an "X".

Then they put us in the bathrooms and I remember they gave us some clothes to wear – not clothes, just like robes. And they washed our clothes and disinfect them, and they gave us a bath. So there we are, all clean. We probably even had *piojos,*[5] *yo no sé.* That I don't know. I don't remember.

But I do know that all of this was on the fourteenth of June in nineteen sixteen. My mom told us more or less when we passed, but when I became a citizen in nineteen sixty-seven, they ask me if I knew the date when we passed. I think it was to see if I was telling a lie.

---

[5] 'lice'.

5

I told the examiner, "No, I don't remember. My mother only told me that it was in nineteen sixteen, sometime in June. We passed in those days, but I don't know exactly."

But they found the record. The man told me, "Well, you passed on the fourteenth of June. They have the mark there for *Jacobo Chávez Rodarte*[6](i) from *Chalchihuites, Zacatecas.*"

The fourteenth? I didn't know they still had those records! We registered, and that's how they found out when we passed. So, I have my record over there. I'm still there *en la garita*. Look how many years!

El Traque

Anyway, my dad signed, and we finally crossed but I don't remember how, if in a car or walking, I don't know. And everyone – all the people coming in – they was there all bunched up in *El Paso*. They passed the border, but then they couldn't leave from there unless somebody took 'em. Nobody thought, 'I'm going to a certain place in the United States.' They had to go *enganchados* to some place[7](ii) – to California, to Pennsylvania, to Kansas. Any place.

That's how they took people to other parts of the United States – *puros enganches*. You could see the offices at the Santa Fe railroad there in *El Paso* full of *enganchistas* saying, "Come over here." And another one, "No, I'll send you over there." And, "No, I'll send you someplace else."

Oh, and so many Mexicans lookin' for work. Because in *El Paso* they came in free. They didn't have requirements like they

---

[6] See *Comment* (i) on p. 14 at the end of this chapter for an explanation of surnames in Spanish.

  Note to the reader: These side comments – at the ends of chapters – will be indicated in the text with small subscript roman numerals enclosed in parentheses. They are intended for readers who may have a particular interest in a topic but which they don't need to access immediately. These *Comments on Language and Culture* may be referred to at any convenient time.

[7] 'They had to be recruited (*enganchados*) to go to some (particular) place.'

6

do now. They registered, they paid their ten cents, and that was it. And people kept on comin' from Mexico because, well, the war was really bad.

Anyway, we passed, and my dad and the other ones who came – my uncles and other men – right away they got work on the railroad. There was a lotta families, and they put us all *en carros de ferrocarril.* Everybody still said *'ferrocarril'* for the 'railroad' because we barely came in from Mexico and we didn't know the words that they used over here.

And they stopped the trains outside of the towns in camps that they had for the railroad workers. When the train stopped, they left us there in one place for two or three weeks, and they brought railroad cars with water and food. Then they would take us to a different place.

But the train always stopped close to an irrigation ditch. Mom gave us a bath in there, and she washed clothes in there, too. Well, there wasn't no other place. And if we had to go to the bathroom, well we went behind a tree. Oooh!

Us girls really enjoyed it, though, but not Mom and Dad. It was in the summer, and besides it was in Texas where it got really hot. They were all working, so as soon as the train stopped we jumped out. We would go play in the ditch or go running around in the fields. Then, we went inside and laid down on the mattresses. Except Ruth because she was too little. She was one year old when we passed.

So then after they finished in Texas, they sent everybody to Pennsylvania and New York – Buffalo, New York. They needed people to work on the tracks. The men worked over there all winter.

But we stayed there in a railroad camp in *El Paso.*We were two families that lived in a boxcar – my *tía Pola* and us. Her name was *Telésfora*, but we called her *tía Pola*(iii). She was my *tío Santos'* wife. She lived there with us and she had just as big a family – four children. And we were four also – *Cuca* who was the youngest, Alta, Jobita, and me who was the oldest – five with my mom.

7

So, everybody together we were ten, and all of us in one boxcar, one of those that had four little windows, two on each side. And it had big doors that opened where there was steps to climb up. They gave us one half of the boxcar to each family. *¡Fíjate!* Half of one car – one family over here, and the other family over there.

We slept in there and cooked in there. We put some sheets to divide the rooms. It had a coal stove right in the middle for both families. Both of 'em cooked on that stove, and the one that got it first, that's the one that cooked first. We had to go out to the ditch to wash clothes – a big irrigation ditch that was there close.

My mom told us afterwards how she suffered with my aunt who was mean to her. She didn't hardly let her cook. And when she cooked, she had to make *tacos* that we took outside to eat. My mom got a lotta sores on her face, I think from that.

And then the men hardly sent us any money. Very little. The railroad took away for their expenses. And the rest, *pos, ¿quién sabe?* What was left they sent by telegram from the office. My dad didn't know how to read or write, so the clerks there were in charge of sending the money.

And my mom and my *tía Pola* went to the bank any way they could to cash it. It was so little. And at that time, who was gonna help us? The railroad didn't help at all, and the government even less.

That's why Mom went to work on the other side of town as a maid. They paid her one dollar and gave 'er ten cents for the bus. Ten cents each way. But she didn't spend it. She went over there walking, and she walked back so she could save twenty cents because we didn't have no money even to eat. It was a dollar twenty for ten people. God knows how we must'a lived. I don't know. That was in nineteen sixteen, nineteen seventeen. By then I was already seven years old.

My *tía Pola* was the one who took care of us. I think she had a real hard time 'cause there was eight kids, and I guess we fought a lot. But my aunt was very strict. Oh, she was strict! She spanked us with a strap just for nothing. I think we were scared of her.

8

The Red Poncho

One time that my dad wrote to us, he sent a picture of the four brothers. They were all dressed in a suit and wearing a *bombín* – those little hats New York style. I saw that picture, and my mom took it with her to Mexico, but they lost it over there. Darn it, I don't know what happened to that picture.

My dad told us that when they first got to New York, one of his brothers – maybe it was my *tío Daniel* – was wearing a red *poncho*, the kind they only wear for the cold. It was all wool, real warm, and over there it was really cold because it was in the winter. He didn't take it off at all because he was so scared that he would freeze to death. He was working on the tracks with that *poncho*.

A lotta times his *poncho* would fly in the wind. The ones who drove the train saw it and they thought it was a red flag and stopped because from far away it looked like a red sign that meant 'danger'. Right away, the supervisor went over to tell him to take that off. "*No*," he said. "*No, no, no. ¡Hace mucho frío!*" That it was too cold. He didn't want to let go of that *poncho*. My dad argued with them so much for that *poncho*. He didn't want 'em to take it away from his brother.

So then, they took 'im a mackinaw, one of those heavy overcoats. But he told 'em, "*¡No, no, no!*" And he couldn't talk English, and the other ones didn't know Spanish. Finally, they both understood each other, that he had to take off that *poncho* because two or three times the trains had to stop 'cause they saw the red sign. So, they gave 'im the mackinaw to put on.

Enganche to Kansas

Well, Dad didn't come back from New York until after the winter passed. Then, after they got back, they were hired to go to Kansas. They gave them the jobs to go over there because they needed people. I don't know who hired them. The *revisadores,*[8](iv) I think.

So, that's why we went to Kansas. It was in the summer because I was almost eight years old.

We all lived there *en la sección* – on the part of the tracks far away from the towns. That's when everybody started to talk about '*el traque*' this and '*el traque*' that,[9] and who knows what else.

When we got to Lawrence, Kansas, they put us in some *tejabanes* outside of town where they put the workers. They were like trailers with two rooms, but they were ugly. The floors had wide boards on them that were all *astillosas*.[10] Ugly, and without linoleum or nothing. The families were all separate now. Every person with their own family. Dad in his house and the other ones in their house.

Cuca was two years old. I was playing with her on a big cardboard box. She was inside, and I pulled on it and made her laugh. I pulled on it, and I hit my foot on a board. I got an *astilla* way up inside my toe.

Oh! My dad tried to take it out but he couldn't do it and couldn't do it. He put me some medicine, but Mom and Dad had to be up with me all night. *A llore y llore y llore.*[11] I was older already – almost eight years old. *Pero, a llore y llore y llore.* It was night time, and us without a car, there was no place to go. Where could we? Oh, if they could just give me a shot or something to put my foot to sleep!

The next day they had go see the *mayordomo* to take me to the doctor. He took out everything. *Toda,* even the toenail. Ooh! The toe was white, all white. He put on some medicine, but I lasted a long time for it to get better.

---

[8] In Elvira's lexicon, 'recruiters'. See Comment (iv) on p. 15 for a fuller explanation.
[9] Pronounced [TRAH-kay].
[10] 'full of splinters (*astillas*)'.
[11] 'crying and crying and crying.'

Finally, it grew out again. It came out all purple, and every year it got more and more curved, *toda chueca*. I never went to the doctor no more, so that's how it stayed, crooked. It looked like a cow hoof, all hard, hard. *¡Ay!* I have so much trouble cutting that nail.

I remember that in that year we went to school from the *sección* all the way to town. We went in a little car, like a bus, but it was electric. I think it was a streetcar. We went running to catch it, and then we waited for it and got on.

I don't know what school we went to. I think just me and Jobita went. We're the ones that was old enough to go. That was the first school I had in the United States, but I don't remember it. I think that's where we learned English.

ELVIRA CHÁVEZ' BAPTISMAL CERTIFICATE

Parroquia de San Juan Bautista

Hidalgo y Rotarismo s/n   Apdo Postal # 12
Tel. (433)935-01-45   Sombrerete, Zac., Mèxico.C.P. 99100

CERTIFICADO DE BAUTISMO

El día catorce *de*   Agosto   *de* 1909
fue bautizad a   *en esta Parroquia un* a   *niñ* a   *a quien se le*
puso por nombre Elvira Chávez Castillo - - - - - -
- -
nació el día 27 *de*   Junio   *de* - - - - - -
en   Sombrerete, - - - - - - - - - -.- *hij* a· Leg.
del Sr. Jacob Chávez - - - - - - - - - - - - - - -.
y de la Sra. Jacinta Castillo - - - - - - - - - - -
Padrinos: El Sr.   Ygnacio Ybarra - - - - - - - - -
y la Sra.   Margarita Ybarra - - - - - - - - - - - -

EL PARROCO   EL BAUTIZANTE
                          Pbro. Rafael Arenas, Vicario

Notas Marginales:
No tiene notas.
Libro Núm. 55
Acta Núm. 443

Es copia fiel tomada de su
original expedida el día 03
de Agosto
de 2005

FIGURE 1. THE FAMILY OF MARÍA RODARTE DE CHÁVEZ (MAMÁ MARIQUITA)

Antonio Rodarte (Jacobo's Grandfather, don Antonio)

Mariquita + Carlos Chávez
(the first Chávez)

┌Carlos Chávez

└Daniel Chávez

Mariquita + José Ventura Chávez
(the second Chávez)

┌Santos Chávez + Telésfora (Pola)
　Magallanes

├Jacobo Chávez + Jacinta Castillo

└Adela Chavez + José Valdez

The homeland of the *Chávezes* and the *Castillos*.

Clockwise from the Top: *Jacinta* with *Refugio* (*Cuca*) in her arms, *Elvira*, *Jovita*, *Altagracia*.

Portrait taken in Chalchihuites just prior to leaving for El Paso.

Elvira in her First Communion dress, 1916.

The crown worn by *Elvira* for her First Communion.

13

Comments on Language and Culture

i   Jacobo's paternal surname was *Chávez;* his maternal surname was *Rodarte.* The Mexican naming system uses the father's surname after the first and middle names, followed by the mother's maiden name, often resulting in a fairly lengthy full name (e.g. Her husband *Maique's* full name in Spanish was *Miguel Félix Hernández Fonseca*). In formal documents, often just the initial of the mother's name is used (*Miguel Félix Hernández F.*) Elvira's maiden name was *Elvira Chávez Castillo.* When a woman married, she retained her paternal maiden name and added her husband's surname, sometimes with *de.* So, Elvira's married name was *Elvira C. Hernández,* since she habitually abbreviated the *Chávez.*
   In the U.S., since the final name in a list is considered the legal surname, Mexicans often resorted to either dropping the maternal surname entirely or placing it before the paternal name, in effect making it into a middle name. Occasionally, the mother's surname is kept as the legal surname. More recently, some people, wishing to keep the two surnames in the original order, have taken to hyphenating the two or leaving the two unhyphenated but having to explain to one and all that both are "last names".

ii   *Enganchados*, 'recruited', is formed on the base *gancho* which means a 'hook' and so has the sense of being hooked for a job by a recruiter, like a fish. It was all voluntary, of course. Other words formed from this root are *enganchista*, 'recruiter' and the various forms of the verb *'enganchar'* 'to recruit'.

iii   Nicknames (hypocorisms) in Spanish are often reductions and phonetic (sometimes grammatical) adaptations of the full given name. (Compare English *Bob* (and *Bobby)* from *Robert,* although in Spanish, the adaptations are considerably more complex.)
   Initially, perhaps, they were active phonetic processes – most probably based on adults attempting to mimic child pronunciations. These have over the centuries become conventional nicknames. I suspect that some of these, like *Lola* from *Dolores* or *Pepe* from *José,* go back even to Hispano-Romance (popular Latin) since they are found not only across the Iberian peninsula and Latin America but also in places like Italy.

Endnotes continue on the following page:

14

Thus, the processes described in the examples that follow are historical-linguistic in nature only and are most certainly not active psychological-phonetic processes for speakers today (if they ever were), except possibly for the change of [s] to [ch]. In this case, many adults speaking to babies today will convert many of their [s] sounds to [ch]. (Compare the "baby talk" change in English of [w] for [l] and [r] as in *a widdow wabbit*.) Also, what are presented here as sequences of phonetic changes with intermediate forms were most likely, even initially, produced simultaneously. Some rather technical examples of these processes are described in later endnotes.

To derive the nickname *Pola,* the name *Telésfora* drops the first two syllables in a process called *apheresis*, leaving *fora* (as an intermediate, not-yet-pronounced, form). The consonant *f* is produced with friction at the lips and is converted to a different consonant, also pronounced at the lips but with complete stoppage of air. This new consonant is pronounced *p*, leaving another intermediate form *pora*. (In general, consonants pronounced with complete stoppage of air are considered by linguists to be less complex than those pronounced with friction, thus more 'baby like'.) The *r* is converted to *l*, to which it is very closely related, resulting in *Pola*.

iv   *Revisadores* were nominally officials of the sugar companies who oversaw the irrigation systems, the distribution of water to farmers, and the allocation of acreage for the planting of sugar beets. They also enforced work rules and were intermediaries in disputes between workers and farmers. In English, they were referred to as 'fieldmen' or 'ditch riders'.

Elvira expands the use of the term *revisadores* to mean company officials who were traveling 'labor recruiters'. These were also sugar company employees, and in fact may have been the same individuals who, during the growing season, were the field men. Elvira further expands the meaning of *'revisadores'* to include recruiters for the railroad and meat packing companies.

15

Chapter Two

QUIANSES[1]

*The truth is that we all worked, not just the men.
Mom had four boarders. She did everything for them.
She cooked their food, she washed their clothes,
and cleaned up their rooms.*

El Caris

I think my dad only worked less than a year on the railroad there, *y los engancharon otra vez* to the packing houses in Kansas City, like Cudahy's and Swift's. It was in the time of the war, and there was no people to work. They needed workers, and they were taking Mexican people all over.

Well, when they came to the big city, a lot of 'em quit the railroad where they paid them fifty cents an hour or something like that. People always look for a better job. The packing houses had better pay and the work wasn't as hard as on the railroad, so they went there.

So that's why my dad went to look for work at the packing houses where they paid more money. Right away he got work *en el Caris*. That's the way they said it, "We're working at *Caris* – Cudahy's."(i) And that's why we went to live in Kansas City.

We rented a pretty nice home in Kansas. It had three bedrooms upstairs. It was big and had stairs. The little kids went

---

[1] The common Spanish pronunciation of 'Kansas' by Mexicans in Kansas and Nebraska, pronounced [KYAN-ses].

up the steps and slid all the way down on the – how do you call it? – the *barandal.* But it was funny – it didn't have no bathroom. It had water inside, *pero los escusados* were outdoors. It had a real nice porch in front.

Home Schooling

There was a big park close to the house where the four of us went to run around. It was me, Jobita, Alta, and *Luz* – one of my *tío Santos'* daughters that was always there with us. I was the oldest one, so I took care of 'em. After a while, I told 'em, "Hey, we better quit. Mom is gonna call us now. We have to go in and pray. Let's go in." They all mind me.

Mom always called us in every day to go pray. Every day at noon. "Come in to pray. Because right at twelve o'clock*," nos decía,* "that's when they caught Our Lord God to crucify him, and he lasted three hours. So kneel down here until we pray one mystery." Just one place of the rosary. "Then you can sit down and think about who Jesus Christ was. You can't go out and play for three hours."

Oh, Mom, *¡qué va!*[2] She taught us how to pray and to be good in the church. She was a very good Catholic. But we didn't always go to Mass. How could we? It was far. Once in a while, when my dad was there to take care of the little kids, we walked to church with my mom. It was *Nuestra Señora del Carmen.* That's where we went.

Sometimes, we were playing outside the house, and I told the girls, "Let's go ask Mom and see if she can give us a penny." 'Cause my mom gave each one a penny to go buy a candy. Not every day 'cause she didn't have any. But we had to tell her what she taught us – the *Padre Nuestro,* the *Ave María,* the *Credo* – all those little prayers we learned when we went to confession or to make our first communion.

---

[2] Something like 'really' or 'for sure'.

I remember a lotta those things. If you have a good memory, you don't forget to have Our Lord God in your heart and in your mind.

Mom also taught us the letters – *el abecedario*. She didn't want us to grow up and not know how to read in Spanish because here they didn't teach us. *Nada*. Well, I already knew a little bit because I went to school with the sisters in Mexico. But the other ones were too little. So, she used to take her time with us because she thought we were gonna be *sin educación del lenguaje* at all.

My mom knew a lot. She came from Mexico with all her books – especially *la biblia*. She taught us a lot. So afterward, when the government sent them all back to Mexico(ii) I wrote to my mother and my sisters in Spanish.

She taught us some tongue twisters, too, so we could practice our pronounciation. *Nos decía*, "Come on. I'll give you a penny, but you have to say these. Let me see if you say them right."

Jobita learned them real good. Me, too, but not like her. There was a lot of 'em, but one of 'em said,

'Yo tenía una tablita muy intinbilitinguladita, y el que me la desintinbilitingulare será un buen desintinbilitingulador.'[3]

All of us said them. Then, she gave us our penny. There we go to the drugstore that was right across the street. She told us, "Go on. But come back soon." She had to be there inside to take care of the small children, but every little while she came out to the porch to see if we were comin' back.

Las Manitas

We loved *manitas*. They were two popsicles on one stick, one on one side and another on the other side. They were *'paletas'* but we didn't know about *'paletas'*, just *'manitas'*. We grabbed 'em with our hand in the middle. I think that's why they called 'em *'manitas'*. Both of 'em for one penny.

---

[3] The word, of course, is meaningless. In English it would be something like: 'I had a little board that was *intinbilitingul*-ated. And whoever can dis-*intinbilitingul*-ate it will be a good dis-*intinbilitingul*-ator.'

We came out of the drugstore with our *manitas*. Mmm! We were so happy. There we go, just walkin' slow with our *manitas*. Then, all of a sudden, somebody came up. It was a man. He was tall. "Oh," he said. "¿What you got there?"

"Manitas."

"You know, right here close by they're selling four *manitas* for a penny. I can take you. ¿You wanna come? *Dije*, "Let's go. All four of us."

He got my hand, and I went with him. "Come through here. Let's go over there. We'll turn over there, and there it is. Oh, they sell a lotta candies for just a little bit. You can buy more *manitas* for a penny than what you have."

So there we go with him, when all of a sudden it came to my head. 'Uh-uh! It's scary over there.' I turned around and said, "Jobita! Alta! *Luz!* Run to my mom and tell 'er!"

Then the man squeezed my hand. I began to yell, "Mom! Mom!" Loud. But he still had ahold of me.

Then, I turned my foot, and bam! I kicked 'im in the leg. He yelled and let me go. He bent over to grab his leg, and I run!

They was all yelling, "Mom! Mom!" The drugstore man came out right away. "¿What's the matter? ¿*Qué tienen?*"

Dije, "¡A man wanna take us!"

"¿Where is he?"

Dije, "He went. He ran over there and went in there."

"¿See? You didn't go straight back to your mom."

"No, the man said that over there on that corner there's a store where we can buy a lotta candy for a penny."

He just shook his head. He said, "From now on, you know you have to go straight home."

I said, "Thanks. We're not gonna come out no more."

My mom was on the porch crying. I ran.

Dijo, "¡Ay! Thank God you're here." She was so glad to see me. She hugged me, and went in crying. I was crying, too, 'cause I was scared.

But it's a good thing that I been real strong since I was little. If they tried to do something, I fought back.

John J. Ingalls School

Our house was in Armourdale, close by to John J. Ingalls school – right there close. It was on Fifth, and I think we were on Fourth. I went to that school up to the third grade.

Oh, they were so discriminating in Kansas City. No, not 'discriminating'. They were 'racist'! At John J. Ingalls school, they kept all the Mexicans separate because they had *güeros*[4] there, too, and the parents didn't want us to be together. I don't know why. Maybe because it was during the war and there was a lotta discrimination. The Mexicans and the Negroes were all downstairs, and sometimes we had to sit two of us on one chair. *Los americanos* were upstairs and they didn't get together with us.

Outside, the *güeras* would throw rocks at us. I would tell 'em, "Why do you hit us? It hurts us as much as you. We're the same." Then, they didn't do it no more. Ever since I was little, I stood up for myself.

Oh, Kansas City was terrible. A Mexican was nobody. He wasn't a resident from here. Even if we lived here, they didn't claim him a resident. There was signs that said NO NEGROES, MEXICANS, OR DOGS ALLOWED.

When a Mexican was born, it was like if he was an animal. They didn't register him. That happened to *Eduardo.* The doctor went to the house when he was born, but he never sent us a birth certificate. That's why, in Scottsbluff, we had to prove that he was born so they could give him his birth certificate.

---

4 Pronounced [WED-ose]. A common term among Mexicans in the U.S. for 'Anglo-Americans'; more generally it means 'white persons' or any light-skinned person.

21

And then, we didn't get along with the *negros*, either. I don't know why, but they didn't like Mexicans. And us, we were afraid of them because they pushed us and hit us.

Los Hernández

By that time, the *Hernández* were in Kansas City, too, and the *Chávez* and the *Hernández*[5] knew each other from over there because in Armourdale, it was all *colonia mexicana*. My *tío Santos* was the one who knew *don Juan Hernández*, Mike's[6] father. They got to be good friends because they both worked at Swift's – *en la Suis*, like they called it.

Mike was also at John J. Ingalls, but I never met him because he was in a higher grade. He went there to the sixth grade. His brothers Johnny, *Cesáreo*, and *Moisés*[7] went there, too, because they were young. But afterward, they all went to school in Scottsbluff.

I don't know much about that family because Mike and I never talked about that after we got married – about how he came, and even about how we came. Nothing. We never sat down to talk about the families. The only one was *Chole*(iii), his mom, who told me a little bit when we lived with them – that they would go and come back, and they had a house there in Mexico, and stuff like that.

On one of their trips from Mexico, they brought *Chole's* sister *Coni*. She married *Chente* – *Vicente Velásquez* – in Kansas, and they lived there until she died, in nineteen fifty-nine more or less, I think.

Anyway, *don Juan* never worked in Texas. They came to Wichita first to work in the railroad in nineteen ten, and Johnny was born there. I think *don Juan* had relations or something there.

---

[5] Surnames in Spanish generally have no overt plural marking. So, they do not change from singular to plural.

[6] *Miguel Hernández*, Elvira's future husband. Also known as 'Mike' or '*Maique*', pronounced [*MY-kay*].

[7] See *Figure 5*, *The Family of Juan Hernández and Soledad Fonseca*, page 154.

Mike wasn't two years old yet because he was born in *León, Guanajuato.* They went back and forth to Mexico. They went to Mexico for a while 'cause they had a house there, and then they came again. *Cesáreo* was born in *León* in nineteen fifteen, and *Moisés* was born in Kansas City in nineteen eighteen.

The boys all looked like their dad, except Johnny Mack[8] who looked like *Chole.* She was pretty. She looked very Spanish – white, kind of pinkish. That's how Johnny was. He wasn't too dark, but he was the shortest one of the four boys.

By the time *Moisés* was born, *don Juan* was working in the packing house at Swift's, and my dad was at Cudahy's. The last time *don Juan* went back to Mexico was in nineteen twenty-three because afterward they began to go from Kansas to Scottsbluff for the time of the beets. They didn't go back anymore until nineteen thirty-five when the government was sending everybody back to Mexico.

The Fly and the Plow

I think we worked there in Kansas City for about two or three years, because we was in the section in Lawrence, Kansas in nineteen seventeen and we went to Nebraska in nineteen twenty.

I said 'we worked there', like the fly said. The story is that a Mexican farmer was plowing with his *bueyes.*[9] And that's when a fly came over and sat on the plow. The farmer scared it away, but it came back again. All day long, he was plowing one row and then another one, and the fly was still there on the plow.

Finally, there comes another fly, and she asked the first one, "¡Hey! ¿What are you doin'?" The first one just looks at 'er, and told 'er, *"Pos, ¿qué no ves?* We're plowing."

So that's why I said 'we worked' about two or three years in Kansas City. But really the truth is that we all worked, not just the men. Mom had four boarders, men that was also workin' in the

---

[8] *Juan, Jr.* was a boxer who took 'Johnny Mack' as his ring name. Later, everyone continued to call him that, and he made it his legal name. See photo album at the end of this chapter.

[9] 'oxen.'

packin' house. She did everything for them. She cooked their food, she washed their clothes, and cleaned up their rooms. And then with us four girls and *Juan,* who was just born, *no se daba abasto con nosotros.* She just couldn't keep up.

That's why one day she told me, "*Hija,* you're the oldest and have to help me fold the *tacos* for the workers."[10] I was barely nine years old.

She told me, "¿You wanna learn to make *tortillas?* Come on. I'll show you how to make 'em." So, she taught me how to make the *masa* and the *testales* and how to use the *pa lote.* Then she showed me how to cook them on the *comal.*[11] "Don't let them burn," she told me. 'Cause I had to cook one and turn it while I was rolling another one. And so on.

I remember that, at first, my *tortillas* came out all crooked. But I learned pretty quick, and from then on, that was my job. We made a great big pan of *masa,* then the next day we had to do it all over again. In that time, I had to make about six or seven dozen every day. Because there was six adults plus all the children. Then, we had to make all the *tacos* for the workers. In those times, we ate everything with *tortillas.* We didn't use forks to eat with.

Sometimes in the morning, I couldn't wake up 'cause we had to start real early before the men went to work. My mom told me, "*Elvira,* ¡get up!" She would grab my hands and turned me around and around so I would wake up.

No. Afterwards, I got used to getting up early in the morning.

---

[10] In the north of Mexico and in the U.S., tortillas were made, and are still made, from white flour, and 'tacos' were what are now called 'burritos'.

[11] *masa,* 'dough'; *testales,* 'flat balls of dough for making each tortilla'(from Náhuatl *teshtli); palote,* 'rolling pin'; *comal,* ' metal griddle on which tortillas are cooked' (from Náhuatl *comal-li),* originally made of clay.

John J. Ingalls School, Armourdale area, Kansas City, Kansas.

Miguel (Maique),
and don Juan

Kansas City, 1924.

The *Hernández* family, Kansas City 1919.
<u>Back Row</u>: *Maique, Soledad, Concepción* (*Soledad's* sister).

<u>Front Row</u>: *Cesáreo, don Juan* seated with *Moisés*, Johnny Mack.

Racist sign in Kansas City, 1920.
NO DOGS, NEGROES, MEXICANS.

Johnny Mack as a boxer in Scottsbluff.

Comments on Language and Culture

i The colloquial pronunciation of *Cudahy's* in English is something like [kádₑïz]. (The [h] in this context is not pronounced.) The [d] between two vowels, when the first one is accented or stressed, is pronounced in a relaxed manner very similar to the Spanish [r]. The [ₑï] is simplified to [i], and the [z] is pronounced [s]. Voilà: *caris.*

Comments continue on the next page

27

It's important to note that adaptations (technically, *borrowings*) such as this are not 'corruptions' of speech, but are governed by systematic correspondences – the overlaying of the sounds of the source language onto the sound system of the receiving language. The adaptations are performed unconsciously by the original "adapters" in an attempt to copy the foreign sounds that they hear through the filter of their own language. With use, the words become a conventional part of the vocabulary repertoire in the receiving language and are no longer actively adapted by speakers by means of the correspondences between sounds. Such words eventually become integrated into the receiving language and by most speakers are no longer considered part of the donor language. Examples are *tomato* and *avocado*, borrowed into English from Spanish but originally from Náhuatl *tomatl* and *ahuacatl*. They are now seen as 'borrowings' only in a historical sense by linguists.

ii   During the Great Depression of the 1930's, a long period of xenophobia and racism continued as a consequence of the First World War and the Mexican Revolution which was thought to be communist inspired. The U.S. established a policy of "repatriation", i.e. of returning as many Mexicans as possible to Mexico, including persons born in the U.S., accusing Mexicans of taking American jobs. They pushed many to leave 'voluntarily', offering the incentive of taking whatever possessions they wanted free of taxes or duties. That's how the *Chavezes* and the *Hernandezes* and many other Nebraskans left. Others, especially in states like California and Texas, were expelled forcibly on trainloads full of repatriates.

iii   'Chole' is derived from *Soledad* by dropping the final syllable –*dad* (apocope), then changing the s̲ to ch̲. This latter change is extremely common in adult speech to children as well as in nicknames. In a similar way, *Vicente,* pronounced [visente], becomes *Chente* after dropping the first syllable (aphaeresis), which is the most common modification.

Chapter Three

OFF TO NEBRASKA

"¡Oh, qué va! Over there, they have little kids working,
and my family can help me. Not like here.
We're going to Nebraska now for sure."
— Jacobo Chávez

Again, the *Revisadores*

But then, here come those dang *revisadores* from Nebraska to Kansas to find people for the beets. They made meetings with the workers, offering them so many acres and that they would make so much money, and this and that.

And, well, not only that. In the packin' house, the man worked by himself but he had three, four, or five in the family, and all of 'em could work in the field. They needed more people for the beets.That's why you could see the fields here full of families. They didn't pay too much either, but still it was better for them. That was the advantage for the Mexicans to come from the big city to work in the beets.

The *revisador* told my dad that over here they would give us a house and that everybody in the family could work. Even six- and seven-year-old children helped out. That's why he came by himself first, in nineteen nineteen, in October, when topping started. He came from Kansas to see what kind of help it was.

My dad said he was going to Nebraska to see what kind of work that was in the beets. *Nos dijo,* "They tell me you can make

29

good money in the beets. I wanna see what that work is like."
That's when he came here to Scottsbluff. He saw what the
tapeo[1] was, and that everybody was topping by hand. They didn't
have machines yet.(i)

It was at the time of the flu there in Kansas. Not just there – all
over.(ii) My brother *Carlos* was dying. He was just skin and bones.
He was a little baby 'cause he was just born on July 5th. There was
a lotta nurses going everywhere takin' care of people. One of 'em
came to see *Carlos* almost every day.

Dijo mi papá, "If the baby dies, don't even call me or nothing.
Well, ¿how can I come? ¿How would I even know when he died?
If he dies, well, bury him." No. He finally got better, but he was
real sick.

Then, in November, my dad came back real excited. *"¡Oh, qué
va!" dice.* "Over there, the little kids work too, and my family can
help me. Not like here. We're going to Nebraska now for sure."

He told my *tio Santos,* "Andale, take your family. They're big
already. Over there, you can squeeze the juice out of 'em."
Pancha was already married, but my *tío Santos* still had *Manuel*
and *María.* They were about my age, and then *Luz* was about as
old as Jobita. They're the ones that could help. The other ones
were too little yet.

My uncle told him, "Well, you squeeze the juice outta your own
kids. I'm not going."

My dad said, "There's bunches of *güeros* and *rusos* with all
their kids working and helping them."

Oh, yeah. In those times, there was still a lotta Russians
working – German-Russians. Oh! there was bunches of Germans
comin' over from Russia. 'Cause Russia went over to get a lotta
Germans, and they were supposed to get real good jobs in
Russia. But when they saw it wasn't true, they started to leave.

---

[1] Spanish adaptation of English *top(ping)*, 'sugar-beet topping', cutting the
tops off the beets during harvest. The same root has verb forms like *tapear*
'to top beets' and *tapeando* 'topping beets'.

Where'd they go? Over here. Oh! Bunches of 'em came to work just like us.(iii)

Over there by where the church is, they called it Russian Town, and that's where all the Russians lived. Now, it's all Mexican people, but a lot of 'em still call it 'Russian Town'. But they just worked four or five years, and then they asked for a farm. And they rent(iv) to 'em because they were *güeros*. Us, it was a long time afterward before we could get a farm.

Many years later when we were already married, Mike and Manuel[2] went to a meeting that the beet farmers made. They wanted to see if there was a chance to rent a farm. They sat way in back, and I don't think the other ones saw them.

One of the farmers was talkin', "Mexicans now want to rent farms, but we shouldn't rent to 'em. We need 'em to work for us." Mike and *Manuel* just listened, and then they got up and left.[3]

But a few years later, *Manuel* rented a farm at Schubert's in Gering 'cause he worked for 'im, and Schubert knew him. Also, Summerfield knew us real well because we bought gas from his filling station for a long time. So, we rented from him in nineteen fifty-one, and since then we started to farm. *Nabor Guzmán* also got a farm, so little by little they started to see Mexicans as farmers instead of just field laborers.

But when we first came, the Mexicans lived in little one-room houses right in front of that big hole over by the sugar factory. They use to fill it up with beet pulp from the factory. All of that belonged to the sugar factory. But when they made the houses, they didn't put pulp in it no more. It was too smelly. They called it *'la Colonia'* – *la Colonia mexicana*, I guess, 'cause that's where the Mexicans lived.

Also, a lot of 'em lived in a big building that looks like a hotel that's over there going on East Overland, about two blocks from where we turn to go to church. Made of bricks. The sugar factory

---

[2] *Manuel Ramirez*, Jobita's husband and *Elvira's* brother-in-law. See *Figure 4. The Family of Jacobo Chávez and Jacinta Castillo*, p. 108.

[3] This incident was related to me by Joe Ramirez, Manuel's son.

put people in there, too. That one is still there, *pero ahora es rentataria* for low-income people.

'White City' was a big place, too. It had a lotta rooms and a long, long hallway. In the middle there was a big room, with the hallway on one side and on the other side, with doors, doors, and more doors on both sides. They were apartments that had two or three rooms with a little kitchen and everything. It was made of wood, but it was real big. Maybe it was a whole block long. And they put a bunch of Mexican people in there. It was painted all white, and that's why everybody called it 'White City'.

Right in the middle, it had a great big room where they made dances. They had fights, too! They say that the women grabbed each other by the hair and the men fought with knives. I knew about all that because *doña*[4] *Lola García* and *Ramona Quevedo* lived there. I met them later, and they told me about it. *Ramona* was a *manita* from New Mexico,(v) so I think the *revisadores* went over there to find people, too. They brought 'em from everywhere, not just Kansas. *Mexicanos*, naturally.

White City was on the other side of Overland, over there in a field about a half a mile north of the sugar factory. We called it the 'Sugar House'. They tore it down already. Now, they have big hotels and a lotta buildings.

Dice mi papá, "But over there Nebraska we're not gonna live in a house like we have here. Over there, we're gonna live in *chantes.*" We didn't know what a '*chante*' was.(vi) If we only knew! Because a lotta Mexicans went to live out on the farms where they worked.

They put 'em in dirty little houses without springs[5](vii) and full of flies. On top, they just had boards for a roof. But in Kansas City, our house was big and real nice.

---

[4] The title doña (*don* for men) is used with first names as a form of respect or deference for persons of mature age.

[5] 'screens'; also, 'springs' in other contexts. See Comment (vii) p. 43 for an explanation of this convergence.

My mom said, *"¡Válgame!* So we're gonna get in there like little animals. ¿Is that it? ¿What are we gonna do over there? 'Cause we're just fine here. ¿Why are we going?"

"No," dice mi papá. "¡We're going, and that's it! The girls are big enough to help." I was the oldest. By then I was ten years old.

Lawrence, Kansas

So, my dad stayed working *en el Caris* until about March because they didn't start thinning beets until the last of May or the first of June. Then we left Kansas City. The fieldman paid for everything. We rode free on the train. They gave us tickets because they needed people to come and work. A lotta Mexican people were coming from over there in Kansas. That's how the farmers did the beets.

But the work didn't start yet in Nebraska – thinning the beets. So first they stopped us where they needed track workers, over there on a camp outside of Lawrence, Kansas.

Oh! That was so ugly. They put us in some little shacks – little old trailers the same like the one where I got that *astilla* in my foot. There was one trailer for each family that had a stove with two little *comales.*

We stayed there for two months. That's why me and the girls didn't go to school no more that year. How could we? We went to John J. Ingalls until we left Kansas City, and then no more until afterward in Scottsbluff.

My mom got sick in Kansas City, and she was still sick when we stopped. I think it was the flu that was goin' around because she got a real bad fever. My dad went to the *mayordomo*, the man that was the boss there, and right away they took her to the doctor.

The doctor said, "It doesn't look good. We can't cure her." He gave her a medicine, but he told her that she wasn't gonna live, that she was gonna die!

And what about us? Oh, my gosh!

"*¡Válgame Dios!*" *decía mi mamá.* "*¿Cómo?* ¿How can I go and leave all of my family? ¿What will my children do? *¡Dios mío!*" We were all very young. I wasn't eleven years old yet. And my mom was crying. I saw her cry.

Le dijo a mi papá, "I'm just going to ask you one thing." *Dice,* "If I die, *bueno, sea por Dios.*[6] But take care of my children."

Le dice, "*¿*Can you take me with *doña Eleuteria?*" She was a *curandera* – from Mexico, I guess. She was in Topeka, or I don't know what town. *Dijo mi mamá,* "I want to see if she can cure me. So I can stay with my children."

My mom knew about her because she was a *Rentería,* a family she knew in Kansas City. She's *Ernesto's* mom, a man my age that came to live here in Scottsbluff. When he got old, I used to go give him communion at the Center.[7]

So, my dad went to the *mayordomo* again. He lived close-by in a great big house. He's the one who took Mom to the doctor. He had a little girl about eight or nine that used to go play with us until her mom called 'er.

So, they stopped the train that was going to Topeka. They put my mom on a little bed, and they took her away. Oh! We cried so much when we saw her go.

'No, we're not gonna see Mom no more!'

My dad went with her on the train. He was over there for a week. Who took care of us? Well, we did ourselves. My dad told a woman who lived close-by to take care of us. She never did. We stayed by ourselves. I was ten, Jobita was eight, Alta six, and *Cuca* was gonna be five in April. *Juan* was born in nineteen eighteen, so he was gonna be two years old in May, and *Carlos* was still a little baby. I was the one that took care of everybody. But I was still real little, too.

---

[6] 'it's God's will'.
[7] This is how *Elvira* referred to the nursing home, i.e. the 'Center' for old people.

Carlos was still sick, and he cried and cried and cried. Jobita picked him up to get him to quiet down, and she started to jump on the bed to rock 'im. Ooh! *Carlos* fell over, and she grabbed 'is leg, and it twisted. He didn't break nothing, but he got hurt.

All the time that my mom was with *doña Eleuteria*, all we did was cry and fight and play. We took out all the food and the dishes from inside to play house and to play store outside on the dirt. All of us were real dirty. Well, who was gonna wash? They washed with a *lavadero*, so how could we do that? The beds were all dirty 'cause how long was my mom sick? I don't know how long it was, but for us it seemed like a month.

Well, finally Dad told us that Mom was gonna come home. I think they sent 'im a telegram through the railroad or something 'cause, well, who else was gonna let us know? My mom couldn't write to us, and we couldn't either.

So, *doña Eleuteria* cured her. *Le dice,* "I'll get you well, you'll see. God willing," dice, "we don't need a doctor."

So, you see? She cured her.

Well, the *mayordomo* came to tell us that the train from Topeka was there and for us to go get 'er. The depot was about a mile away.

Eee! We were playing outside, and we threw everything! There we go running, *greñudas,*[8] dirty. We were probably full of *piojos.* I think we were, 'cause our heads were itching a lot.

Mom was sitting outside of the depot, where they left her. When she saw us, she came running. Ooh! She hugged us and was crying a lot. Well, of course. Especially because she saw us all so dirty!

After we got back to our little house, *mi mamá le dice a mi papá,* "Look. I can't wash clothes. Take this to town and see if they can wash 'em." She had a big bag of dirty clothes – a great big one. He took 'em to wash.

---

[8] 'having disheveled hair'.

Arriving in Scottsbluff

So, we came from there on the train to Nebraska. We got to Scottsbluff in May of nineteen twenty. I don't know why we didn't keep on goin', so we didn't have to be Nebraskans – Colorado or California or any other place to go.

But we didn't stop at the houses where the sugar company put the people they hired. My dad arranged with a farmer that we was gonna stop at his place, and he was waiting for us. I don't remember his name.

We went to live in a one-room school, way out on the farm, in a school they didn't use no more – a country school. It was all alone in the middle of a field that they had beets planted there. It didn't even have a single tree. They told us that they started to plant in April, but the beets wasn't gonna be ready to thin until about June.

So, we started to fix our house. The school we lived in was just one room. It had a stage like for a piano and so the school children could go up to sing and things like that. On the stage, my dad put a stove and the kitchen. Right away, he put up some ropes to hang sheets to make bedrooms.

Oh! Coming here from such a nice home! Because we had a real good home in Kansas City. Our house wasn't too bad. That's why my mom didn't want to come.

When the thinning started, all of us were out there in the field with my dad. The farmer was the one who showed us how to do the work – which ones were the beets and the ones that wasn't. The leaves of the beets had little red lines on them, and the weeds didn't. And we were suppose to leave just one plant, twelve inches apart. We used a short hoe to do the work.(viii)

The farmer told us, "Your mom can use a long hoe, and she can leave little bunches of two or three plants. One of the children can follow her, and where the hoe leaves a little bunch, they can take out the other ones and leave just one."

I remember my mom so much because she was expecting *Joaquín*. He was born in August, but he died a few months later from diphtheria. As soon as she finished her house work, she went out to the field that was right outside the door of the little school.

Nos dijo, "I'm gonna see if I can help a little bit." 'Cause she didn't know nothin' about working outside the house. In Mexico, women don't go out looking for work. A woman belongs in the house, no matter where she lives. Her work is in the kitchen. But here, she used a long hoe to thin, and she put Jobita behind her picking the doubles. Jobita was barely nine years old.

Mi mamá le dijo, "Look, pull out the weeds and the doubles so you leave just one little plant." So, there goes Jobita, picking the doubles.

Until the farmer comes to look. "Hey!" he said when he saw her, "She's not doing right here. She's leaving only one leaf." But he just laughed. Because they told her just one *matita,* but I think she didn't understand that it meant just one plant.

¡Y fíjate! Alta was just seven years old, so my dad had to teach her. She was so little, so they gave her a short hoe, and there she goes, thinning on the rows behind the house however she could.

Cuca was five years old, but she had to take care of *Juan* and *Carlos* that was still little babies. Mom hoeing and hoeing, and the little kids sitting there in the hot sun. It was so sad to see them over there on the end of the rows.

So there goes Mom, little by little, takin' 'er time. She did a round on the rows, then she went right away to see how the kids were. At noon, she left 'er hoe and hurried up to make dinner. In the afternoon, the same thing to make supper for everybody.(ix)

She worked like that until we finished the thinning. On that first year, my mom thinned five acres all by herself.

Then, there was so much clothes to wash! Well, we didn't have a machine, so we washed everything on a *lavadero.* And so many clothes to iron! In those days, there wasn't no electric irons. We had to put three or four irons on the stove, real hot, and then iron with one of 'em until it got too cold, and put it back on the fire and get another one.

37

I didn't iron yet, but I helped 'er wash whenever I could and to make *tortillas*. I was the oldest, so the other ones, how could they? I was gonna be eleven in June. Jobita was just nine, and the rest were still little.

Here in Nebraska we really suffered a lot – a lot a lot a lot. We worked so hard! Ever since we were little until we left the farm when we got old.

We were about ten miles from town, but my dad used to come walking to town. He walked the whole way. Nobody to give 'im a ride. Every week he came to buy groceries, and then there he goes, bringing everything back. But on the way back, he took a taxi because he had so much groceries. My mom always stayed at home. With so many children, she almost never went out.

Then, the first year after the topping, my dad moved us to town. We didn't stay in the winter because there was no way to go out of the farm because of the snow.

At least he didn't move us to White City 'cause over there we were gonna be real crowded. It's a wonder he didn't because it was free. And we couldn't go to the *Colonia* because our family was too big for those little houses.

That's why he rented a little house on Seventh Street, on the end of Russian Town. Seventh is close by the tracks where the trains passed, full of cows or who knows what. But we got used to it.

The house only had two little rooms and one room in the basement, but at least we didn't have to stay so far away on that farm in the winter, all alone and without a car or anything.

There on Seventh Street there was a few Mexican people, but not too many because almost all the people were over there in the factory buildings. Later on, a lotta those families moved to town.

A little while after we moved, *Joaquín* got sick, the little baby that was just born in August. He got diphtheria, which was real catching at that time. It was everywhere – all over. The policemens came and put us a sign on the house: DIPHTHERIA. STAY OUT. Everyone had to be sprayed. Everyone.

38

But the baby didn't live too long. In about two weeks, he died. The police came over again and said that nobody could go out of the house until the quarantine was over. That was forty days that we couldn't go out so we didn't give the sickness to other people. They didn't let anybody go to the cemetery. Here in Scottsbluff. Nobody.

The only ones that went to bury the baby was my mom, me, and my dad. It was so sad.

"There's bunches of *güeros* out there."
–Jacobo Chávez

Photo courtesy of David and Nancy Zimmerer. Huntley. Wyoming.

Left: *don Másimo García* thinning beets.

Below: *don Másimo* topping beets

Photos courtesy of Hector Rojas, don Másimo's grandson

Elvira's short hoe that she used for thinning beets.

The beet knife that *Maique* used for topping.

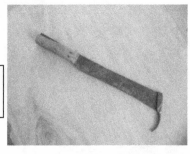

Loading topped beets in Huntley, Wyoming,1936.

Photo courtesy of David and Nancy Zimmerer.

Comments on Language and Culture

i   A sugar beet ready for harvest has the shape somewhat like a carrot, but it is white and is from ten to fourteen inches long and about six or seven inches in diameter. To top the beets, they are first pulled out of the earth with a specialized machine. Then the workers pile the plants all with the same orientation to facilitate the topping. The worker uses a knife, called a *machete,* that is about 15 inches in length and has a hook on the end to pick up each beet. Holding the beet with one hand, the worker cuts off the top. Then it is thrown into a pile for loading into trucks.

In the last half of the 20th Century, machines were invented that performed all these operations in a single pass, eliminating the need to top the beets by hand.

ii   This was the flu pandemic of 1918-1920. It was called the "Spanish flu" because of the fact that the Spaniards, more than in other countries, were the ones who documented and reported the general death rates caused by this disease. In order not to cause panic during WW I, other European countries either hid or minimized the effects of the pandemic which affected 500,000,000 people worldwide. The flu was especially spread by soldiers fighting in that war who were much more susceptible to it because of their crowded living conditions. In Kansas, the military camps near Kansas City almost certainly contributed to the propagation of the pandemic in that region.

Endnotes continue on the following page:

iii   The Germans of Nebraska, Kansas, and the Dakotas of that era were immigrants who arrived from the Volga region of Russia in the last decades of the 19th Century. In 1763, following a period of famine, the Russian Empress Tsarina Catherine II the Great invited Germans to repopulate those lands, offering them the right to maintain their language, culture, and religion (rights which were later abrogated).

Between 1875 and the eve of World War I, responding to the offer of free land by the U.S. under the *Homestead Act,* tens of thousands of these Russian-Germans immigrated to the Midwest. Because of anti-German, and in general anti-immigrant sentiments stirred by the War as well as by World War II against the Germans, many of these immigrants abandoned the German language and identified themselves simply as Russians or Russian-Americans.

For these reasons, even to the present day, many Scottsbluff Mexicans call these folks '*rusos*' or 'Russians', extending these designations to all Anglo-Americans, regardless of their national ancestry. Following WW II, the anti-communist and anti-Russian hysteria led many of these Russians once again to identify as Germans.

iv   In those years, "renting" a farm was essentially share cropping. The owner provided the land, and the renter provided all the equipment and the labor, plus the costs for water, fertilizer, etc. The proceeds from the sale of the crops were split, with 75% going to the renter and 25% to the owner.

v   Among certain groups, especially the *Penitentes*, a traditional religion of New Mexico and Colorado, there exists the custom of using the term *mano* or *mana* as a form of address with a given name, for example *Mano Pablo* or *Mana Teresa*. It is a shortened form for *hermano/hermana*, 'brother/sister' in which the first syllable is omitted in a process called *aphaeresis*.

Because of this usage, many outsiders apply the diminutive of the term, i.e. *manito/a,* to refer to the inhabitants of the region or to their distinctive variety of Spanish. Its use by outsiders is considered somewhat belittling. *Elvira* used the term to refer to any person that uses a variety of Spanish that she considered rather strange.

Endnotes continue on the following page:

vi   *Chante* is not found in the *Diccionario de Mejicanismos* (F.J. Santamaría), but other sources give the origin as Náhuatl *chantli* 'home' (*The Tongue of the Tirilones* by Lurline Coltharp); 'house', 'lodging', 'abode' (*Llave del Náhuatl* by Angel Mª Garibay); and 'house, building, lodging' (*Diccionario en Línea Español-Náhuatl* by Manuel Rodríguez Villegas).

In Southern Mexico among *náhuatl* speakers, there is a well-known rural commune, *Chanti Ollin,* meaning 'House in Movement'. This modern form *chanti* almost certainly derives from *chantli,* noted above, and may be the direct source of *chante.*

Another possible origin of the word is Irish-English *shanty,* whose own origin is probably to be found in the Irish phrase *sean tig,* 'old house'. After considering the various possibilities, *shanty* is the preferred etymology of *The Spanish Language of New Mexico and Southern Colorado: A linguistic atlas* by Garland D. Bills and Neddy A. Vigil.

In the Spanish of the U.S., *chante* refers to a *shack.* The word is also used in Chicano *caló* in a more general sense, closer to the original meaning, e.g. *–¿Pa' onde la tiras, carnal?* 'Where you goin', bro?' *–Pos pa'l chante a planchar oreja.* 'Home, to get some shut-eye (literally, 'to iron out my ears').'

vii   Spanish speakers in the midwest adapted both *screen* and *spring* as esprín because of their phonetic similarity: the Spanish language has only the vowel [i], pronounced like the the ee of screen. It does not have a sound corresponding to the i of spring. So, both converge as the [i] of esprín. Similarly, at the ends of words, Mexican Spanish only has [n], but not [ng]. So, both English [n] and [ng] are pronounced as [n]. (The vowel [e] at the beginning of the word is common in Spanish for words that begin in the consonant combinations [sp, st, sk].)

Also because screen doors were usually equipped with springs for closing, the two English words were not distinguished and were integrated into Spanish as a single word, though one with both meanings, i.e. a homonym.

In *Elvira's* English and that of the Mexican community general, the use of *spring* for both *spring* and *screen* is probably not due to confusion of the two words. Rather, it seems to be the result of a complex process of adaptation from English to Spanish, as noted above, and then "back-borrowing" from Spanish to English.

Endnotes continue on the following page:

Since in local Spanish, _esprín_ is now the common word used for both _spring_ and _screen,_ it is natural that it should be used this way in the English acquired by the newcomers. But now as English speakers, they have acquired the pronunciations of both the [i] and the [ng] of spring, and the recently formed Spanish word _esprín_ is re-borrowed back into English as a single word spring which carries both original meanings.

viii   'Thinning' was the process of cutting the unproductive plants out of the row. In those years, the sugar-beet seeds were planted thickly in the rows to insure that enough plants sprouted to allow for one plant every twelve inches or so. The worker used a short hoe to thin the beets, cutting all the unnecessary beets (and weeds) between the plants that were to be left.

Generally, two or three plants remained close together that the hoe could not cut. So, the worker plucked the unwanted plants, or "doubles", with the other hand, leaving just one.

To accomplish this task, workers had to walk bent over and sideways down the length of each row. Certain persons who could not tolerate this position used a long hoe, but then a second person, generally a child, followed behind the thinner, on hands and knees, plucking the doubles.

In recent times, better seeds have been developed that do not require such closely spaced planting. This allows workers to use just a long hoe, or even specialized machines to thin the beets, eliminating the need for plucking the doubles.

ix   In Scottsbluff, and certainly in other parts of that region, _dinner_ referred to the mid-day meal, while _supper_ was for the evening meal. The use of _dinner_ for an evening meal was mostly reserved for a more formal event. This usage continues today, especially among the older generation, but many people now use _dinner_ for the evening meal and have _lunch_ at midday, adhering to the more general American-English usage.

Chapter Four

OREJEL[1]

They didn't like the Mexican people here.
There was a lotta racism. Everywhere.
'Cause in those times that's the way the people were.

The next year, which was nineteen twenty-one, we went to work for another farmer named Jacob Dorn. My dad always found a farm by himself. He went where he wanted to and where there was better work.

Ever since we got here, he wasn't registered in the company. Oh, Dad was real smart about getting work. The other people, the sugar factory found 'em farms. We didn't live in the company houses either because we rented a house in town. When we were working, we lived there with Dorn, and then in the winter, we moved to town.

But we only worked one summer for that *caracho*.[2] Oh, how I remember that dumb guy because he made my dad so mad when he blamed 'im for stealing some chickens.

---

[1] *Jacobo's* Spanish pronunciation of "Go-to-hell".
[2] Euphemism for *carajo* meaning something like '*damn person*' (which *Elvira* would never utter).

45

Bars of Gold.

No way was my dad a stealer. *¡Ni lo mande Dios!*[3] Never. Especially after they punished 'im when he was young that he stole gold or money from his grandfather.

What happened that time was that my dad and his brothers were orphans, and they had to work hard to support themselves. They grew up there in *Zacatecas* with *Mamá Mariquita,* their mom. She was a widow, so she lived with her father. His name was *don Antonio Rodarte,* and he was my dad's grandfather. My dad told me that the *Rodartes* had money, probably because they stole from the poor people. They were very Spanish. That's why my dad was so white, after his grandfather.

That man was so mean. If my dad didn't do it right what he said, toom! He slapped him and told him, "¡Kneel down there!" For even just a little thing. My dad hated him so much. Whenever he thought about him, he said, "¡That old ta-ta-ta-tá!" But Dad said other words. They sent him to school, but instead my dad used to go to some farmers to help them with their cows or their sheep.

Don Antonio had money, and I think that my dad knew where he hid it. So, one day him and some other boys stole a bunch of gold bars or a bunch of coins *de* gold, something like that. And when the grandfather noticed, he didn't know who stole the money. But then they went and got a lotta boys from around there and made 'em all go to confession. I think that man even told the church what to do.

The boys probably thought that a priest would never say what he heard in confession. They say that a priest should never divulge a confession. No, and in those times I think they were more religious than they are now, anyway.

So, everybody told their sins. And the priest turned my dad in! They punished 'im real hard. But he wasn't the only one who stole because there was three or four boys together. So, how did they really know it was just him? I think that the other ones didn't tell about that sin.

---

[3] 'God forbid!' Literally, *May God not command it!*

From that time, my dad despised the priests, and he went away from the church. But he still went, just once in a while. One time, here in Scottsbluff, Father Portray told Mike to read the Passion of Christ during Lent, on Holy Thursday. My dad went to Mass that day 'cause he still believed in the church but not in the priests. Afterwards he told me, "Oye. Miguel speaks really good." Dice, "¡He even made me cry!"

That's why I say that after they punished 'im for that, I never heard that my dad stole or cheated anybody.

So, for my mom's birth'ay, my dad always made a fiesta. Even if he treated Mom bad, or whatever – because he was real mean to her – every year he brought musicians and made a dance for her birth'ay. He looked for somebody to come and play the guitars because my dad was a dancer and he loved music.

Well, on September 11, 1921 – my mom's birth'ay – on that day my dad went to another farmer and bought a dozen chickens because he invited a lotta people to come and eat. Dorn, where we lived, went to a vacation because topping wasn't started yet. But we were still there, so my dad went to another farmer to buy the chickens.

My dad was the one who killed the chickens. He just grabbed 'em by the head, and ¡pum, pum, pum! He turned 'em around and around, and there goes the chicken flying, with its head in my dad's hand. Oh, I didn't like to see the poor chickens jumping and kicking everywhere without a head.

That's why afterwards I learned to hold 'em so they wouldn't jump. It was so easy. I got my bucket and put it where I was gonna kill it. I got the chicken by the legs. I held it's wings, and I cut it's neck with a real sharp knife. Then I stuck it in the bucket. I didn't let it get all full of dirt.

Well, on my mom's birth'ay, there was a lotta trees where we lived, close to Dorn's house, and in those trees there was a big hole. They peeled the chickens, and they put the feathers and everything in that hole. Then they made the dinner and the dance.

Afterwards, when Dorn got back, he saw that somebody stole his chickens. They stole potatoes – that was the time that they picked potatoes – they stole corn, they stole a lot. Mexican people, I suppose. Well, they were just workers that didn't have nothing, and that's why they took what they could.

Pero mi papá no.

Then they saw the hole with all the feathers and stuff, and the men came on horses. I think they wanna scare us, or I don't know what.

The farmer told me, "Is your father here?" He said, "You know, somebody stole a lotta things. Do you know who it was?"

"No." I told him, "We don't know who. Nobody." I told him, "We're over here, and you're way up the road." It was about a quarter mile. They had so many tractors and other things there that we couldn't see, anyway. "No, we didn't see anybody."

Then they said, "You're the ones who stole 'em."

My dad told 'im, *"No, nosotros no fuimos a robar a nadie."*

The man said, "Yes. We saw the feathers and intestines over there. You stole the chickens."

I told him, "No, my dad went and bought them with that other farmer. You can go and ask 'im." I told 'im who it was, but right now I don't remember his name.

Boy! My dad really got mad! *Dice, "¡Frega'o ranchero! ¡Now* we're not gonna do his work for 'im!"

It was almost time for topping because the factory was already open, and there wasn't enough workers.

Dijo, "And we're gonna leave. Don't tell 'im nothin'. He'll see. Let that son of a so-and-so stay without workers."

He went walking, and he found another farm right away. All the way to Gering! We were ten miles to the north of Scottsbluff, and he went to Gering to a farmer that the factory told him that needed people.

My dad went to see. He had eighty acres. My dad said, "I can't do it all by myself, but I have my family to help, and you can hire more people if you want." But in broken English.

"Oh, yes. Of course," they told him.

He came back and told us, "I got a place. And over there they have a better house." That one was pretty nice. With a stove – it already had a stove – and then it had a little porch and three rooms, so at least we all had a place to sleep.

I don't know where my dad got a wagon so we could move – a wagon with horses to put in everything that we had.

Then, when Dorn saw the wagon there, oh! There he comes, saying "Jake. Don't go."

I think Dorn went and asked the other farmer, and he found out we didn't steal nothin'. He was saying, "Okay, okay, Jake. You stay." Telling 'im not to go.

"No. No. No. ¡Orejel!" my dad told him. He stuck out his arm and pointed his finger to 'im, *"¡Orejel!* No stay here. No steal. *No robé."*

I was so scared 'cause my dad was so mad. Oh! He could'a hit him with a rock he was so mad.

I told 'im, "He said he didn't steal from nobody, and he's not going to work for you anymore."

"Jake. We're sorry. We're sorry."

My dad just pointed his finger, *"¡Orejel! ¡Guirao, guirao!"*[4]

My dad didn't let the farmers tell 'im nothing. That's what everybody should do with the farmers, 'We don't work for you no more!' If my dad had a little more education, he would'a done that with other workers. He would'a said, "¡Don't take nothin' from those farmers!" I think that's why I turned out so *renegada*. I was the same as my dad.

Then, we all got on the wagon with all our stuff, and there we go to Gering, putting on a parade. We left Dorn with his beets, and we did the topping for another farmer. His name was Burbach, and that was in nineteen twenty-one. We did his beets and potatoes for two or three years before we moved to another farmer. My dad was always looking to see where there was better work.

---

[4] *Jacobo's* Spanish pronunciation of *get out,* "We're getting out!", pron. [gid-DOW].

The House on Seventh Street

After topping, when Burbach paid us all the work we did, we were gonna move back to town. My dad went by himself and bought the same house that we rented on Seventh Street. That's the last street before the tracks because that's the only place we could buy a house.

We didn't know how much we made or how much money my dad had. He was the only one with the money. He came back and told us, "I bought the house. *Me costó novecientos pesos.*" Nine hundred dollars.

The house had a big yard in back, but it only had two rooms upstairs and one in the basement. The girls slept downstairs, and the little kids and my mom and dad slept right by the kitchen. By that time, they had *Juan* and *Carlos*, and *Teresa* who was just born. Me and Jobita had two beds in the living room.

What a big family! But we were finally in a house that was our own. That house is still there. They sold it a lotta times, but it's the same. Except that it has a porch with posts to park the car, and it has a great big window in front and it's all painted up.

That first year, we fixed up the house real nice. You should see how nice my dad fixed it up. There was two little rooms, but he took out the wall, and he made a great big room for the living room. Then he had 'em build two rooms in the back, big ones so we could all fit. Then, he made some more big rooms – the kitchen, almost as big as my kitchen here, and then another room for a bedroom. Five rooms. That's what it had upstairs. The basement was just one room, but it was real big. Then, we built a big porch, and we had two windows that we could see out to the street. Oh, we were so happy there! We thought we were rich with that house.

But again, *mi papá trajo bordantes.* You know, boarders to help us out for the winter. But, how could they help? They didn't help nothing!

The boarders came over to eat, and we had to do everything for them, especially the *tortillas*, which was my job. Besides that, we had to do all the housework – washing and ironing for everyone and cleaning the house. It was a lot.

We didn't like having those people there at all. And that made us so mad. But, what could we do? My dad had to go buy groceries there at Diers. That was a store there on Eighth Street. He came back with boxes and boxes of groceries.

My dad, it didn't matter how strict he was with us or how much he hit my mom, we were never hungry, *gracias a Dios*. Never. You never saw him just sitting, without doing nothing. No. Shoom! Out he goes to see what he could find. He was up and down, here and there. He brought food, and it didn't matter what it cost.

We had work over there with Burbach, so he got credit at Diers – all that we want. And he didn't let 'em cheat 'im because my dad, even if he didn't know how to read, he was good at numbers. Everybody knew Jake because in the winter he always paid when we got our money after topping.

So, we came over here to Seventh to pass the winter. Because every year after topping, we moved to the house in town and then, when thinning started, we had to move to the farm again. With all our furniture. And we stayed over there all summer. Well, the farm was too far to go and come every day – about seven or eight miles – and then we didn't have a car. A lotta people did it like that. We were like migrants, except right here in Scottsbluff. Some people went back all the way to Kansas.

My dad always went and got us a wagon to move, and we put everything in that wagon. I remember *las payaseras* we did[5] through town. Two times every year, there we go with the wagons full, the kids on top of the wagons with the mattresses and chairs and all our stuff.

One time, we were on our way back to the farm. We were all on top of the wagons there on Broadway, and we stopped there to buy something. I don't know what.

---

[5] 'the show we put on'. Literally, 'the clowish acts we did'.

51

Juan was little. Real little. He still had a bottle. *¡Válgame Dios!* We must'a been like crazy people there. *Juan* took off running. Running and running with his baby bottle. He climbed on some steps goin' up. And then, he fell down the steps. He cut all his chest with the bottle.[6]

'Oh! Let's get him!' It so happened that upstairs was a doctor's office. 'Take 'im upstairs!' He cut all his chest. I think he still has the scar there.

Oh! Goin' right through the middle of town! 'There goes the parade.'

Anyway, that's how we moved. I remember all that, *y me da vergüenza.*[7] Of the Mexican people. The other people were just amazed.

'Well, what's all that?'

'Oh, they're just Mexicans – beet workers.'

When they moved, they moved on trucks, but not all the time, and without any children on top. Their furniture and that's all. But us, we moved on wagons and with all the kids on top. And two times every year.

We took everything from the house on the wagons because the farms were far away. Eight or nine miles. And we stayed there all summer. Over here, the house stayed all alone because in those times, nobody did any damage in town – only on the farms, stealing from the farmers. Chickens and potatoes and beans. They told us that sometimes, when the beans were ready, somebody would pull out three or four rows. Who did it? The workers, naturally. Well, who else?

Discrimination

That's why at first, they didn't like the Mexican people here. But not just because of that, because the majority of us was just

---

[6] Baby bottles were made of glass at that time because plastic hadn't been invented yet.
[7] 'and I feel ashamed'.

workers. Poor people. But we didn't go around stealing. There was a lotta racism here. Everywhere. 'Cause in those times that's the way the people were.

The Ku Klux Klan(i) burned crosses up on the Bluffs.[8] *Mi mamá decía,* "Oh, look. ¡How pretty! They're lighting a cross for Our Lord. ¡*Bendito sea Dios!*"

We didn't know what that was until later. We were so dumb. The same way on the Fourth of July. *Decía mi mamá,* "I didn't know they celebrated *Nuestra Señora del Refugio* here. They celebrate it so pretty with lights and parades." Because it so happened that the Fourth of July was the same day as the *Virgen del Refugio.*

My dad called the Ku Klux Klan *"Los Cocos".* Because he heard 'Ku Klux' but he couldn't say it. *"Son los Cocos* that don't want the Mexican people here." They were everywhere. They put signs in the restaurants with green, white, and red on 'em to make sure we noticed 'em. They said, NO MEXICANS OR DOGS ALLOWED. Oh, yeah. It was pretty bad here.

At school, too. They didn't let us talk Spanish, even on the playground. *¡Qué esperanzas!*[9] At East Ward, there was a real mean teacher, *la* Miss Ames. She didn't let us get together and talk Spanish. We had to hide to talk to each other. If she caught us talking, she grabbed us and shook us. Just because we were visiting in Spanish. But there was a lotta students who didn't know English yet, and for us, Spanish was what we speak.

Once in a while, we went to the show at the Bluffs because they wouldn't let us go to the Egyptian. Even in the Bluffs and in the Grove in Gering, they sat the Mexicans in the rows in back on one side. My dad stayed at home with the kids, and me and the older girls went with my mom, and we took the older kids to see the show.

---

[8] *Scott's Bluff,* the mount which dominates the North Platte river valley.
[9] 'Not a chance!' Literally, "What hopes!"

53

One time that we tried to go in the Egyptian Theater, they told us, "There's no place." *Que no había lugar.* I never went back to that show. That was just before I got married.

Even the church discriminated us. The only church there was St. Agnes. But the Mexican people didn't go to church until some of us started to go.

Not too long ago, my sister *Consuelo* tried to find her baptism certificate there in St. Agnes because she was born here. She didn't find nothing. My mom probably said, 'It's an American church. I'm not gonna baptize her there.'

At first, we went to church only in the winter because in the summer we were working and we lived too far away. There in St. Agnes, they put us about four benches way in the back where the Mexicans were supposed to sit. I was sixteen, and I said, 'I'm not gonna let that priest boss me around. He shouldn't be like that.' It was a Catholic church and they're supposed to treat everybody the same.

The *Rojas* girls were the first ones. They were pretty good-looking girls. They was sister-in-laws of my cousin Lois.

Well, one time, they came in, all dressed up. They looked pretty. They went and sat down right in front.

Then, the Mass was gonna start, and the priest comes out. "You girls! You can't sit here! You go to the back!"

They got so mad, they pushed over the benches and went out. I don't know if they got away from the church or not. 'If that's the way the Catholic church is here, ha!' Afterwards, they left Scottsbluff. Where, I don't know.

After that happened, the girls that were with us said, "Look at what the priest did!"

I told them, "You know what? I'm not gonna let him do that. Next Sunday when we go to church, let's get in front."

"I'm not gonna sit in front." A lot of 'em was embarrassed.

"¡No! They have to get used to seeing Mexicans. *Somos mexicanos,* but we're from here now."

I wasn't scared. "We're equal. *Come on.*"

"If he tells us to get out, ¡we stay there!"

"If he makes us leave, and he tells us to go to the back, ¡we won't listen!"

"If he grabs us by the hand ¡push it away!" That's what we did. Not right in the front, but in front. And he didn't say nothing. He didn't talk to us. But I said, "I don't care. We're Catholics, and we belong to any church. Don't let 'im."

That priest died a long time ago. *Que descanse en paz,*[10] so he doesn't try to chase other ones away.

Afterwards, who was the first one of the group of the Catholic Daughters – *las Hijas de María*? They elected me. We had that society at our house. And there I told them, "Let's go to St. Agnes."

"No, I don't wanna go."

"Come on. Let's go." So, we kept on goin' and goin'. They knew me. I don't know why, but I didn't let nobody treat me bad. I think I was the same way as my dad.

That's how they started to see me in that church. I went to Mass with all the kids, my sisters, *y los García.* "Come on. Let's go," I told 'em. "We're Catholic, and we're going."

The *Garcías* lived close to us, over there on Tenth Avenue. They used to come to our house, and we went over to theirs. We were together like cousins. Like family. They were about five or six of 'em. We weren't related, but we were good, home friends. *Antonia* was a real good friend of mine.

One time, one of them, *Agustín García,* asked if we could do the Christmas play. They made me Our Lady and the Baby Jesus. I said, "Well, okay, if you want to." We fixed everything up real nice with the Christmas trees and everything. A lotta people went to see it, Mexicans and *güeros.*

So, little by little, we started to open St. Agnes for the Mexican people because we're Catholics. We have to go there. Now,

---

[10] 'May he rest in peace'.

there's a lotta Mexicans that go there. It got to be the same church for everybody.

We learned more about religion in this town. Over there in Mexico, I made my first communion, and I went to Catholic school. But I don't remember going to Mass because of what happened to my dad. My mom didn't go very often, either.

Then, when they saw that we were here, and that we wasn't gonna leave, the bishop ordered them to build churches all around here for the missions for the Mexican people. He made a mission in Minatare, Scottsbluff, Mitchell, Morrill, and Lyman. Those were all missions. Little missions like they make for the Indians on the reservations to teach 'em the religion. But here, we were Mexicans, and we were already Catholics.

We helped build that little church, and we named it Our Lady of *Guadalupe* – naturally. The first priest was Father McDade. That's when we started doing some things. I started the first choir 'cause I liked to sing. We also made the society of the *Guadalupanas*. Some of the boys became altar boys – *acólitos*. And we cooked food to make money to decorate the altar and things like that.

Me and Mike were the first ones to get married in that church.

Elvira with her children next to Our Lady of Guadalupe church where she
and Maique were married ten years earlier. Elvira, Jr. is to her right.
In front of them are Bobby, Bill and Terry.

Photo taken in 1939.

Scott's Bluff seen from the Neil Barbour farm.
Shown are young sugar beets being irrigated

Photo courtesy of Lee Hernandez
Elvira's granddaughter (Bobby and Betty's daughter)

Comments on Language and Culture

i   The Ku Klux Klan was founded in the 1860's to forcibly resist the emancipation of the Black slaves. Since then, it has re-emerged several times, whenever Whites have felt attacked by socio-economic conditions for which they blame other ethnic groups. This was the case between 1910 and 1940 because of the great immigration of Mexicans, and after WW II with the large migrations of blacks to northern cities. Their racist activities continue today in opposition to the continuous Mexican immigration and the influx of Middle Eastern refugees.

Chapter Five

LOS CHAVEZ(i)

In those years, tuberculosis never got better.
When they got tuberculosis, that was it.
Well, lack of eating good, that's why tuberculosis came.

Santos Chávez[1]

After we moved to town, my *tío Santos* and my *tía Pola* came from Kansas City. I think that was in nineteen twenty-two, in the winter. My *tío Carlos,* my *tío Daniel,* and my cousin *Teófilo* all came with 'em.

But the next year right away after we finished the thinning, *dice mi tío Daniel,* "¿Who's gonna do this kind of work? You work like animals here. I'm not staying."

He took off. Him and my *tío Carlos* went to Mexico, and we didn't hear from them no more. *Teófilo* stayed here, but in nineteen thirty-five he got killed in an accident in Torrington.

My *tío Santos* came with six children because *Aurelio* and *Aurora* were born in Kansas. No. I don't think it went too good for them over there, so he brought 'em "to squeeze the juice out of 'em", like my dad said. Maybe because they didn't have no more family over there in Kansas.

---

[1] Jacobo's older brother. See *Figure 2. The Family of Santos Chávez and Telésfora Magallanes* , page 65 at the end of this chapter.

Pancha(ii) was the oldest, but she was with her husband, *Benito González*. They all went to live close to *las casas de adobe* that were on the other side of the ditch, over on Eighth Street by the *Colonia*.

The Mexicans who came here first were the ones who built those homes *de adobe*, like *Manuel y Micaelita Huerta* who got to be good friends with us. Not too long ago, the government was going to make those houses into historical landmarks or something like that, but I don't know what happened. I don't think they got money for that, so they knocked 'em down now. They were just Mexican houses, anyway.

I remember *Pancha* so much because her husband left her. He was always running around. He left *Pancha* with a lotta kids. In those times, there wasn't no help from the government. Nothing. They wouldn't help with anything. So, *Pancha* went to live with my *tío Santos*.

But my uncle didn't have nothing either because they just got here from Kansas, and there wasn't no work in the winter. And they had so many kids! My uncle had *Manuel, Aurora, María, Aurelio y Luz*. And then, *Pancha* herself had five.

Ooh! That's why my dad would take 'em boxes of groceries. Oh, Dad was real generous. He could take off his shirt from his back to give it to one that didn't have any, and he stayed without a shirt. That's the way my dad was. He was very charitable with people that didn't have it, and he took what he could to his brother.

Tuberculosis!

Not too long after, *Pancha* died from tuberculosis 'cause they didn't have enough to eat. She didn't last long. There was a lotta that sickness in those years, I think because there was so many poor people.

So when *Pancha* died, she left Esther, Mike, and Jessie. They were the oldest ones, so my *tío Santos* raised them with him. After he died, they went back to Kansas City. When she got older,

Esther came to Denver for *Pablo's*[2] funeral, but she never came back.

Pancha also left *Aurora* and *Irene,* who were still babies. She gave the two babies away. *Las dos niñas las dio* because she didn't have any money to support them.

She gave *Irene* to a couple that didn't have no kids. A soon as she gave her to them, they took off to Mexico so nobody would know who she was. They wanted to say that she was their daughter.

She grew up and went to California and over there she found out she had family here. I don't know who told her that couple wasn't her parents. She didn't know until then. So, she came to see us, to see who was her family. When she left, she said she would write to us. I don't know what happened. We never heard from her no more.

The other girl they gave to some friends that lived on a farm. She was still a baby, maybe less than one year old. They were already middle age, but they didn't have any children. They were so crazy about that baby, they wouldn't leave her alone for a minute. The were so happy with her, they didn't know what to do. They loved her like a sweet candy. They loved her so much, they said that God sent her to them.

One night they went to bed, and in the morning she was dead! She suffocated. Oh, what her parents must have felt like! I would've gone crazy. But, at least she would'a known they weren't her parents. She didn't have to be asking, 'Who are my parents? Who are they?'

Then, *Pancha's* sister *María* also got TB, and she died from that, too. She was real, real young, 'cause she just had her sixteenth birth'ay. That was so sad for my uncle. For all of us.

There was a priest from St. Agnes that came every day to see her. He told her about Our Lord God, and for her to don't worry,

---

[2] 'Paul Acevedo', husband of Ruth *(Cuca) Chávez,* Elvira's sister.
See *Figure 4. The Family of Jacobo Chávez and Jacinta Castillo,* p. 108.

'cause she was going to a more beautiful place than here. She looked real sick.

There was times that *María* asked my *tía Pola,* "Mamá. Mamá. *¿Cuándo me voy a mi casa?"*

"Hija, this is your home."

"This is not my home no more." *Que le decía,* "No, Mom. I'm very tired here. I'm going now to God, because that's where my home is."

She saw she was going to die. *Que Dios la guarde en el cielo.*[3]

Oh, God! So many poor people. Poor *Pancha.* Poor *María.* They died from tuberculosis because they didn't have enough to eat.

My *tía Adela* stayed in *Zacatecas* when we left. Afterwards, her and her husband came to live in Wichita. His name was *José Valdez.* But their life was too hard in Kansas, so in nineteen twenty-three they came to live with us in Scottsbluff because my *tía Adela* was my *tío Santos'* and my dad's sister.

They came to work, but my aunt knew she had TB, so she just came here to die where her brothers were. She told her husband, "Take me over there. I'm real sick."

They had three children. My *tía* got married way after my dad, so her kids were still little. We were little, too. I wasn't even fourteen yet when she died.

That was in nineteen twenty-three, *en el 'veintitrés.* I think it was around April or May. It was in the spring, before we went to look for a farm to start working. I remember that because I took care of my aunt when she was dying.

When she got real sick, my dad right away got a doctor to come. She had TB. In those years, tuberculosis never got better. When they got tuberculosis, that was it. Well, lack of eating good, that's why tuberculosis came.

The doctor said, "Take her out of here! Out of your home! Tell your dad to take her out because you're all going to get it." He

---

[3] 'May God keep her in heaven'.

said, "It's tuberculosis. It's catching." Right away, my dad rented her a house across the street.

My dad was real 'Go, go, go.' He'd get whatever he wanted. I don't know how he did it, but he would get it. *Luego-luego* he went and rented that house. Right away, and wiithout no money, but he rented it.

The doctor said he didn't want nobody to go in there with her. Nobody. Not even her husband who lived there with us. The doctor only let me go in with her, for me to be the one to take care of her. I don't know why! I think because I was the only one who could talk English to him.

I was fourteen – not yet 'cause that was in 'twenty-three, and she died in April. We were still in the house in town. We always changed to the farm in May.

The doctor said, "I don't want nobody to eat from her plate." He told me, he said, "You neither. You don't eat from that. Tell 'em to bring boiling water, and the plate she eats from, you wash it outside to throw the water. Then you give her again in the same plate. Don't get no other plates." I was the one who took her the food.

Oh, the day she died! I took her supper, but she didn't want any. She was too sick. She screamed so much! *¡Ay!* She just yelled and cried and yelled.

I remember *don Másimo* who was there. The older people could come in now because she was dying. But not everyone, just the family. He was so scared!

I told him, *"Don Másimo*, kneel down and pray." He got the prayer book and he kneeled down. He was shaking.

Dice, "But I can't see it." He had the book upside down.

Le dije, "¿What do you mean you can't see it? Look." And I turned it over for him.

Oh, how my *tía* suffered to die. All night long. She yelled that she saw the Devil coming to take her. She kicked her feet and turned and hit herself. We had to tie her. Oh! I was so scared that I think I saw the Devil, too! She suffered a lot to die.

He took care of her kids, her husband did. He went to a farm to work so he could go back to Mexico. I think maybe him and my dad had an argument, I don't know. But when my *tía Adela* died, he went to that farm and we didn't see him no more.

The Death of Santos

A long time afterwards – I think it was in nineteen thirty-three – my *tio Santos* and two friends found a bottle in a ditch. They thought it was a bottle of whiskey and they got poisoned. That was during the Prohibition when the whiskey was homemade. I think it was that. *Sea por Dios.*

After my uncle died, his children all went back to live in Kansas City. They were all grown up, and they didn't like it here. *Manuel* told me one day, "¡Oh, it's terrible to work so hard! I can't stand it anymore. ¡All night long, I dreamed that I was picking potatoes!"(iii) *Manuel,* he hated it here like the dickens. So, they took all the little kids and my *tía Pola* and left. My aunt died in Kansas. *Qué Dios la tenga en su santo descanso.*[4]

Afterwards, *Manuel* went to California, and he died over there. I think he probably got killed. He was about my age. I think he was a year older. But it's been about twenty years that he died. *Luz* was Jobita's age. I don't know if she's still alive.

Aurelio was the youngest one, but one day we talked on the phone, and I told him to come and visit. He told me, "*Pos no,*" *dice.* "I'm still working." He got to be a waiter en Meulbachs, a big hotel there in Kansas City. He's probably around 83 or 84, if he's still alive. *Aurelio* and *Manuel* looked just like twins.

Some of the *Chávez* are buried in the cemetery here in Scottsbluff. My *tía Adela* is here. So is my dad, my *tío Santos* and his daughters *Pancha* and *María.* I don't know where they are all buried. My dad, yes, but not the rest. It would be good to see if somebody could find them, to see where they are buried. We don't

---

[4] 'May God keep her in his holy rest'.

know nothing about them anymore. There's nobody to tell me!
Nobody to remember them. So many *Chávez*! Only God knows how all those people are.

FIGURE 2. THE FAMILY OF SANTOS CHÁVEZ AND TELÉSFORA MAGALLANES

Mariquita Rodarte + José Ventura Chávez (the second Chávez)

Santos Chávez + Telésfora (Pola) Magallanes

┌Francisca (Pancha) + Benito González

├Ester, Mike, Jessie, and
  two others that Pancha gave away

├Manuel
├María
├Luz
├Aurelio
└Aurora

65

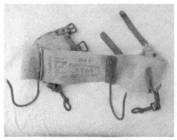

Belt used to pull
the sacks of potatoes.

Workers picking potatoes.

Loading sacks of potatoes
to take to the cellar.

Manuel Chávez, Tío
Santos' son, who
couldn't stand the work
of picking potatoes.

Comments on Language and Culture

i   Spanish surnames are normally not pluralized although the article *'los'* is. So, *'los Chávez'* has a meaning like 'the *Chávez* family' or 'the *Chávezes'*. Capital letters usually do not carry a written accent.

ii   The nickname *Pancha* involves a complex reduction of the name *Francisca*. The <u>fr</u> changes to <u>p</u> (both <u>f</u> and <u>p</u> are pronounced labially); the combined sounds of <u>cisc</u> are reduced to a simple <u>s</u>, which undergoes the common change to <u>ch</u> resulting in *Pancha*.

    In Chicano *caló,* cities are often given nicknames reminiscent of nicknames for persons. In this vein, the city of San Francisco is often referred to in *caló* as *'San Pancho'.*

iii   Picking potatoes was another back-breaking job. Pickers wore a wide canvas belt with two large hooks in back to hold up to 25 or 30 burlap sacks. They placed each of these sacks, one by one, on smaller hooks in front and placed the bag between the legs.

    The potatoes, tubers which grow underground, were dug up with a special machine and left lying on top of the row attached to the large vine on which they grow. The workers shook the vine to remove the potatoes and threw it aside, then they picked the potatoes into the burlap sack, filling it to approximately a bushel (60 pounds). These operations required workers to drag the sacks bent over along the row between their legs until each sack was filled to the appropriate weight. The full sack was then stood up at the side of the row, to be loaded on trucks by other workers and taken to special cellars for storage. A fast picker could fill up to 200 bushel sacks per day.

    Some workers used metal wire baskets into which they picked the potatoes and then emptied them into the burlap sacks. This allowed them to pick on their knees, but they were not able to pick nearly as much per day as were workers who used a belt.

    Children too young to pick potatoes were often enlisted to shake the potatoes off the vines, allowing the picker to fill many more bags of potatoes in a given time period. During the years referred to by Elvira, pickers were paid between $.05 and $.07 per bushel. By the 1950's the entire process had become automated.

Chapter Six

LOS CASTILLO

And all these relations –
my aunts and uncles and my grandparents –
they're always part of us, the ones that follow them.

Papá Lolo

And so many *Castillos!*[1]

My mom was the first one of the *Castillos* to come over here. Other ones came afterwards. My grandpa, the father of all of 'em, his name was *Ysidoro Castillo.* His mother was *Ysidra Pérez,* and I think that's why they named him *Ysidoro.* He was my grandpa, but we never called him *abuelito.* Everybody called him *Papá Lolo.*[2] He was born there in *Chalchihuites* on April 4th, 1850.

My mom says that when *Papá Lolo* was young, he heard about President *Benito Juárez,* even though the only thing he knew about him was *que era indio.*

My mom said, *"¡Imagínate! ¡Un indio como presidente de México!"* In *Chalchihuites,* they also heard about a war by Indian

---

[1] See *Figure 3. The Family of Ysidoro Castillo (Papá Lolo) and María Ortiz* on page 83, at the end of this chapter.

[2] *Lolo* is the conventional nickname for *Ysidoro. Papá* is the title of deference used with the first name of a grandfather. See Comment (i), p. 87, for the phonetic derivation of *Lolo* from *Ysidoro.*

soldiers against the ones from Europe, and they beat 'em.[3] *Papá Lolo* knew about that, too.

Papá Lolo must'a been real impressed because he was an Indian, too. He was *trigueño*, all brown, and he had a big mustache. No. Now he was a Mexican. He wasn't Indian no more, but he had Indian blood. He always wore his big hat, the ones they call *Estetson*.

I think his wife was more white, but I don't remember her. I think so because one of their sons, *José,* wasn't dark. He was kind of light brown, not like *Papá Lolo.* His daughters weren't brown, either, and that's why I think that my grandma was a little more white.

My mom never told me about *Papá Lolo's* family or nothing. The only thing she told me was about an uncle who had a farm there in *Chalchihuites. Papá Lolo* worked with that brother of his, but I don't know what brother. My mom told me that he married my grandma in 1878, and they lived in *Chalchihuites* until she died in nineteen twenty-three. Her name was *María Ortiz.* They had nine children.

The oldest one was named *Miguel,* and he was born one year after my *abuelos* got married. In nineteen oh-three, he went to *Parral, Chihuahua a trabajar en las minas.* My *tío José* told us that some men were hitting one of the carpenters from the mine, and my *tío Miguel* tried to defend 'im. Instead of one of them getting killed, my uncle is the one that got shot. Like they say, *"El que mete paz, saca más".*[4] *Sea por Dios.* He was real young, about 24 or 25 years old.

Papá Lolo didn't find out until I don't know how long afterwards, when a man from over there came to say they had killed *Miguel Castillo.* When they told *Papá Lolo,* right away he

---

[3] The Battle of Puebla, 1862, in which a ragtag army, mostly Mexican Indians under the command of General Ignacio Zaragoza, defeated French invaders led by the Archduke Maximillian. This victory is commemorated as the *Cinco de Mayo.*

[4] "The one who tries to make peace gets more (than he bargained for)".

went to investigate, to see who killed him and why and when and, well, where he was buried, and to know everything.

But he didn't go on the train. He went walking from way over there in *Chalchihuites* to *Parral*,[5] a town that's over here in *Chihuahua*. Far. At least seven hundred miles round trip. *Papá Lolo* could walk a long way because he was still young. Well, this was in nineteen oh-three, and he was fifty-three years old. He was real strong. They say he did the whole trip in about a month.

He went walking so far because *Papá Lolo* was afraid of the train. He lived when they started to have trains, and he told us that those things were made by the Devil. My *tío José* said that when he heard the train coming, he went way up to the hills because the train was gonna pass by where he was.

He never got to see *Miguel* because he didn't find out until two or three months after they killed him. But he got some things that *Miguel* left, clothes or things that he had.

Afterwards, when Papá Lolo's wife died in nineteen twenty-three, he went to live with my *tío José allí en Chalchihuites*. When my *tío José* came with his family to Nebraska, *Papá Lolo* came with 'em. That was in 'twenty-four because my *abuelito* was seventy four when they came. They all passed together.

My *tío José* told us that they didn't want to let *Papá Lolo* cross because they said, "Your father is too old." They said he couldn't work no more. They only wanted to let workers come in.

They took my uncle to the office and told 'im, "But if you want to be in charge of him, and you support him, well, we'll let him in."

Les dijo mi tío, "¡Pos sí. I'll be in charge of him! I'll support him. But he still works."

The man told 'im to prove that *Papá Lolo* still works, so he asked him where he was working.

---

5 Officially, it's known as *Hidalgo del Parral*, about midway between Durango and Ciudad Chihuahua. See *Map 1. Principal Destinations in Elvira's Narrative,* on p. x.

71

Le dijo mi tío, "We were working over here in Velardeña. He worked there in the tunnels where they unload the metal."

"¿De veras?" dice el hombre.

"Sí."

Then they took my uncle outside and took in *Papá Lolo* to the office, and they asked him the same questions. "¿Where did you work? ¿What were you working in?"

He told them where he was working, and both of 'em said the same thing. So they didn't lie, and they let 'im pass. They crossed *en el mero Dieciséis de Septiembre.*[6]

When they got to Scottsbluff, my *tío José* and my *Papá Lolo* came to live with us *en la Siete,* in a little *chante* that my dad made behind the house. That's where we really got to know *Papá Lolo* because in *Chalchihuites* we were all too little.

Oh, how *Papá Lolo* loved his grandchildren! He was so good to everybody, especially the younger ones. Alta remembered how *Papá Lolo* would take them all the way to town – to Montgomery Ward or the show or the stores. They went walkin', 'cause he didn't know how to drive. He got each one of 'em by the hand, he washed their face and combed their hair, and there they all go for their walk. *Carlos,* Jimmy, *Consuelo, Teresa, Juan.* All the young ones. There was so many of 'em, he got a rope and tied 'em all together. There go the bunch of grandkids, all tied up but real happy.

They even showed him some words in English. He would say, *"¡Yu charap!"* They answered him, "No, *Papá Lolo,* you shut up!" They all laughed. Alta said they was naughty with him, but it was all in fun.

My mom *le preguntaba,* "¿Why do you take them?"

Dice, "Pos, so they can get a lot to eat over there." *Papá Lolo* used to buy them candies and ice cream. And after the show, he talked to them about the cartoons they saw. He never got tired, even if we lived far away from town.

---

[6] 'right on September 16th (Mexican Independence Day)'.

Papá Lolo and my uncle Joe lived there at Seventh Street for about two years, but afterwards my uncle got work over here with Charley Barbour, Neil's brother, who gave them a little *chante*. Charley and Neil had two farms that before belonged to their father. Afterwards, my mom and dad went to work for Neil. They lived in a *chante* across the ditch where my *tío José* had his little house. That's the reason that afterwards, Mike and me got work on that same farm, and we lived there for many years. It's funny how things happen.

When both of our families lived there with the Barbour's, *Papá Lolo* went out to help us on the field. He didn't thin beets 'cause he was too old to do that work, but he stayed at the end of the row, cutting the weeds with his hoe, little by little.

I remember him so much when we lived there. Every day, he came over to see my mom. He came in and said, *"Buenos días le dé Dios."*

And my mom said, *"Y la Virgen que lo parió, en gracia de Dios fue concebida."*[7] That's how my mom and *Papá Lolo* said 'good morning'. They never said hello just with *'¿Cómo estás?'*

Always, God was in the middle, no matter what we said. When we said goodbye, we said *"Dios te ayude"* or *"Ve con Dios."*[8] And when we mentioned somebody that was dead, we said, *"Que Dios lo tenga en su santo descanso* – May God have him in His holy rest". When we said anything, we always remembered Our Lord. *"Si Dios es servido* – If God is served", *"¡Válgame Dios!* – God help me", o *"Jesús te ayude* – Jesus help you".

Papá Lolo told us so many things. To pray the rosary, he told us, *"Miren, en la mañana* when the sun is coming up, you get up right away. You pray the rosary to the side of the sun because it's the glory of the day and God will take care of you all day. In the afternoon, you turn to the other side. You pray the rosary to that

---

7 'God give you a good morning.' And my mom said, 'And the Virgin who gave him birth, conceived in the grace of God.'
8 'May God help you' or 'Go with God.'

side because the sun is going down, and it's the guardian of the night." But we don't have that no more.(i)

When we were little, I even got scared because *Papá Lolo* told us a lotta stories about ghosts. One time, he almost caught a witch. *Decía*, "I almost caught her, but she got away. I was sitting outside the kitchen, and I saw her coming. It was a real big bird, black with a red mouth." *Dice,* "Those are the *brujas.* They're coming to put a curse on somebody."

Dice, "Then, I grabbed a basket, and that *bruja* that's been bothering us is gonna fall in there. So I got my rosary, and I start praying to bring her down. There she comes, there she comes. And I'm praying and praying for that *bruja* to go in the basket."

I don't know how many *Our Fathers* and how many *Credos* he was supposed to pray.

Entonces dijo, "And then, just when she was comin' down to go in the basket, ¡I forgot one of the prayers! That dang *bruja* just peeped and flew away."

Just because he forgot one part of the *Credo.* That's the only part he had left.

One day he went to visit *don Juan Hernández,* Mike's father, who lived over there close to the sugar factory, and *Papá Lolo* was telling him about the witch.

Don Juan tells him, *"Don Ysidoro,* ¿you know what? You believe in witches," he said, "but there aren't any witches. Those are lies. They don't exist."

"Ay, señor Hernández," dice *Papá Lolo.* "You haven't seen 'em, and that's why you don't believe it. I almost caught one."

Dice don Juan, "Don't believe it. No, it's not good to believe in witches. *No es parte de nuestra religión."*

Dice Papá Lolo, "Yo sé, señor Hernández. I know it's not good to believe in that." Dice, *"Pos ¿sabe qué?* I don't believe in witches, either. ¿But do they exist? ¡They do!"

Papá Lolo's Family

After they killed my *tío Miguel,* my *tío Hijinio* was then the oldest son. Him and his wife *Carmen* came from *Chalchihuites,* and my aunt *Petra* and her two kids came with them. They all came to Scottsbluff in nineteen twenty-four. My cousin *Luz* was nine, and *Luis* was eight. *Petra* and her children came to live with us on Seventh Street, *en el chante* where my *tío José* and *Papá Lolo* were living. She didn't have a husband, so where else could she go?

She was just there for two or three months, and shoom! Right away she eloped with *don Másimo.*

She came back and told us she got married, *"Ya me casé."*

Oh, Dad was so mad. He was very mad. He wasn't mad because she got married, but because she didn't tell us that 'I'm gonna get married' or something. Nothing.

See, before she came from Mexico, she told my dad to send her some money and she would pay him when she got work here. First, he sent her some. She spent that. And he sent her again. She never gave back one cent, and he sent her so much money. Besides, we barely had any, either.

She eloped like a young girl. How old was she? Well, that was in 'twenty-four, and she was born in eighteen ninety-five. That was still in the other century. So, twenty-nine years old. Yes, she was a grown woman, but at least she should have said, 'Well, I'm going to marry *don Másimo'*.

Anyway, that's her business.

Hijinio and *Carmen* went to live *en la Colonia.* Oh, that *Colonia!* My uncle lived in one of those *chantes* that was just one little room. The little kitchen on one side, and they had their beds and everything in the same room.

One day, *Chole* and I went over there. That was after I got married. We went to visit my *tío Hijinio* and *Carmen.*

"Andele," le dije a Chole. "Come with me.*"

"Okay. Let's go together, if you want"

So we went. We had a car then, and I was the one that drove it.

We knocked on the door for *Carmen,* and she came out, and she was so happy that we went to visit her.

*Dijo, "Espérame, espérame tantito...*wait. Just a minute... Wait for me a little bit. I'll be right back." She closed the door and went in.

Oh, how I remember that time!

No. In a little while she came to the door. *"Pásense."* We went in.

We were in there talking when we saw a big shape sticking out right in the middle of the room.

*Le dice Chole, "¿*What's that?"

Dice, "Es Hijinio. He's taking a bath."

All she did was go in and cover him with a blanket, and then she told us to go in!

It didn't have any closets, no other rooms, nothing except just one room. Yeah. Just so she wouldn't feel bad 'cause she shut the door on us, she went and threw my uncle a blanket there in the tub(ii). '¡Here! ¡Here you go!'

What was he feeling like under there, inside the tub of water? Poor man. But, what was she thinking?

She should'a told 'im, 'Hurry up. Finish.' Then, she could'a come out with us.

*Le digo, "Pero, ¿*why didn't you tell us? We would'a waited until he finished."

We left right after that. Oh, what it's like to be poor!

They stayed here a few years, but I don't remember how many. A while after I got married, they went to Mexico. My *tío Hijinio* died over there. They lived up in the mountains *en un aserradero.* Those are the places where they cut trees to make lumber. That's why they lived in that place. *Carmen* said it was a sad place. She had a little restaurant in the *plaza* close to the movie theater where she sold *tacos.* She died already, but her daughter *Lola* still lives in California. Over there, she's the only one left from my *tío Hijinio.*

So, one by one, my aunts and uncles came from Mexico to Scottsbluff, I think because my mom and *Papá Lolo* were already here. Some of 'em stayed, and others didn't, like my *tío Hijinio* who worked here a few years, and then he went back.

I remember my *tía Feliciana* a lot. She got married in *Chalchihuites* to a man named *Rafael Blanco.* He was from a pretty rich family, but he was a drunkard and he treated my aunt real bad. He beat her and didn't give her money for food. They had three children, poor things. Sometimes those little kids were starving. When we still lived in Chalchihuites, my mom stole food from my dad to take to her sister, sometimes even money. She got it from the room where my dad had it full of *provisiones.*

My aunt wanted to come to Scottsbluff, just with her children, but before they crossed, they stayed a while in *Juárez.* One day, her son *Nieves* was playing with a rifle. I don't know where he got it. He got careless and the gun went off. It killed my aunt. They buried her there in *Juárez.*

Afterwards, the oldest daughter *Cuca* came with her brothers to Scottsbluff. She was a little bit older than me. I think all of this happened in nineteen twenty-four or nineteen twenty-five because we already lived in the house on Seventh Street. *Cuca* started a little *chilistencito*[9] for the Mexican people. But she just stayed one year, and then they went back to Mexico. We didn't hear no more from them.

Another one that came was my *tía Camila.* She was married with a half-French named *Couturier.* They came to Nebraska to work, but they didn't like it, so they went to California.

That was real sad for *Papá Lolo* because he said he was never gonna see his daughter no more. And he didn't because she got run over by a car in nineteen thirty-two. She was going home from work in Los Angeles. It was raining. The car passed by and,

---

[9] 'a little Mexican-food stand'. (*Chilistén* is Elvira's own word, adapted in Spanish from *chile* plus English *stand,* on the pattern of *hotdog stand.*)

¡Tómala! The car hit her, and left her laying there. They say the driver was drunk.

Camila's daughters were my cousins *Englantina, Raquel,* and Ruth, and her son was *Genaro.* I think Genaro got killed, but I don't remember.

Ruth was the one that came when we made the reunion for *Papá Lolo.* That was in two-thousand six.

Raquel is the one that came to Scottsbluff to take care of my *tío José* and *Chuy* when they got old. She lived across from where they lived, on Eleventh. She took care of them for about six or seven years.

Afterwards, she went to California. She writes to me once in a while. I do too, but I'm real lazy to write. She wrote and told me that *Englantina* died. *Englantina* was the oldest of *Camila's* four children. She's the one who had the triplets that still live there in Los Angeles somewhere.

I haven't heard from Raquel for a while. She's the only one I keep in contact with. She came about five years ago, just for a visit.

I have some cousins in Chicago that are daughters of my *tía María de Jesús*(iii). They were *Graciela, Trinidad,* and *Jovita*, but I don't know when they came to the United States. One of them started a *tortilla* factory. So, in Chicago they had *tortillas* there when they came! Here, there wasn't no *tortillas* made in a factory. We did everything with a *palote.*

I knew them when they were little and came to Scottsbluff, so I probably also knew my *tía María*, but I don't remember. I saw my cousins afterwards when they came for my ninetieth birth'ay with some of their daughters. After so many years!

Another aunt also lived in Mexico. *Eloisa.* She was the youngest one of *Papá Lolo's* daughters. She was the only one of my aunts that never came to Scottsbluff. She got married to a man named *Olloqui,* and they had three daughters. Two of them went to live in Mexico City, and my sister *Teresa* knew them over there. But after they went to *Mexicali*, we never heard from them no more.

From all the *Castillos,* only my *tío José* and *Petra, mi Papá Lolo y mi mamá,* they're the only ones buried here. Well, who else?

So, in my family, everybody came from *Chalchihuites.* That's where we're from. It's our hometown. But now, Scottsbluff is our hometown. We finally settled down here after living like tramps up and down, my dad always looking. But now we're from here, both the *Chávezes* and the *Castillos.*

And all these relations – my aunts and uncles and my grandparents – they're always part of us, the ones that follow them. The ones that are left, they're buried here. Me, too, because here is where I'm gonna be.

PAPÁ LOLO WITH EIGHT OF HIS YOUNGEST GRANDCHILDREN CHILDREN OF JACINTA.

Back: Juan, Teresa, Carlos.

Front: Jim, Papá Lolo with Ramiro, Linda, Consuelo, Arthur.

Photo taken in 1931 behind the house that Jacobo bought on Seventh Street in Scottsbluff.

Ysidoro Castillo con Maria Ortiz

E

En la Sta. Yglecia Parrog.l de S. Pedro de Chalchit. a los
dos dias del mes de Mayo de mil ochocts. setenta y ocho, pre
via la correspondiente informacion matrimonial de libertad
y soltería, y publicadas las tres canonicas moniciones inter
missarum solemnia prescritas por el Sto. concilio de Trento
que lo fueron el veinticuatro y treintaiuno de Marzo y siete del
ppo. Dom. 3o. y 4o. Quadrages. y la de Pasción de N. S. J. C. y no
habiendo resultado impedimto. alguno aun despues de pa-
sadas veinticuatro horas despues de la ultima monicion,
Yo el Pbro. Fran.co Lujan cura encargado de esta Parroq.a
casé y velé á Ysidoro Castillo, de veinticinco años de eda
soltero, originario y vecino de aqui hijo legitimo de Ramon
Castillo y de Ysidra Perez = con Ma. Ortiz de diez y seis
años de edad, celiba, orig.a y vecina de aqui hija legitima
de Ramon Ortiz y de Fermina Ortega, fueron testigos
Pedro Castillo é Ildefo. Samaniega. Y pa. q. conste lo firmé

Franco. Lujan

On the preceding page is a photocopy of the Marriage Certificate of Ysidoro Castillo Peréz and María Ortiz Ortega, archived in the church of San Pedro in Chalchihuites, Zacatecas. The parish priest was so generous as to permit me (Eduardo Hernández), my wife Ysaura Bernal-Enriquez, and my aunt Consuelo Chávez Viuda de Piedra to examine the books of the historical registers of the parish. We sought documents pertaining to the sacramental certificates of Elvira's parents and siblings. One can only imagine our surprise and elation on hearing Ysaura exclaim, "Could this one be Papá Lolo?' And indeed it was.

For the reader's convenience, we include here the translation of the ancient document.

"In the holy parish church of San Pedro in Chalchihuites on the second day of the month of May of eighteen hundred seventy eight, with prior matrimonial information corresponding to their freedom and unmarried state, and having published the three canonical announcements Intermissarum Solemnia prescribed by the Holy Council of Trent, done on the twenty-fourth and thirty-first of March and the seventh of last month, the third and fourth Sundays of Lent and on the Passion of O.L.J.C., and there not having resulted any impediment, even after the passage of twenty-four hours following the final announcement, I, the Presbyter Francisco Luján, priest in charge of this parish, married and gave the sacrament to Ysidoro Castillo, twenty-five years of age, single, native and resident of this place, legitimate son of Ramón Castillo and of Ysidra Pérez, with María Ortiz sixteen years of age, single, native and resident here legitimate daughter of Ramón Ortiz and Fermina Ortega, witnesses were Pedro Castillo and Yldefonso Sariñana. Let it be affirmed that I signed,

Fran^{co} Lujan"

Los Castillo

THE CASTILLO FAMILY OF SCOTTSBLUFF
A FEW OF PAPÁ LOLO'S DESCENDANTS

Back Row: Juan Chávez, Miguel Castillo, Ruth (Cuca) Chávez, Petra Castillo, Jesús (Chuy) Castillo.

Middle Row: Jobita Chávez, Elvira Chávez Hernández, Carlos Chávez, Altagracia Chávez, Luz Rojas (with son Hector), Teresa Chávez, José Castillo, Timotea Castillo (with daughter Nellie).

Front Row: Ramiro Chávez, Eduardo Hernández, Elvira Hernández, Jr., Hermelinda Chávez, Joaquín Chávez, Constancia Rojas, Arturo Chávez, Jacinta Chávez (with daughter María)

FIGURE 3. THE FAMILY OF YSIDORO CASTILLO
(PAPÁ LOLO) AND MARIA ORTIZ

Ramón Castillo + Ysidra Pérez
|
Ysidoro Castillo Pérez (Papá Lolo) + María Ortiz Ortega
|
- Miguel (unmarried)
- Hijinio + Carmen Simental
- Jacinta +Jacobo Chávez
- Feliciana + Rafael Blanco
- Camila +José Mª Couturier
- José + Timotea Castañeda
- Petra + Másimo García
- Mª de Jesús + Gonzalo Hernández
- Eloísa + Miguel Olloqui

SOME OF THE CHILDREN
AND OTHER DESCENDENTS OF PAPÁ LOLO

Papá Lolo's son, Hijinio Castillo, and his wife Carmen.

Papá Lolo's son, José Castillo pictured with his niece Altagracia, Elvira's sister.

Papá Lolo's daughter Petra Castillo and her husband Másimo García.

Photo courtesy of their grandson, Hector Rojas.

Papá Lolo's granddaughters Jobita Ríos, Gracia Lira, and Trinidad Urdiales: Daughters of Mª de Jesús Castillo de Hernández.

Raquel, daughter of Camila Couturier and grandaughter of Papá Lolo. Pictured with her husband, Ernesto Vega

The *chantes* where the Chavezes and the Castillos lived. José Castillo y Papá Lolo lived in the one in back; Jacobo Chávez and his family lived in the one in front. Later, Elvira and her family lived there, too. The child is César (Bill) Hernández.

Photo taken in 1938.

The headstone installed on the grave of Ysidoro Castillo Pérez by his great-grandchildren on the 3ʳᵈ of September, 2006 on the occasion of the Castillo family reunion in Scottsbluff, Nebraska. The image of Papá Lolo was designed by his great-grandson Carlos Hernández Chávez, based on the photo on page 85, and was sculpted by laser.

Below. The original headstone, placed on his grave after his death in 1934. It was always buried in the grass, so it was taken out and incorporated into the base of the new headstone.

Comments on Language and Culture

i   As noted by Elvira, Papá Lolo was racially and, at least in this way, culturally, an *indio*. So, this custom is almost certainly a syncretism of Catholicism and the widespread, if not universal, indigenous reverence for the Four Directions and veneration of the Sun as God. In Native ceremonies, participants face North, South, East, and West in turn, then to the Sun, as a central aspect of their devotion. Lolo is derived from *Ysidoro* by the familiar dropping of the first two syllables, leaving *doro*. [r] changes to the closely related [l] and the [d] follows suit by a process of consonantal harmony.

ii   Farmworkers generally did not have running water in their houses. They got water from a hand pump located outside the house, and they heated it on wood stoves. They bathed in portable galvanized metal tubs that were also used to wash clothes. These tubs were about three feet in diameter and eighteen inches or so deep. As is seen in the incident described, the "bathroom" was the kitchen.

iii   Like Kansas City, Chicago was an important destination for Mexican migrations in the latter decades of the 19th Century and the early decades of the 20th. Although emigrants from *Zacatecas, Durango,* and *Guanajuato* tended to cross the border at El Paso, Texas, on their way to Kansas and Nebraska, those who left from *Nuevo León* or *Tamaulipas,* further to the northeast, crossed through Laredo, Texas. Many of these followed the railroad and the cattle industry to St. Louis, Missouri and Chicago, Illinois.

Elvira's aunt, *María de Jesús*, married *Gonzalo Hernández* with whom she went to live in *Monterrey, Nuevo León*. Later, they followed the same route as others and established themselves in Chicago

MAP 2

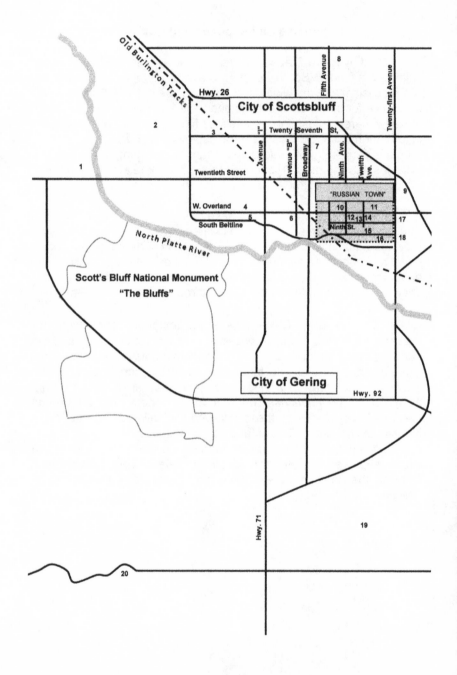

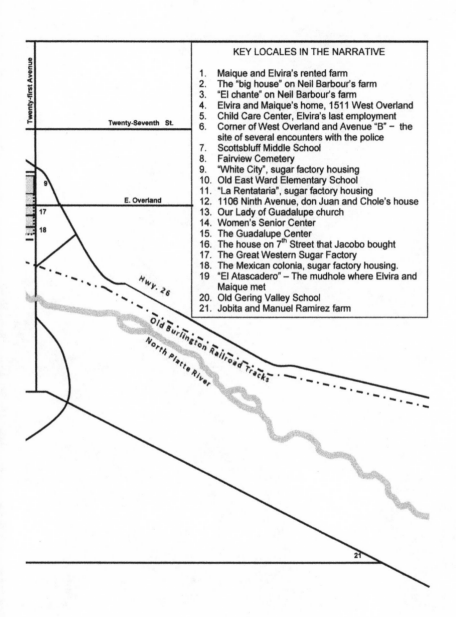

KEY LOCALES IN THE NARRATIVE

1. Maique and Elvira's rented farm
2. The "big house" on Neil Barbour's farm
3. "El chante" on Neil Barbour's farm
4. Elvira and Maique's home, 1511 West Overland
5. Child Care Center, Elvira's last employment
6. Corner of West Overland and Avenue "B" – the site of several encounters with the police
7. Scottsbluff Middle School
8. Fairview Cemetery
9. "White City", sugar factory housing
10. Old East Ward Elementary School
11. "La Rentataria", sugar factory housing
12. 1106 Ninth Avenue, don Juan and Chole's house
13. Our Lady of Guadalupe church
14. Women's Senior Center
15. The Guadalupe Center
16. The house on 7th Street that Jacobo bought
17. The Great Western Sugar Factory
18. The Mexican colonia, sugar factory housing.
19. "El Atascadero" – The mudhole where Elvira and Maique met
20. Old Gering Valley School
21. Jobita and Manuel Ramirez farm

Chapter Seven

A NEW LIFE

*Me, I always liked art and music, if I only had the chance.
"¡Ha!" dijo mi papá. "¿Now you wanna be an artist?
Women are just supposed to work in the house."*

The New Ford

Don Másimo was the first one in the family to buy a car, *en el veinticinco,* in nineteen twenty-five. He used to go visit us with his car.

'Ooh! ¡Look at *don Másimo!'* And us, we were so anxious to have a car so we could go to town from the farm.

Then, a year later was when my dad bought his first car. I was the one that went around everywhere with him because he didn't know English, so I went with him to order the car. When we went to town, he went first walking by himself, and then he came in a taxi to take both of us.

So, we ordered the car, but they had to send to the factory to make it. The man told us, "It will take a while for it to get here." That was in the summer, but I don't remember the month.

Well, in August my dad went to see if they got the car yet. A few hours later, he came back in a taxi.

He said, *"Andale, vámonos.* The car's here already."

Le dije, "¿But who's gonna bring it?"

He said, "*Pos,* you have to learn because we have to bring the car." Ha! How am I supposed to learn to drive the car if I never did that?

I told him, "I could do it if you didn't yell so much. But you always yell." 'Cause he yelled for everything. '¡Don't do it like this! Do it like that!'

Le dije, "I'm not going."

So, he told me, "*Bueno.* I won't yell at you."

"Okay."

But I was scared. Well, I was only seventeen years old.

No. The car was already there at the store. The Ford garage was there right in the middle of Broadway. Oh, what a pretty car! It was kind of greenish – dark green. Square, with windows.

So, when it was time to take the car, the man said, "Who's gonna drive it, your dad?"

"No, he doesn't know how."

"Then you."

"No, I don't know how."

He said, "You don't?"

I told him, "No, I don't know."

He said, "Come on. Let's go. We're gonna ride around town. I'll show you how to drive."

He showed me. "With this – we drive it with this. Just underneath, we have the stop and go. You turn this up. Down. That's all. And then the gas is here, and then the clutch, and then the brake, and then you give it gas again."

And over here I was supposed to do I don't know what, and then with this hand over here! And the clutch again, then the brake.

The poor guy was just, "Now! Do it! Do it! The other one! Now. This is for this! This is for that! Now!"

¡Uy! Válgame Santo Niño de mi vida. He's telling me over here, and my dad's sitting in back. "*Hazlo. Hazlo.* Do it like he tells you."

And I'm seventeen, and I wanna learn so bad! Well, that's how he took me around for more than an hour, and I learned how to drive. Just with only that. I was the first one to drive it – nobody else could. The other ones were too young.

We left the garage about ten o'clock, and I drove it to the farm. In nineteen twenty-six we were working with McKennan, about seven miles outta town. I drove all the way over there. But I was so scared.

Y mi papá telling me, "¡Not so much gas! ¡Don't push the brakes so hard!"

¡Híjole! I didn't say nothin'. But I drove it as best as I could. I gave it the gas. And then the brakes, and then the clutch. But the good thing is there was no stop signs.

We were so happy with our new car! It was prettier than *don Másimo's* that was one of those cars that had curtains, an old-fashion car. And it was cold in the winter. Ours was better 'cause now they had windows, and we were real comfortable inside.

Not too long ago when I went to the bank, they were selling little model cars of old cars. And then I looked at 'em. 'Oh!' I said. 'A 1926 Ford. Just like the one we had!' Well, I bought it, and I have it there.

Cheap Soap

After we bought the car, they knew my dad everywhere here in Scottsbluff. "Hey, Jake. You want some wind?" That's what they said to him when we went in the filling stations for them to put air in the tires. In those times, you went in, and they did everything. They even washed your windshield.

We went in, and he told 'em, "Hey! Put me some wind." But he didn't know there was two words for 'air' in English. For him, they were the same. But he could make himself understood, *a señas y en inglés todo mocho.*[1]

---

[1] 'signing with his hands, and in broken English'.

One day, he went to the store to buy some soap. Oh, how I remember the 'cheap soap'. My mom told him to go get some soap for her because she didn't have any to wash. He was the one with the money, so he bought everything. So, he went over here to Diers Brothers to get some soap.

He told Diers, "Hey. Gimme soap." In those times, you asked the clerk what you needed, and they brought it to you.

"Uh-huh. What kind?"

"Cheap soap."

"Cheap soap?" There goes Diers to look for it. He brought him some chips, soap that comes in little pieces.

"No, no, no. Cheap soap!"

"This is the cheapest I got."

"Come on! Cheap!"

There goes Diers to go look. He told him, "Come on. Show me."

So there goes my dad to go show him what he was looking for. Finally Diers saw what it was.

"Oh, sheep soap! Okay. Sheep. You're right, Jake, you're right. Sheep soap." It was Crystal Soap, but it had a picture of a sheep on it.

My dad made himself understood. But in those times you had to ask for everything in the stores. It wasn't like now when you go get it and you take it to the cash register.

My dad wanted to learn how to drive, too, but he wrecked it. That was the first wreck. I think he was drunk. He didn't wanna drive it no more. From then on, he made me the driver.

Afterward, when I was with him, I told him, "*Mire, Papá. ¿Sabe qué?* You like to drink too much." *Le dije,* "One of these times, if I wreck or something and you're drunk, they're gonna put you in jail, and they'll take my driving license away."

He listened and little by little, he started not being so drunk.

Jake's Temper

When he was drinking, my dad was real mean to us. We were really afraid of him. He came home drunk, and he would hit my mom, and he hit the boys, too. If they didn't do what he said, wham! He hit the boys with the belt. Not the girls, though.

But he didn't hit 'em like *don Juan* did. Never! That man was a beater more than anything. No, my dad was more yelling and noise than anything.

He'd go over to one of 'em, or he'd go to another one, *"¡Muchacho carajo!"* And he'd kick at 'im. And as soon as he lifted 'is foot, the boy would run. But he was just mean with *Juan, Carlos,* and Jim. The young ones, they didn't even pay attention to 'im.[2]

When my brothers grew up, they were terrible, too. Not all of 'em. Some. The worst one was *Arturo,* but because he went to the army, and he used to get drunk over there. When he got back and got married, ooh! He was worse than anything.

Arturo was really bad with Ruth. She finally left him. Until she started to lose her mind, and her children took her to the Center. Then, finally, *Arturo* began to think about how she was and how he was, and then he was real good to her. He went to the Center every day to see her and give her to eat. Poor Ruth. At the end, she didn't know nothing. Before she died, she was almost blind and couldn't talk.

Carlos was the same with *Lola,*(i) because *Carlos* was just like my dad – a drunkard and a hitter. He hit *Lola* a lot. He came home drunk just to treat her bad. He would yell at her, "¡You so-and-so woman!" He'd grab her and *¡tan, tan, tan!* There she goes, down on the floor.

I wouldn't get married to a man like that. Even if we argued and got mad, Mike never hit me. My children never saw that. *Nunca.*

---

[2] See *Figure 4. The Family of Jacobo Chávez and Jacinta Castillo,* page 108 at the end of this chapter.

95

But that's the way the men were. They grow up seeing their father, and they're the same. Just *Juan* with *Chita* and *Joaquín* with Onie, they weren't like that. I don't think *Ramiro* was, either.

When my dad wasn't drinking, he was real good, but he was mean with my mom, though. He never hit the girls. But my mom, he hit her a lot.

One time he hit me. That's why I was afraid of him. I was sweeping the floor, and my dad was sitting over there. *Teresa* was running around there in the kitchen. She was little. She was about five years old.

"Get out of the way," *le dije.* "¿Can't you see I'm sweeping?" So then, when I had a pile of dirt, I told her, *"Tere,* go get me the dust pan."

Dijo, "¡Tráelo tú!" She was little, so she never mind me, anyway.

I told her again, *"¡Dame el recogedor!"* Me too, I was stubborn.

Dijo, "¡No!"

So I got the broom and I hit her with it.

"¡Yaaa!"

And then, my dad stands up. *Me dio unos fajillazos!* He hit me with a strap 'cause I made her cry, 'cause I hit her with a broom. 'Cause she wouldn't bring me the *recogedor. ¡Shu!*

Me dijo mi papá, "That'll teach you to hit someone." *Dijo,* "¿What'd you hit her for? She's so little."

I didn't say nothing. Well, what could I say?

One other time, Jobita and I were in the kitchen drinking a cup of *atole.*[3] My mom had given Jobita un condolchito. These were like fried *masa de tortillas* with sugar. We'd stick 'em in the *atole* to get 'em wet. They was really good. They were like *buñuelos,* but softer.

I told her, *"Oye,* you already had one. *Dame ese condolchito."*(ii) And I took it away from her.

---

[3] *Atole* is a hot drink made of corn meal or the meal of other grains.

Ooh! My dad heard me, and right away he got up and took the *condolchito* and the *atole* away from me.

"*Oye.* ¿What'd you take that away from her for? It's not yours. Go in the other room, and leave 'er alone." He didn't hit me that time, but he sure scolded me good.

Another time I remember a lot, *Juan, Carlos,* and the girls went to the show. My cousin *Luz Chávez* was with 'em. By then, the girls could go if the boys went along, too. I was already married, and we lived with *don Juan* and *Chole.* The boys brought my mom and dad over to visit us while they went to the show.

My dad told the boys to come home early, as soon as the show was done. The first show was over about ten. But then, the second show started because it was a double feature.

Well, they liked it so much, they stayed to see it. They didn't get out until about twelve thirty. At night. Yeah, 'cause the first one stopped at ten, and then the other one didn't start until afterwards.

Over there where we were, my dad said, "¿Where are these people?" *Dice,* "They left us here like fools."

Entons', le dice a Maique, "Miguel" – that's what he called 'im – "Miguel, take us home. I don't know where these people are." He was madder than heck.

So, we took 'em home. My mom was real scared.

No. When the kids finally got home, eeee!

"*Pos ¿¡'ónde estaban!?*" Oooh! He goes after them. He was trying to hit 'em with his hands.

But *Juan* grabbed my dad's hands when he tried to hit him, and he said, "*Papá, no hicimos nada. No hicimos . . .*"

"¡What do you mean you didn't do nothing! ¡You come home at this hour, and here I am waiting and waiting like a dang fool!" But he used another word.

And Luz Chávez keeps saying, "*¡Tiyito, tiyito! ¡Por favor, tiyito, tiyito!*"

¡*Qué 'tiyito' ni que nada!*[4] She was scared like the dickens.

And then, Jobita got scared when Dad was over there goin' after *Carlos* or I don't know which one. ¡*Paaun!* She fainted. He just looked at her, and he turned to my mom, "Hey, come an pick this girl up." *Dice*, "She fell down over here." But he was madder than anything.

Girls' Behavior

My dad was always very strict. With all of us, but more with the girls. Before I got married, we couldn't go out of the house for nothing. He sent the boys to the store, but not the girls – only if my mom went with us. Diers was real close, and sometimes we went walking with Mom. We also went walking to town, but only once in a while if *Papá Lolo* or my mom took us to the show.

And we're not supposed to talk to no boys. Never. Not even in church. When the girls went to Mass, my dad went with us. He didn't let us go by ourselves.

He told us, *"Andenle. Vámonos."* We would go, and he would stay way in back sitting down, to see that we didn't talk to nobody.

The only boy we could talk to was *Agustín García,* who was my same age. *Don Simón* and *doña Lola* were *compadres de mis papás,*(iii) and that's why their children were almost like they were family. But to no other boys.

When we went out to go to Mass or to school, or even if just to the store, he never let us go without stockings. Not even with just socks. If we wanted to wear socks, we had to put on our stockings first and put the socks on top. But not without stockings.

---

[4] "Please, *tiyito, tiyito.*"
'*Tiyito*', hah!' ('*Tiyito* is the diminutive form of *tío*, 'uncle').

Flour from a Different Sack

And Dad never let us cut our hair. No way he would tell us we could cut our hair! No, the girls should have their hair long. Girls shouldn't have their hair cut. No, no! My dad, never! That was just for different kind of women, not for us girls.

I really wanted to have my hair short because that was the style – short hair for girls. But I was too afraid of my dad, so I didn't cut it.

Altagracia y Cuca *sí*, they cut their hair, down to here, just on top of the shoulder. Short like that so they could put it in little curls.

"*¡Ay!*" *Mi mamá dice,* "*¡Válgame Dios de mi vida!*" *Dice,* "*¿What's your father gonna do if he sees you?*"

They cut it anyway, but they hid away from Dad as much as they could. When he was at home, they were always real busy, and they tied their hair up with a bandanna.

Anyway, after I got married, Mike told me, "Do you want to cut your hair?" He said, "I'd like it if you want it."

"Oh, goodness, yes."

He said, "Go ahead. *Córtatelo así* real pretty the way you like it."

So I cut it all bob, short like this so it was just over my ears. Just real short hair, without kisses. They called that a shingle bob.

Later on, I went over to my mom and dad's for a visit. He didn't know I cut it. Mom was making *tortillas*, and I was cooking them. Helping her.

That's when my dad came in. He sat down in a chair behind us with his legs crossed. I was turned around to the stove.

So, there he is, "¡Uh-huh! ¡Uh-huh! ¡Just look at you! ¡How beautiful you look!" *Dice,* "You look like a bald sheep. If you was mine, I would chop it all off ." *Dice,* "¡That way you'd really look pretty!"

¡Ah, caramba! I didn't say nothing.

Then my mom turns around and tells him, *"¡Ja, ja! Pero como ya es harina de otro costal,*[5] you can't do nothing to her."

My dad just ran out real mad. But that's the way he was. You couldn't change him.

No. When I lived at home, he watched us like an eagle. The school we went to was over on East Overland, and to get there, we had to go across Ninth Street because we lived on Seventh. On the other end of Ninth Street they had a lotta bars and other places that wasn't very nice.

My dad would say, *"La Nueve es un ta-ta-tá,"* but he said a bad word. "I don't want the girls goin' through Ninth Street." That's why we had to go around through another way, over there close by where the church is.

He went a different way, and us four girls went over here by another street where we were supposed to cross Ninth Street to go to school.

My mom told us to be careful, *"Cuídense, hijas.* Because when you go, your father goes to see what street you're goin' on. If you don't go on the one he says, he'll hit you with the strap."

Ooh! We were scared of him. Real scared, until he took us out of school at the sixth grade. 'Out!' He didn't want us to go to school.

Girlish Dreams

Cuca really wanted to go to school. She was gonna pass to seventh, to junior high school. Everybody says that the one who passed to seventh, it's better. But my dad didn't let her go. He said she was fourteen now. She was just gonna go so she could talk with the dumb boys. That's all she wanted to go to school for. Girls weren't going to study or nothing. Women are for the house and that's all. To work at home.

She went and told the principal that she wanted to go to school but my dad didn't wanna let her go.

---

[5] "Ha, ha! But because now she's flour from a different sack, . . ."

The principal said, "If you want to go to school, you can come because you're still entitled to go to school. And your dad cannot stop you from going to school if you want."

Then, the police came to my dad, that why he didn't want to let *Cuca* go to school? He said, *"No. Ya no.* I don't want her to go to school no more."

They told him, "Well, you either let her go to school or you're gonna pay a hundred-dollar fine or go to jail for a month. And besides, she has to go to school anyway."

"Oh," *dice.* "¡That's real nice! Now they want to put me in jail, ¿do they? *¡Estas fregadas mulas!"*[6]

Le dijo mi mamá a Cuca, " It's up to you. ¿Do you want your dad to go to jail, for a month or two or whatever they give 'im?"

Ooh! *Cuca* got too scared. We didn't have no money to pay a hundred dollars. How could we put my dad in jail? *¡Ay, Dios mío! ¡Ni lo mande Dios!*

"No," she said. "Dad will beat me up." No. *Cuca* didn't want to go no more. It was her decision. She was fourteen or fifteen. She still had up to eighteen that she could go to school. She said no, that it was better for her to help my mom. She didn't go no more. None of us four older girls went.

And *Cuca* always regretted it. I told her, "Forget it, Ruth(iv) It's over with. You can't cry over spilt milk. Nothing. Forget it. Saying, 'I should have this, or they should'a let me do that,' it doesn't matter. That's what happened to all of us."

But when Mom and Dad went to Mexico, *Consuelo,* Linda, and *Teresa* went to school over there. They learned how to read, and they already knew English, so they did real good in English. With that, they could get some good positions because they spoke both languages. They stayed over there. Linda came back later. She lived here with us for a little while, then she went to other places to look for better jobs. Afterwards, she went to Denver and got married with Robert Brabo.

---

[6] 'These dang stubborn girls (mules)'.

101

The Artist

Me, I always liked art and music, if I only had the chance. But my dad never let me.

When I was in school, I got a prize to study for being an artist. I think I was about twelve years old. I was probably in fifth grade at East Ward. I went to third grade in Kansas City, and when we came here I went into fourth.

I got to sixth grade – and it took us a long time to get to sixth grade 'cause working in the farm we didn't go to school. My dad only let us all go to sixth grade, no more. Just to sixth grade, and that's it. To go to seventh, we would have to go walking to the high school that was all the way on the other side of town. No way he would let us go way over there!

Anyway, I made two little paintings, one of them with a river, mountains, and trees, and I won first prize. I made it in school, but I don't know where they took it – to an exhibition.[7]

I made that one, and then I made another one – it had a river, too, but it also had a boat, one of those big ones. It was a boat with two of those – how do they call 'em? – those sails that boats have, one of 'em a small one, and the other one bigger. I remember they were yellow. I got first prize again.

So then, the principal told me, "Look at your pictures. I want you to talk to your dad. We'll give you free lessons to learn the better way of painting."

'Cause I painted those by memory. We didn't have lessons just so that we could paint. At painting time, the teacher told us, "When you want to do this, do it on your own." Well, that's the way it was in those times.

Then I told my dad, *"El* principal *de la escuela* told me he wanted to give me free lessons.

"¡Ja!" dijo mi papá. "¿Now you wanna be an artist? Well, now. ¿You don't like working anymore? What you have to do is learn

---

[7] Probably at the Scottsbluff County Fair where this kind of work was shown.

how to work, not paint. Anyway, you'll get married and have a family, and that's all you're gonna do."

'Cause he said school was no good. It was just to learn to read and write, and that's all. That's it. Only that.

I didn't do any more painting.

But, for the principal to say he wanted to give me free lessons so I can do better. And for him to tell me, "You did wonderful. Wonderful." If my dad gave me permission to go to painting school, I think I would have changed my life. That they would send me to school free if I wanted to go. If my dad would let me. I was born ignorant with my parents being the way they were.

But my dad didn't like school. He never went 'cause all he'd get was a whipping from his grandpa if he got home late or did something. He was raised by his grandpa.

Another time, a Mexican musician came, I think from Denver. He wanted to make a girls' orchestra. All girls. He said it at the church that he wanted to start with girls. Oh, I was about fifteen years old, and some were lower age and some were higher, some of them younger and some of them older.

No. This time my dad let me. He said, "*Las que quieran entrar.*" Right away, I took the violin. Oh, how I loved it! But it ended real soon. I think the musician's wife got jealous because he had just girls. They separated or divorced. Then, she left, and he did, too. And all of that was finished.

But I always liked those kind of things. For the Sixteenth of September, they always said poems. They did plays, and they had dances – everything. And I was right in the middle of it.

No. I had to forget about art, about music, about plays. It was a different life now. But if my dad would'a let me, I would'a liked it.

Buying *Hule* [8](v)

We never had any money at home. My dad always gave us for whatever we needed. *Decía, "Toma,"* for this. *"Toma,"* for something else.

One time, the girls were all in the kitchen, and we were seeing how ugly the floor was. Just boards, *y todo astillado.*

Dije, "¡Oh! Let's go buy an *hule* for this floor."

Dijeron, "¿How are we gonna buy it? Dad isn't gonna let us. He won't give us the money."

I told 'em, "We'll tell 'im a lie what we want the money for. Then we'll go and buy it." No. He gave us the money to buy shoes for one of the boys, or something. We just told Mom we were gonna use the money *para el hule.*

Dice mi mamá, "Your father's gonna get mad." That's how she called him, 'your father'. "'Cause you're gonna spend the money on the linoleum and not on the shoes."

"But we need *hule* for the kitchen."

There we go to McCrear's to find a linoleum, the big furniture store here in Scottsbluff, and we bought it. My dad didn't know nothing about it until we put it on.

And then he walks in! *¡Uúpale!* Stepping here and stepping over there. Ooh! Taking big steps so he didn't have to put his feet on it.

"*¡Ay!" dice.* "¡Now you wanna be bigshots! There's no place to step." He was mad.

Afterwards, he didn't say no more. Well, we had already put the *hule.*

Then, it was about a year after we bought the *hule* for the kitchen. We told him, *"Papá,* ¿Why don't we buy a linoleum for the front rooms? A real nice hule."

Dice, "Bueno, we have to go to McCrear, to see if they'll give us credit. If they do, we'll get it. Let's go see if we can buy it."

---

[8] 'linoleum floor cover', also 'rubber'.

I told him that if they give us credit, why don't we buy a dresser or something for the bedroom.Yeah, they gave us credit. We bought the linoleum and the chest of drawers. It was big, and it had shelves on the side and a mirror in the middle. They sold us all of that.

I still have the chest, but it's been so many years. The mirror was getting cloudy, so I took it off and the other things, too. I don't know why. ¡Dummy! There was a lotta prettier things in the stores, so we didn't care for the older ones. I still have it there, though, the first chest of drawers we bought. I was eighteen, one year before I got married. I didn't even know Mike yet.

La Apapachada[9]

I was always goin' around everywhere with my dad 'cause I was the one that drove the car. I think that's why I was like my dad. No, I was always like him since I was little. And since he was the one with the money, he always told me to buy this or that for myself, "Cómprate esto. Cómprate unos zapatos."

Pos, ¡qué bueno! One time, he bought me a dress. Oh, so pretty. "Oye," dice. "Let's go to the store so you can buy yourself a dress."

Oh, I really remember that dress! It was fuchsia. Fuchsia is dark, real dark pink, that they call hot pink. And it had long sleeves, and on top of the sleeves they had loose little pieces. 'Cause I went to dances, and the little pieces went from one side to the other when I moved my arms. On the belt it had a sobrefalda that we call it, over the skirt. But with gajos – like strips. So, when I danced, the gajos they blew out real pretty. I used to be thin then. Oh, how I loved that dress.

That's why Jobita says, "No. Vera[10] was always la apapachada. Dad bought her everything." She has always been jealous. But I never paid attention to her, and she got madder.

---

[9] 'the spoiled child.' The root word is papás, 'parents' who presumably did the spoiling. Note the childlike use of ch for s as in nicknames.
[10] Elvira's usual English nickname. Pronounced [VEER–a].

'Cause I went out with my dad, and he was the one with the money. We went to a store, and he said, *"Mira, ¿You like that dress? Buy it."* Then afterwards, I gave the girls what I didn't like no more. No. Sometimes they bought dresses, too.

I didn't go around with none of my sisters. Well, I was always the oldest one, and now I was by myself taking my dad over here and over there. We didn't visit with each other until we got older. But the girls – Jobita, Alta, and *Cuca* – all got together with the two *Luces*, my cousins. I didn't go with them.

The Dances

My dad didn't let us go out with nobody. He said, "You don't go outta the house until you get married. *Nada."* But he did take us to the dances. He was a good dancer. He really enjoyed the music, the singing, and the dances. My mom, too.

You should see them in the dances! I can just picture them together. Eee! They were so good dancing *el choclo. ¡Chun, chun, chun!* They turned, and there they go. They turned some more, *el chotís.* Oh, so many. Another one was *la varsoviana,* turning and turning. They danced everything. They was good dancers! That's why we loved dancing so much.

And that's why he said he would take us to the dances. But he didn't take us until after fifteen years old. When the Mexican girl is fifteen and up, she's a woman. *Ya es mujer.* They can get married at sixteen or seventeen if someone asks for them.

They made dances in a hall that was there close to the Burbach store. Dad would ask us, *"¿Quieren ir?"*

Oh, we were so happy! Of course we did. Except Jobita. She didn't want to.

He took us, but he stayed over there sitting down. *Decía,* "You aren't gonna talk to nobody. And the one that asks you, that's the one you dance with. Not always with the same one."

Not with the same boy. We couldn't dance with the same one. With everybody.

"And if I see you talkin' with somebody or that you're laughing and having fun with one of 'em, *nos vamos luego-luego*. I'm taking you home." He didn't want us to look at anybody with goo-goo eyes. We went just to dance.

The men stood over there on one side, and the women over here sitting down on chairs. As soon as the music started, bang! The men ran to see if they could ask the one they wanted.

We would hide on one side, and my dad was over on the other side. No. My dad watched us like an eagle. But after a while, he got up to dance. Oh, he really liked to dance. He asked an older girl, and there he goes dancing. He didn't see us no more. We talked in the dark place, and when we went by where he was, we stayed quiet. We really liked to dance.

But, everything ends.

FIGURE 4. THE FAMILY OF JACOBO CHÁVEZ AND JACINTA CASTILLO

Jacobo Chávez + Jacinta Castillo

- Miguel (died in infancy)
- Elvira (Vera)+Michael (Maique, Mike) Hernández
- Jobita (Jovita)+Manuel Ramírez
- Altagracia (Alta)+Basilio (Bise) Durán
- Refugio (Cuca, Ruth)+Pablo (Paul) Acevedo
- Juan+María de los Angeles (Chita) Barragán
- Carlos+Dolores (Lola) Lugo
- Joaquín I (died in infancy)
- Teresa (Tere)+Cesáreo (Chayo) Hernández
- Joaquín II (Jimmy)+Onie Price
- Consuelo (Chelo)+José Luis Piedra
- Arturo (Arthur)+Ruth Sánchez
- Hermelina (Linda)+Robert Brabo
- Ramiro+Theresa Hernandez
- María+Mike Martínez

The Chávez Family, 1931.

<u>Back Row</u>: Ruth, Jobita, Elvira, Alta, Juan.
<u>Front Row</u>: Carlos, Consuelo, Teresa, Arthur, Jacobo with Linda,
Jacinta with Ramiro, Jim.

Elvira as a newlywed –
and since she's now
'flour from a different
sack' – flaunting her
shingle bob hairdo that
Maique suggested to
her.

A clay jar that Jacobo bought at the "Diers" store (note the label). It was originally used by Jacinta for baking powder.

Above: The 1926 Ford that Jacobo bought. Seated on the running board are Freddy (Johnny Mack and Ramona's son), Elvira, Jr. and Eddie (Elvira's children).

Right: The model car of the same make and year that Elvira encountered at a bank much later.

Comments on Language and Culture

i   *Lola* is derived from *Dolores* by dropping the initial syllable
(*aphaeresis*). As with *Ysidoro* and *Telésfora*, the *r* is changed to *l*, in
this case harmonizing with the preceding *l*. As is often the case (cf.
Cuca), the name is made more transparently feminine gender by
substituting the final syllable with - *a*.

ii   *Condolchito*, '*a little sweet confection*', is composed of *con* + *dulce*
+ *ito*. *-ito* is the diminutive form. The *c* of *dulce* ('sweet') is
pronounced *s* and undergoes the now familiar change to *ch*.

iii   The relationship between godparents (*padrino* and *madrina*) and
godchildren (*ahijados*) is very special within the Mexican Catholic
community. Note that the roots of these words are the same as for
padre (father), *madre* (mother), and *hijo* or *hija* (son or daughter).
The *padrinos* sponsor a person – the *ahijado* – in receiving a
sacrament such as baptism or matrimony. By this act, the *padrinos*
and the parents of the *ahijados* become *compadres* (co-parents). As
a consequence, the *padrinos,* who now have a quasi-familial
relationship with the parents, have the formal obligation to care for
the *ahijados* in case anything happens to the parents.

iv   For immigrants, the principal goal of American schools was, and
always has been, not the academic education of students but their
Anglicization and Americanization, under the theory that only in this
way can they learn their subject matter and become good and loyal
American citizens.

A critical detail in this effort was (and is) to change the identity of
the student from that of his/her community of origin to American
culture and social life. The first step has always been to Americanize
the names. In simple cases, this involves merely changing the
pronunciation or the spelling, as in *Robert* for *Roberto* or *Therese* for
Teresa. In other cases, The translations are not as transparent, as in
William for *Guillermo* or *Phillip* for *Felipe*.

However, some names do not lend themselves to such facile
strategies. Nevertheless, the ideological imperative to Anglicize the
names is so strong that teachers find very creative means to
accomplish their objective.

Endnotes continue on the following page:

This is why *Refugio* can be changed to *Ruth* where only the minimal phonetic content of the original name is retained. Other examples of these brusque substitutions are *Jim* for *Joaquín*, *Richard* for *Ramiro*, *Harry* or *Gene* for *Genaro (*pronounced *hen-ah-ro)*, *Stanley* for *Estanislao*, *Sally* for *Chole*, or *Phyllis* for *Feliciana*. Then these Anglo-sounding names form an integral part of the subsequent cultural identity of the individual.

v   In Mexican Spanish, *hule* means 'rubber'. The word is also used to refer to 'linoleum', the rubberized material used to make floor coverings. This particular semantic change is through a process of *metonymy* by which the name of a material is used to designate an object made from it. *Hule* derives from the Náhuatl *ul-li,* 'tree gum'.

Chapter Eight

EL ATASCADERO

*Girls were not supposed to talk to no boys
until they asked for them. ¡No way!
I don't know how we were supposed to meet each other.*

¡Dale Gas!

I met Mike *en un atascadero* – in a mudhole.

'Cause my *tío* Santos bought a car – a Chevy two-door that was real pretty. Prettier than ours. It was a nineteen twenty-seven. They said that he wrecked with the mailman and he didn't want to drive no more. Anyway, there he goes for me to take him over here and to take him over there, 'cause I was the one that drove ours.

So, there we go. I was real happy 'cause sometimes we were at home, and we were gonna do this or that, and my uncle would come.

My mom said, *"¡Ay! Dios de mi vida.* I'm tired of don Santos. Here he comes to take you. I'm not gonna let you go. You never stay home."

"Listen," Mom told 'im, *"Elvira* has a lotta housework to do."

"No," dice mi tío. "I'll bring her right back. You got the other girls there that can help you." Then I would go with him.

So, the time I met Mike, it was nineteen twenty-eight. It was the third of August. How could I forget? They were irrigating the beets, and in that time the roads were really bad – all dirt.

At night after supper, my uncle came and said, "I'm gonna go see Valenzuela. Take me over there." They lived on a farm a long ways away, south of Gering.

So, we went to visit, and it was late when we were coming back, about nine or ten at night. And we came to a great big mudhole! From the irrigation.

"*¡Ay!*" *decía mi tío*. "*Dale gas*. Go fast so you can cross in a hurry." Right in the middle, we got stuck right up to the running boards. And my uncle is still telling me, "*Dale gas. Dale gas.*"

Yeah, '*Dale gas!*' The more gas I gave it, the more it got stuck. It was real wet. It looked like a lake. *¡Válgame Dios!*

So, there we are. We couldn't do nothing, until we saw some lights coming.

"Here comes a car," *decía mi tío*. "*Dale la luz, dale la luz.*"

I turned on the lights, but the car turned around and went back. He didn't want to go in the mudhole.

Then, after a while another one came. This one stopped and said, "Let's see if I can get you out." He had a rope and he put it on, but when he started to pull, it broke. No. He got out, and he went. So we stayed there, real stuck.

My *tía Pola* was with us, too, and *Luz* her daughter, and I don't know who else. My aunt was just laughing so hard. She was very funny.

So then my uncle said, "*Ahora sí.* ¿You know what I'm gonna do? It's about a mile and a half or two miles from here to where *don Juan* lives. I'll just go get *Miguel* and *Juanecito* so they can help us get out." He already knew *don Juan* since we lived in Kansas – *Juan Hernández*. So he went to get them.

I already knew about Mike, and Mike knew about me, because we saw ourselves in church and in the dances. But in the dances he never came to ask me 'cause he was too bashful. He wouldn't dare come over.

All the girls wanted to know him. 'Oh, Mike *Hernández*, this, and Mike *Hernández* that!'

They asked me, "Haven't you met him? He's so nice and he's good-looking."

I told 'em, "I know, but I haven't." Even if I was really anxious to meet him.

I almost met 'im at a birthday party. It was *Ester's* birth'ay, one of the *Castañedas*, and she invited everybody she knew. They lived *en las casas de adobe*, on the end of Seventh Street. *Doña Narcisa* and *don Santos, Ester's* mother and father went to our house to invite us. That's why my dad let me go, because it was a family they knew, and it was a *fiesta*.

Ester was after Mike, and he tried to sneak out of his house through a window, because *don Juan* didn't let them go out. They lived over by the sugar factory. But *Chole* heard 'im and told 'im to get back inside, because if his dad caught 'im, he would give 'im a good whipping.

But that was better anyway, 'cause afterwards we met at the *atascadero* by ourselves. We waited about an hour until my uncle went and brought the *Hernández* – until they got dressed and came, because they were already in bed. Johnny Mack and Mike wore their boots because my uncle told them where we were. *Don Juan* came, too, and so did *Cesáreo*, but he was younger.

My heart was really pounding. So was Mike's pounding, because he wanted to meet me, too, and he didn't know me. He came fast.

Afterwards, when the men took the car out, we all got off, and everybody started to visit. Mike was on one side of the car, and I was on the other one. We looked at each other, and when he looked at me, it was like a lightning that put our hearts together. I don't know why. I liked him. He liked me. Just like that. Just by seeing each other, that's all we needed.

Mike and I started to talk, too. That he had heard about me, and I heard about him. He said, "I've been wanting to meet you." And I said, "I've been wanting to meet you." So, we met ourselves.

That was the first time that we met, and we made a 'date' right away, to see each other again. Where? Until there was a dance. Make sure that he'd go and I'd go.

He said, "Can I write to you?"

I told him, "Well, there's a post on the corner of the house. You can put a letter there, under a rock."

My aunt was standing next to me. She said, "Hey, hey! I see how you're looking at each other."

"No, we're not doing anything, *Tía*. I don't know him and he doesn't, either."

Dice, "But you know each other now, *¿verdad?* Well, I don't understand you. You're just talkin' and talkin' in English."

"No. We're just talking about the car, *Tía*."

But from then on, we couldn't take our eyes away from each other. And our hearts, either. I liked him. He liked me. We looked at each other, and that was it.

"Adios."

"Adios." That's all. And he wrote to me. He told me that the minute he saw me, he loved me.

The Sixteenth of September

When we had the parade for the Sixteenth of September,(i) *Libradita* and her husband came to ask if they would let me be the princess, to ride on top of the *carro alegórico.*[1] *Concha Quevedo* was gonna be the queen, *y la princesa* was the one that went with the queen.

Librada Chávez, she was the main one – she's the one that started the Sixteenth. My parents knew her. She also started a school 'cause she was a Mexican teacher and wanted to teach us.

But they were Protestants, and my dad said, "They'll go to your school, but I don't want you to teach them about your

---

[1] 'parade float'.

religion." My dad wanted us to learn to speak Spanish a little better than what they spoke.

"No, sir. I'm not going to teach them my religion. I'm going to educate them."

So, they let me go and be the princess. But they were gonna put *Agustín García* for the prince, and I didn't want *Agustín.* I wanted them to put Mike. So, they asked Mike, and he said yes.

I told *Libradita,* "Let me go ask my dad."

Right away, he said, *"Oye, ¿who you goin' with?"*

Dije, "I don't know. Whoever they put me with." That was just a white lie 'cause there was no harm in that.

So I told *Libradita.* She said, "Oh, okay. *Está bien.* "

My dad told me, "Bueno, if you're gonna be in that fiesta, let's go so you can buy yourself a dress." My dad, even if he got drunk and mad with the other ones, he always treated me good.

So, we went to buy a dress. Oh, the dress I bought! *Era de pura chaquira. ¡'Taba tan bonito! Color de rosa.*[2]

Oh, Jobita got so jealous! *Pero, ahi que siga.*[3]

So, there we go, Mike and me *en el carro alegórico,* and the queen in between. The parade went all the way on Broadway. Mike and me didn't say nothing to each other 'cause my dad was looking. That was after *el atascadero,* but *Maique* didn't tell me nothing about nothing yet.

That night, we had a dance with plays and poems, and everything. They did it on First Avenue in a big hall where they had shows. I think it was the Otoe Theater. At the dance, because I was the princess, I got to give a speech about *la Independencia de México.*

Then we made a play, *de La Mujer Adultera.* I really remember that play! I was the main one, *la mujer adultera.* Her husband had a gun, and I was kneeling down, begging him not to kill me. I thought it was funny, *pero* the *Rojas* girls – the sister-in-laws of

---

[2] 'it was all *chaquira* (shiny beading). It was so pretty! Pink'.
[3] 'But, she had to deal with it'.

my cousin *Luz* – they was cryin' and cryin' 'cause he was gonna shoot me, and I was crying, begging him not to. I used to be in the plays, and I liked it a lot.

At the dance, Mike was selling pop. He had a little table on the side. After a while, I went over to buy one, and he said, "Can you come and drink a pop with me?"

"I don't know. My dad won't let me." 'Cause my dad was sitting over there close. I said, "I'd better go. I'll let you know."

So I went to my dad and told 'im, "*Maique* wants to know if I can drink a soda with him."

"*Sí, sí.* Tell 'im to bring it over and to sit down next to me here."

So, I went and told Mike, and he got a pop for my dad and he brought some for himself and for the other ones that was there – me, Alta and Jobita. But we didn't talk no more. We were all quiet, drinking our pops.

Afterward, they played the music, and Mike and I danced together. There we go, dancing and dancing. He never told me anything. Nothing. Quiet.

They was playing the song, "*Let Me Call You Sweetheart*". That's my record. That's my song. He just leaned over – he was real tall, and me so short – and he told me real quiet, "Can I call you that?" He was so bashful. That was it. That's how he proposed.

And I said, "Yes." And that was our engagement.

Afterwards, we used to write to each other – but in secret – where he gave a letter to somebody to give to me, and I did, too. We showed ourselves where to put a little note, underneath a rock. Nobody knew except me and him.

Yeah!

La Pedida[4]

Mike asked me that when could he ask for me.

I told him, "I'll let you know. When we finish the work, then I'll let you know. But not now."

Oh! I couldn't think of when to tell him to ask for me. *Le dije que sí, pero no le dije cuando. Se me hacía 'cuis, cuis'.*[5]

Then, in November *don Juan* was getting ready to go back to Kansas City. *Los Hernández* came first to Scottsbluff in 'twenty-five, just for the time of the work. In winter, they went back to Kansas. They came in 'twenty-six, and left. Every year since 'twenty-five.

Well, after *el atascadero* and everything, Mike didn't want to go, but he didn't know how to tell his dad. He was really afraid of him. Well, finally he went and told him he wanna get married. *Don Juan* asked him with who. He was surprised, 'cause they didn't know.

Luego-luego le dice a Maique, "¿Did she tell you that's what she wants?"

"*Sí.*"

"*¿Y cuándo dijo?*

"To go ask for her when the *tapeo* was all done."

Don Juan said that on such-and-such a day, they was leaving. They was going back to Kansas.

Dijo, "And if you don't get married by then, you won't get married. So we know once and for all, we'll go ask for her now."

They went to ask for me all of a sudden, because *don Juan* didn't want him to get married. And they went without me knowing, 'cause we were still on the farm, and I told him that I would let him know after the work finished.

Don Juan le dijo a mi papá, "We're gettin' ready to go to Kansas. So, if they're gonna get married, it has to be soon or else

---

[4] 'Asking for her hand'.
[5] "I told him 'yes', but I didn't say 'when'." (The words of a popular song.) I got all nervous.'

they won't." Putting him his condition. That's the way don Juan was.

My dad said, *"Está bien.* Now, I'm gonna put down my own time. Come back in two weeks. And if she says 'yes', then whatever she says. *Es todo."* He told him clear and strong. And *don Juan* just kept quiet. He didn't say nothing then. Well, what could he say?

Anyway, on that day when *don Juan* and the priest first came to ask for me, it so happened that we were moving from the *chante* to town. That was in 'twenty-eight, the first year my dad got work with Neil Barbour, and I got married in 'twenty-nine.

Boy, we were so dumb! It was so close from Barbour's to the house in town. When thinning started, then we had to move to the farm. Our house was on Seventh and Neil's was on Twenty-Seventh, but it was on a farm on the other side of the tracks. It was probably only about three or four miles. Then after topping, when the work was all done, there we go again, moving from the *chante* to town with all our furniture.

I don't know why we couldn't just stay in town and then leave early to go work in the beets. We already had a car. One time every day, we could take us a lunch and eat over there and everything, then come back to eat supper at our house.

But, no! We had to move to the farm. Not to use so much gas, I guess. That's how people did it, and we got used to that. *Don Másimo* and *Petra* moved from the farm to town, too, 'cause they worked at Barbour's.

So, the day they went to ask for me, we were still at the farm. Topping was done, and me and Alta stayed at the farm to say what furniture to take first and to clean the house. My mom, Jobita, and *Cuca* were over there in the house in town waiting for the furniture. So, we're over here, and they're over there, and my dad and the boys with the truck taking all our stuff. They were all over there in town when *don Juan* and the priest got there.

Well, Alta and I finished. We washed the *chante*, we cleaned and we left. I had the car. And when we got over there, my mom was crying and crying and crying. And Jobita, ooh! She looked so mad.

I told her, "¿Why is Mom crying? What happened? ¿Did Dad hit her?"

She said, "¡Tú! ¡Tú!"

"¿Me? ¿What did I do?"

She said, "¡Ay, chiquita! No sabes."

Le dije, "¿Qué?"

Dice, "¡So now you wanna get married!"

Piiing!

I just. . . . I said, "¿When? I didn't tell him I was gonna get married. ¡Oh!" I said, "¿Why did he do that? I didn't tell 'im."

She said, "¡Ay! No sabes. ¡Qué inocente eres! You oughtta be ashamed." She was madder than the dickens because my mom was crying and crying. Mom didn't say nothing.

"¿And Dad?" I said. "¿Where's Dad?"

"He's gone. He's madder than heck."

¡Válgame Dios! Ooh, I was scared to death that my dad was gonna give me a good whipping, even if I was already big. I was nineteen years old.

No. My cousin Luz told me that right after don Juan and the priest left, my dad went to talk to her dad, my tío Santos. When he got there to my uncle, le dijo, "I wanna know what kind'a bums these people are. I don't know anything about that family. ¿Do you know them?"

"Yes. I know 'em, and really well." My tío Santos and don Juan knew each other in Kansas City. He told my dad, "¿Sabes qué? Your daughter is gonna get married sometime. Then, she could get married to somebody that's not for her – with a drunkard or with somebody that's no good for nothin'. Esta es una familia muy buena y muy honrada. They don't go out, they don't drink, they don't go around chasing women. Y si se quiere casar Elvira, let 'er. Don't tell 'er nothing. She's old enough to get married."

121

Dice, "She won't find a better husband than him. *Si a mí* Johnny *me venía a pedir a Luz,* I would hand her over just like that. They're very good sons."

Sure, they was good sons! With their father that beat them all the time!

When my dad got back, they asked me if I wanted to get married. I was really scared. *"Yo no sé,"* *les decía yo.* *"No sé. Yo no sé."* But I was thinking that 'Yes, I'm gonna get married. Yes, I'm gonna get married'. Even if I was afraid. But now, I wasn't scared anymore because my dad didn't say anything. Nothing.

He just put two weeks as the time for them to come and see what I was gonna say. In those two weeks, my mom told me a lotta things − that I was too young, and that I didn't know what marriage is, and for me not to get married yet. Oh, she told me a lot, but it went in one ear and came out the other one. I wanted to get married.

When they came to see what my answer was, they were over there visiting and talking. I was in the other room, in back of a curtain. I was shaking. Then they called me. The priest, my dad, my mom, *don Juan,* all of them was sitting there.

Mike wasn't there. The boy doesn't go. Oh, no, not them. They didn't ask for anybody. The parents did. In those times, the boy didn't ask for the bride. No way! They would beat him up and kick him out. Oh, no.

So, I came out, and they asked me. Ooh! I didn't know what I was gonna say. 'What am I going to say?' So then Father McDade said, "Come on, girl!"

I told them "Sí". That's all I said, "Sí."

My dad just looked down. Nomás dijo, "Okay, that's all we wanted to know." And that was it.

La Presentación

Afterwards, he put together *la presentación* that I was supposed to have. We did a party with girls − just girls there at home − *Luz de la Rosa* and *Ramona* who were gonna be my *madrinas* and some other friends. The boy didn't go. A little party with friends. That's the engagement. That was *la presentación*, to announce that I was getting married, and to tell all of my friends. But there was no gifts then in those times. Nobody gave any gifts. After that, my dad didn't take me out. He didn't take me to the dances. If there was a dance, *me decía*, "No, you don't belong to me no more. I'm not gonna take you."

In those years, after the announcement, the man was supposed to give his salary to the *novia*. Every week. That was to support her. Mike didn't have a salary, but the parents were supposed to give it, anyway. But my dad didn't wanna take it, so he didn't ask 'em for it. The only thing, I wasn't his no more. He said, "If she's gonna get married, then let her wait until she's married."

After *la presentación*, they let Mike go and talk to me. But just a small visit. We stayed there in the living room and they went out.

My dad didn't want us to see each other unless he was there. But my mom told him, "Let her talk with her *novio* alone. ¿Don't you remember us? I was a *señorita* when we met. Remember that. And now, look how many children we have. Leave her."

I think my dad remembered, and that's why he let us be alone. But my sister *Teresa* got under the bed to see what we was gonna do. Well, what were we gonna do if both him and me were so embarrassed? We just sat down to talk.

¿You'll take me? ¡Ha!

But even before *la presentación, Agustín García* was always after me. I told him, "Listen. We're friends from when we were little since we came here." I told him, "Don't talk to me about that. I don't like you in that way. I just like you as a friend." Like we all were.

One day my mom told me, "Go get me some groceries at Hightower." I was already engaged, so I could go by myself, at least to the store. I took *Consuelo* with me. She was little. We both went walking. The store for the Mexicans was right there on Ninth Street. It wasn't far. We went.

Then *Agustín* came over. He lived just up on Tenth Street and he saw us coming. I told him, "¿What are you doing?"

He said, *"Oye. ¿Are you gonna marry me?"*

Le dije, "Estás loco. I already have a *novio."* They all thought they were so nice looking because they were white. That's how the *Garcías* were. All of 'em were real white. Not Antonia. She was kind of dark and she had *cascarita de viruela.*[6] Her and me were good friends.

I told *Agustín,* "You're crazy. You don't think I'm gonna . . ."

Dijo, "I'll take you."

"¿You'll take me? ¡Ha!" *Le dije,* "Let's see. Do it, and see what you get."

Dijo, "Yeah. You can bring the baby with me, too. Both of you, or I'll leave her here crying and I'll take you."

"Go ahead, take me. See if you can."

I don't know why I was like that, ever since I was little. I don't know. I had my dad's strength.

Ooh! If my dad knew that *Agustín* was with me, that he was after me, he would'a grabbed him and throw him I don't know how far.

But I didn't let him get away with it. I told him, "Try it."

Dijo, "I'll put you in my car right now, and I'll take you."

"Go ahead. Try it. See if you can. Mira, I'll just tell the guy in the store to call the police. *Andale, ¿quieres la policía?* ¡Just shut up!" But that's how we talked to each other.

Later, he went and told my mom, "Just look who Elvira is going with. ¿Why does she want to marry him? She doesn't even know 'im."

Yeah, I think he said that because Mike was real dark, and in the summer he got black. Real dark.

My mom just told him, *"Bueno,* he's the one she wants to get married to."

---

[6] 'a pock-marked skin from smallpox'.

That's the way our *noviazgos* were in those times. Everything was secret until somebody asked for them. 'Cause the girls were not supposed to talk to no boys until they asked for them. No way! I don't know how we were supposed to meet each other, but that's the way it was.

I met him in August, and we got married five months later, on the tenth of January, nineteen twenty-nine.

Elvira covers her eyes and weeps with emotion upon hearing the song "Let me Call you Sweetheart" on the music box and on remembering her courtship.

125

Comments on Language and Culture

In the Mexican communities of those times in the U.S., Mexican Independence Day was very much celebrated. They organized parades and *fiestas* at which there was music and patriotic poetry and speeches were recited. Students and workers always took the 16th of September as a holiday and didn't attend school or work.

In Scottsbluff, as part of the festivities, there was also a baseball game, played traditionally between *Los Zorros*, the Scottsbluff team, and the team from Bayard, a neighboring community. Every town in the area had its own Mexican baseball team of which it was very proud.

In Kansas City Mexicans played baseball since the earliest decades of the 20th Century. In all probability, they brought the game from Mexico where it was already a favorite sport. Without a doubt, Mexican youths imported it from Mexico to Kansas City and then to Nebraska.

Chapter Nine

NOVIAZGOS

He told her where to put the letters.
That's how they got to be novios.
When they went to ask for her, the parents were so surprised!
"How can it be that they met?"

Monchi and Johnny Mack

I remember Johnny Mack and Ramona so much. 'Cause before they got married, Ramona was so innocent. Well, she was fifteen, and he liked her. Johnny was in love with her. He was eighteen at that time.

But any time Ramona went outside, there was *doña Paulita,* right behind her. If she sat down outside, her mother sat down next to her. She didn't leave her alone for a minute. *¿Al escusado?* There she goes and stands outside the toilet with Ramona inside.

We invited her to join *Las Hijas de María,* a group of women from the church. Alta invited her. We got together every week. She asked permission from *doña Paulita* to let her join.

Alta told her "It's a Catholic group, and you're a Catholic. You go to Mass, too."

Entons' dijo doña Paulita, "'Stá bien. I'll leave 'er." So, she let her join.

But when Ramona came to our house when we had the meetings, *doña Paulita* waited for her outside so she could go home and so no one came out with her.

127

So then one day, Johnny told Alta, "Hey, ¿will you take Monchi₍ᵢ₎ a note?"

Le dijo Altagracia, "¿Why don't you give it to her yourself?"

Dice Johnny, "¿When do I see her? *Doña Paulita* is always keeping an eye on her."

During that time, the three families all happened to live far away on the Baxter farm – the Ricos, *don Juan,* and my dad and mom. Mike and me were already married. The Ricos lived real close to us, like across the road. That's where Johnny saw Ramona. Our house was on one side of the little road, and their house was over there, right across. The water pump was in between the houses. But right away they put a fence around their yard.

The farm was pretty big, and part of the work was for each family. But they always worked separate. *¡Qué esperanzas* that we would work together! And out there on the field, her father was always behind her, working behind her. They didn't even turn around to look at us, even to say hello or nothing. That's the way that family was. They never said a word to other people. They were over there, and we were over here. That's all.

So then, Alta said, *"Andale pues."* And she gave her the letter. Afterwards, Ramona gave her answer to *Altagracia* to give it to Johnny.

She answered him a letter so in love! Really! *¡Pero enamorada!* Love letter! Johnny even got mad at Alta because he got that letter from Ramona.

Dice Johnny, "Oh, no," *dice.* "She's not like that." *He said, "Tú.* You told her what to say. You wrote this letter."[1]

Dijo Alta, "I didn't write it. Don't lie." And they got in an argument. Alta told him, "Okay. Now, you have to write her. I'm not gonna take it."

---

[1] Ramona gave these love letters to her daughter, Joy Gonzales. One exchange of these letters is reproduced at the end of this chapter, beginning on p. 136. As the compiler, I am extremely grateful for Joy's generous permission to use her mother's very private communications.

Johnny said, "¿How am I gonna give it to her?"

Dice Alta, "Okay. Just so you can see how Ramona is. Don't think she's so innocent. She's not. She's just like us."

She argued a lot with Johnny. Anyway, she told him, "Look, over on that corner, I'm gonna put a rock. Right there on the corner of the fence close by the pump. When *Ramona* comes out, I'll just show her some of the flowers there, and then I'll tell her where your letter is, underneath the rock."

Doña Paulita watched her so she would only be with Alta. *Ramona* picked up the rock real quick, she took the letter, and went. She answered at the same rock. She left her letter there so Johnny could pick it up. He went and got it, and finally he believed Alta.

Johnny told her, "I'm sorry."

Le dice Alta, "¿Ves? Don't think she's such a dummy."

'Cause Ramona kept looking to see if they needed water. Right away, she'd go to the pump to bring a bucket of water. *Doña Paulita* was right behind her. But she right away would reach down and put her letter or get Johnny's letter. That's how their *noviazgo* was.

Well, when Johnny's parents asked for her, Ramona's parents were shocked! 'Well, ¿How could they meet each other? ¿How did they become *novios?'* Amazed.

But they had a reason. They really loved Ramona. They only had two daughters, Ramona and an older sister who had gotten married. But she always had bruises. I think her husband took her with him to Mexico. Over there, he beat 'er to death. *Ramona* told me about it. *Dice,* "I think that's why they didn't want me to get married."

Ramona was real quiet. She never talked much. But one day, after they got married, I was talking with Johnny and *Ramona,* there in their house. I saw that the house needed a lotta work.

Le digo a Johnny, "Oye. ¿Why don't you do something with this house? ¿What are you gonna do with your money? You can't take it with you."

But then, Ramona turns around real quiet *and said,* "Yes, he's gonna take it with 'im. I'm gonna write 'im a check, and I'm gonna put it in his coffin."

Johnny got mad. He said, "*Monchi,* ¿where'd you get that?" And he turns to me, "*¡Tú! ¡Tú!* ¡You told her what to say!"

I told him, "I didn't tell her nothing. The same way I told her to marry you, that's how I'm telling her now." He didn't say anything no more.

Teófilo

One of my cousins, *Teófilo,* who was my *tío Carlos'* son, told us about his wedding in Mexico. When he was ready to get married, there was a man who had five daughters that lived on the other side of the wall. 'Cause the houses had walls all around.

They went to the river to wash clothes at four o'clock in the morning so nobody would see them. There goes the father and the mother with their daughters in front. *Teófilo* said there was a *pirul* on this side of the fence from their yard. Two or three of the boys climbed way up that tree so they could see the girls.

Dice, "Sometimes we saw them when they came out on their way to the toilet."

The other ones asked him, "*¿Cuál?* ¿Which one you like the best?"

So then, he said he picked out the one he liked. There was one girl who was real pretty. They always came out with their heads covered. Quiet, real quiet.

Their parents never went to town. If they went out, it was to go to Mass. They went to Mass early, and the daughters went in front and the parents in back, watching. They came and they went, but not by themselves.

They all came out of their house and went back in, and they never noticed that someone was watching them from up on the *pirul.* One would come out. Then another one came out. So, *Teófilo* wrote a little note. He got on top of the *pirul* and waited for the girl to come out, the one he liked.

Well, one day, the girl came out by herself. She went over there to feed the pigs or the chickens or something. Over there in back of the yard. He threw a rock with the note, and she got scared and ran inside. She didn't know who threw that.

He stayed up there. She went inside and didn't say nothing. But she thought about it. After a little while, she went back out to see the rock, to see what it was. And then she saw him. She told 'im she would answer. So, he told her where to put the letter, in a little hole he made at the very end of the yard, over there where she fed the chickens. That's where they was gonna bury the letters.

That's how they got to be *novios*. Afterwards, when my uncle and my aunt went to ask for her, the parents were so surprised! 'How can it be that they met?' The father got real mad, but he let her get married.

¡Qué Rico![2]

The Ricos had two daughters and three sons. They were *Ramona* and the sister who got killed. Then there was Frank, *Aniseto* who was married to Jenny, and the oldest one who was my *padrino, Esteban.* He's the best man in my wedding picture.

I remember my cousin *Luz Chávez.* She was so in love with Frank Rico. They used to see each other in secret, but he didn't like *Luz* that much. She was after him, and I thought maybe they were gonna get married.

One day, *Luz* was visiting us at the farm at Neil Barbour. *Dice, "¡Ay!* I'm gonna go on a date. But don't say nothing." *Dice, "Voy a ir con* Frank *Rico."*

They was gonna see each other on the corner where Charley Stalnaker lived. Right on the corner.

She said, "It's over there in the trees. But I want you to go with me 'cause I'm afraid to go all the way over there by myself. He

---

[2] 'How rich!' A wordplay on the surname *Rico*.

told me he was gonna wait over there. That's where he's going for me."

So, there she goes, all excited. *Dice, "Andale, corre, corre, y corre.*[3]" There she goes, running and singing, *"Corre-y-corrí, co-rrí-co-Ri-co-Rico."* She was so in love!

And that dumb guy, he just passed by instead of picking 'er up. She went so happy, and all he did was wave to 'er. He stopped there just to say he had a girlfriend, *una güera. ¡Corre-y-corri, co-rri-co-Ri-co-Rico!* Afterward, she came back crying.

Jobita

Jobita really struck gold with *Manuel* and *doña Lázara*! Because they asked for her three times, and she said 'no'.

The first time they asked for her, she said 'no'. About three or four months later, she said 'no' again. Two times she said 'no'. But *Manuel* kept on and kept on. On the third time, she said 'yes'. It took about a year for her to finally say 'yes'.

So, we did a *presentación* to invite the ones that we knew. Her sisters and friends, to make her a little party, to let 'em all know she was gonna get married. With all of that, Mom would feel better and not cry so much that Jobita was gonna get married all of a sudden.

But when Manuel's sister, *María,* and *doña Lázara* went to get her to take 'er to buy *las donas* – her dress, her veil, and everything – then, again, she told them 'no', that she didn't want to get married!

Gee whiz! She already said 'yes'. She already made the reception for her friends to tell them she was gonna get married – *su presentación.* And to have *doña Lázara* and *María* come to get her, and for her to tell them 'no'!? They was so mad when they left. Oh, how they got mad with Jobita!

The priest from here, I think it was Father McDade, he really laughed. Because him and *don Melecio* went to ask for her three

---

[3] "Come on. Run, run, run."

times. They went one time. They asked for her another time. Three times! The priest said, "Well, she doesn't want to get married." He said, "They want to get married, but still they don't. She's the one that doesn't want to."

She was afraid. And after all that, for her to elope!? *Cuca, Altagracia* and I don't know who else made a plan. They knew that Manuel was gonna steal her, but they didn't tell Jobita. They said they was just gonna go for a ride at the airport. Sure! A ride in an aeroplane! Lies!

Bise and Paul[4] got together with Manuel. Everyone took their own car. Then there was *Cuca, Alta,* and one other person. Three and Jobita that was gonna take a ride. All of 'em. Nobody else knew. Naturally, my dad didn't know 'cause they went without saying.

So then, they put *Cuca* in the aeroplane, they put Alta, and then they put the other one. The last one was supposed to be Jobita.

But when the other one got on, *Manuel le dijo a Jobita,* "Sit over here." In his car because they were *novios* again. When everybody got on the aeroplane, choong! *Manuel ganó y se fue con Jobita.* They took off.

Doña Lázara and *don Melecio,* how they must of felt. But then, Manuel called them to tell them he took Jobita and that they were gonna get married.

Doña Lázara told him for them not to get married. *"No se casen."* Que le dijo, "Take her. Stay there a few months, then come back and give her to 'em." For Manuel to come and give 'er back!

Manuel didn't say nothing. They just went to see Father *Onofre* in Denver. That priest had already come over here to say Mass in Our Lady of *Guadalupe.* He knew all of us, and he knew the father from here real good. He called our priest right away.

---

4 Bise (*Basilio) Durán* was Alta's boyfriend; Paul (*Pablo) Acevedo* was Ruth's. Both couples got married later. Refer to *Figure 4, the Family of Jacobo Chávez and Jacinta Castillo, page 108.*

Father McDade told him, "You know what? Just leave them alone. Tell them to go get their marriage license. As soon as they get it, marry them." He said, "I give them the probation[5] because I know them. Just get them married by the church right now, and tell 'em to come home."

They went and got their license, and they didn't get married by the court. They got married with Father *Onofre* who married them in the church.

My dad was really mad. But what could he do? Manuel already took her.

Boy! I had such a pretty wedding, and for Jobita to run off!

But Jobita suffered a lot with *doña Lázara*. I wouldn't of let 'er get away with it, but Jobita was too timid. Pshew! I couldn't of stood that woman. Jobita says that when Manuel went to work and she stayed outside with Mae who was a little baby, they never called her to come in and eat. She went in only when Manuel was there. He would tell her, "You wanna come in and have a *taco?*" He knew how they were treating her. Until they moved out of there(ii). But even after Manuel and Jobita moved out, her in-laws went to live with them.

---

[5] "I'll approve the banns of marriage," announcements in the church of an impending marriage, allowing for any valid objections.

RAMONA AND JOHNNY MACK'S WEDDING AUGUST 30, 1930

Back Row: Bridesmaid Luz Chávez; Groomsman Manuel Chávez;
Best Man Jacinto Raya; Maid of Honor Juanita Raya.

Front Row: Ring Bearer Arthur Chávez; Johnny Mack;
Flower Girl Consuelo Chávez; Ramona.

On the following pages are reproduced two love letters kept by Ramona Rico. In the letter dated May 10, 1930 is Johnny's incredulous response to Ramona's earlier letter in which she agrees to be his sweetheart. He seizes the opportunity to propose marriage to her. Her answer, accepting his proposal, is dated July 10, 1930.

Littlebluff Nebr.
May 10 – 1930

Dearest Ramona:

I am writing these few lines in answer to your wonderful little letter, in which you sent me your lovely picture of which I was overjoyed in receiving. Ramona I am very happy for now I have what I felt I wanted for a long time that is your love and now that I have it I am the happiest boy in the world. Ramona you told me not have a chance to talk with me because your mother goes with you all the time well if you can't. We will do the best we can by writing to each other. Ramona what I wanted to talk to you about is a very important question because my parents want to leave this town soon and if they do I'll have to go with them and if I did I would never be happy being so far away from you and another

thing that it is very hard for me to live without you Ramona. I am going to ask you to make me happy for the rest of my life. I want you to think of this and see if you will marry me. Ramona it is not very long since you are my sweetheart and anything get to marry me perhaps you do not love me enough to want my self. Ramona if you think it is to soon for me to ask you this. Tell me. I will always love you for I think you are the most wonderful girl in the world. I hope you will not become angry on account of what I have asked you Ramona Ramona I will always be true to you. I will forever love you my Ramona that will be yours always.

Ramona when I first received your first letter I could hardly believe my eyes on seeing it and reading that you would be my sweetheart. I thought that some other girl had made it and had put your name to it to have some fun with me by making me

The message in this
Card of mine
Is to the point
and snappy
If you will be
what I ask you
I surely will
be happy.
Love and kisses.

Your faithful lover.
John Hernandez

think you were mine. Ramona
I finally believed it was you who
wrote it when Bertha told me you
wrote it. The night after I returned
your first letter I slept with it
under my pillow kissing it. When
I awoke next morning I remembered
of the letter and looked for it and
I could not find it. I then believed
that I had been dreaming and sure
very sorry then I found the letter
and I were sure you were my girl.
Ramona please answer me at your
earliest convenience. I and your
my heart, kisses and all of my
love.

137

Healtville milla
July 10-1936

Dearest John,

I am write you that you cant no answer
to your letter in which you ask me to if
will marry you this summer, sweetheart
I will marry you any time you want
because I love you John my love all
will yours and it will be yours forever.
John you think I love any boy but I
will never give my love to nobody else
but you. John I think my mamita
will let me marry you John dear I
will always be true to you I will
love your sweetheart I am hoping
to be with you soon and we will be
happy together forever dear I just
think to do is to get married at

soon as possible because I want to
be with you and be happy,
sweetheart I will love you forever
my heart and my love
and many kisses, to you sweetheart

your sweetheart who
will love you truly forever
Romona Rico.

Comments on Language and Culture

i   *'Monchi'* is derived from *Ramoncita* which is the diminutive form of *Ramona*. The nickname involves elision of both the first and the last syllables, leaving *'Monci'*. The c̲, which is pronounced s̲, is changed to c̲h̲.

ii   It was common in this community for newlyweds to live with the groom's parents for a certain time, often several years. The principal reason for this was because the groom lacked the financial resources to set up their own home. Couples tended to marry quite young, often in their teens or early twenties. During his single state, and even later, all of a son's earnings belonged to the *paterfamilias* who controlled these and other aspects of the son's life until, at last, they were able to emancipate themselves.

Chapter Ten

DON JUAN

Oh, don Juan was terrible. He was so mean with his kids.
Que Dios lo perdone. It's not that I'm talking about him.
Pero that's the way he was. It's the truth.

The Wedding

I had a nice wedding there at our house. In the church first because me and Mike was the first ones to get married in Our Lady. Father McDade married us, but the dance and the dinner was at our house on Seventh Street. That's also where I did the *presentación* to tell everybody we was gonna get married. Four months later I was married. On January 10, 1929.

A lotta people came because my dad and my mom already knew lots of people. And some of 'em helped build our church, so we made quite a few friends. Everybody knew my dad. Then, all my friends came from when I was in school.

Yeah, the house was pretty full 'cause it was in winter and we couldn't even go out to the porch. But they made the living room bigger because they took the wall out − like I took mine out here − and it was real big. And then when my dad made two more rooms in back, that gave us more room, and the kitchen was real big, too. There was two, three, four − yeah, four rooms and the basement, which it was just one room, but it was big.

Don Juan and *Chole* made my wedding. They bought my dress, the veil, my shoes − everything I needed for the wedding. That's what they call *'las donas'*. But my dad and mom paid for all the dinner. Everything was there on Seventh Street.

Nobody gave gifts or anything because they didn't do it like they do now where the *novias* want them to give 'em everything real pretty for their home. The only one was my *tío Hijinio* who gave me *diez pesos*. And with that ten dollars I bought a little *petaquita* that I still have here in the basement. I use that for putting away little memories. That's where I have Bobby's[1] boxing gloves and his shorts, and I have in there my little crown and the picture of my first communion. I hope nobody rummage in there to take 'em. I'm not gonna say who!

The *padrinos* made the dance. My *madrina* was Ramona. She wasn't married with Johnny Mack yet, and my *padrino* was her brother *Estevan Rico*. They were the *Padrinos de Boda*, the main ones. The other ones were *Luz de la Rosa* and *Manuel Morales, el concuño de Jovita*[2] after she got married. All of them made me the dance. They got musicians who played here and there. I didn't know them.

Everybody danced a lot. Especially my dad and mom. They was such good dancers, and they danced all the *piezas*. Me and Mike danced a lot, too. But now, we could talk together and my dad couldn't say nothing. But Mike was very bashful, so we didn't say too much. We just looked at each other with goo-goo eyes.

I remember my *padrino Estevan* so much. The one that didn't talk. None of 'em talked. *Ramona* had three brothers, and they never said nothing. Not one word. *Estevan* was the tallest one.

After I got married, *Chole* and me sometimes walked to the store, and we would run into him. He never said one word. It didn't matter if somebody talked to him, he just laughed. Chole said hello, *"Buenos días, Compadre.*[3] *¿Cómo está?"* I said hello, too, but he didn't answer. He just laughed. He smiled and he nodded 'is head to say hello.

---

[1] Elvira's third child.

[2] 'husband of Jobita's sister-in-law', a specific in-law relationship in Spanish based on his being a brother-in-law *(cuñado)* of Jobita's husband.

[3] As her son's best man, Estevan was now Chole's *compadre*, also a formal religious relationship. She was his *comadre*.

One day, we was walkin' to Hightower, and we saw him comin'. So, *Chole* said, *"Mira.* There comes my *compadre.* You watch what I'm gonna do."
This time, she didn't say hello. She just passed by. But when we didn't say nothing, he turned around and said, *"Buenos días."* *Chole* just looked at 'im and smiled and nodded 'er head to 'im to say 'Hello'. We kept on walking, but *Chole* was laughing so hard because she made 'im talk. That's the way she was, *satírica.*

The Honeymoon

So then, the dance finished, the *fiesta* finished, and the wedding was over with. *Don Juan* was just sitting there, serious, with *Chole* and their boys. He said, "Well, let's go then."

But my mom said, "Say, *Maique.* ¿Why don't you leave *Elvira* here tonight? She doesn't have anything except the clothes she has on." *Dijo,* "That way, she can get her suitcase tomorrow and go."

But, right away, *don Juan* said, *"No, Elvira's* leaving right now." Then, he looked at Mike, and told 'im, "She's your wife, and you're taking her right now."

I didn't know nothing about *don Juan,* but that told me everything.

We was gonna go live with them, *en la casa de los Hernández.* It's over there close to the Hightower's store, right across on 1106 Ninth Avenue. In front of some apartments that belong to the church.

Don Juan bought that house right away when he was sure that we was gonna get married. They used to rent a house close to the sugar factory. But they decided not to go back to Kansas, and Mike was their oldest son. So, we had to go live with them.

I don't know why *don Juan* didn't buy a house for us or help us rent one. But he said he had to get a house for everybody because Mike was going to bring them a daughter. Sha! A daughter? Not me!

Well, when we got to the house, everybody went inside. I couldn't go in. I got so I couldn't go in! Oh! I don't know why I wasn't happy. It was so hard for me when I left my home. Instead of bein' happy, Mike couldn't take me inside that house.

I was cryin' an' cryin' an' cryin'. Outside in the cold. Mike was sitting there with me. Oh! I couldn't stop crying.

"Come on," he told me, "*Vente.*"

Mike was so good. That's one thing I always say that I have been so happy to be married to Mike. Very happy. It was a really nice matrimony with us. He was so kind to me. Very much.

Like Father said to us, "When you get married, you aren't two no more. The two become one, because if you have something you wanna talk about it, both of you talk about it. Two have to be the same because you're gonna have a family and you're gonna treat them the same way you are together." And that's true. No way Mike ever got mad at me. Ooh! Because with one word, he said everything.

"Come on," he said. And he put his arms around me.

"No."

They all went inside, but I couldn't go in. I was cryin' an' crying' and cryin'. I couldn't stop. That was my wedding. That was my honeymoon. I don't know what time I stopped cryin'. I couldn't go in the house.

He said, "Dear" – that's what he called me. He said, "Dear, right here is gonna be your house."

I said, "No, this is not my house. I left my house." And there comes the cryin' again.

Finally, I went in. I don't know what time. Cryin' an' cryin' an' cryin'. I woke up cryin'. It was nothing. Nothing. I just didn't want anything with that house. I didn't like it.

At first, they didn't know about my *genio* because I didn't say nothing. I stayed quiet. They didn't know who I was. But they found out later, especially *don Juan*. He found out about me. I always had a *genio* like my dad. Because the word '*genio*' says two things. *Genio* can be either grouchy or nice. 'Oh, what a nice person she is! She's always smiling.' Or else, 'Oh, she's so grouchy. Nobody can stand her.' I was the grouchy one.

Living Arrangements

We lived in that house for five years with the whole family – the boys *Cesáreo, Moisés,* and Johnny.[4] Five years together, and it was really hard because *don Juan* had me up to my head. He was strict as anything. He never liked me, and I didn't either. Ooh, I was so mad. Sometime, not all the time. But I was mad. Mike never told me nothing.

The house had two rooms for the bedrooms – one for them and the other one for us – and the living room and the kitchen. The kitchen was *Chole's.* She made the *tortillas* and cooked everything. I helped her wash dishes and whatever I could, but the kitchen was hers.

The boys all slept downstairs in the basement. They had a door on the floor of the kitchen that they opened and had steps to go down. But when Johnny got married, they put a door on the outside so Johnny and Ramona could live downstairs. They made one room for the boys and two rooms for Johnny – the bedroom and the kitchen, that's all. But they wanted to have everybody there together. Tied up there with them.

I think that was the custom in Mexico because that's what *Consuelo* did with my mom's house *en Durango.* They used to go through the *zaguán,*[5] and outside is where they washed clothes. The yard was big. But now, they made kind of like apartments all the way around where all of her children have their house. They even have a clinic and a drugstore because some of them are doctors. And they made *Consuelo's* house real nice and real big. But they're all still crowded up in there, anyway.

Afterwards, *cuando los Hernández* went back to Mexico, that's how they had *Cesáreo,* too. Him and my sister *Teresa* got married

---

[4] See *Figure 5. The Family of Juan Hernández and Soledad Fonseca,* p. 154 at the end of this chapter.

[5] 'foyer', a common architectural feature of Mexican houses of the period.

over there. That's why their family is *Hernández-Chávez, too.* They lived there with *don Juan* for a long time after they got married. *Teresa* says that they was real strict with her, *Chole* and *don Juan,* both of 'em.

Anyway, when we went to live with them, Mike right away got a job at the sugar factory because the work didn't start yet in the farm. At that time, he earned eighteen dollars a week.

The first check he got, *dijo,* "Here. Here's the check."

Le dije, "¿What do I want it for?"

He said, "Well, you're gonna take care of the money." He said he was gonna work and I was gonna be in charge of the money and the house.

"Me?" I didn't want no money. What money!? I was just surprised.

Le dije, "¿And what am I gonna do with the money?"

"Well, buy what you need, and then put away what we have to save."

So now I was gonna be the boss of Mike's money! That was too hard for me. And it seemed different because the husband was always in charge of the money. We stayed with *don Juan* for five years, and he was the one that had the money.

A Mean Man

Chole decía, "*Papá Yoni,*"[6] – that's how she called *don Juan.* "*Papá Yoni,* I don't have any salt. I'm out of salt."

Then he told *Moisés* or *Cesáreo,* "Go get some salt over at Hightowers." He gave 'em a dollar or whatever.

Both of 'em went, but when they got back, he stuck out his hand, "*La feria.* ¿How much did it cost?" He wanted the change. Oh! He was so stingy.

---

[6] *Chole's* Spanish pronunciation of *Johnny,* 'Juan'.

At least my dad gave Mom money. *"¿You need something? ¡Here!"* He would throw her ten dollars or five dollars or whatever. But even if he threw it, he still gave her.

Yeah. *Don Juan* was really tight. And then, he was the one that got the beet contracts. He got a hundred acres or something like that. When we was working, there was seven of us. Well, it was *don Juan, Moisés, Cesáreo,* Johnny and Ramona, me and Mike. *Moisés* was the youngest one. He was gonna be ten when we got married, but he worked in the beets, too.

We was supposed to get about fourteen, fifteen acres each one. Everybody worked, but I think he just gave us for about four or five acres. We only got about a hundred dollars for the whole winter. He stayed with all the money – to pay for the house expenses and for gas, I suppose. We didn't save when we was there with them.

They wanted me to call them *'Papá' y 'Mamá'*. Uh-uh! *'Mamá'* is just my mom and my dad, too. No *'Papá'* for me 'cause I have my *papá*. No *'Mamá'* for me, either. They was *Chole* and *don Juan*.

Chole, she was an angel. Oh! She treated me like a daughter, and I loved her, too. But I always called her *'Chole'*. And everybody called him *'don Juan'*, and I did, too.

How could I call him *'Papá'*? I didn't like 'im from the first time I met 'im. He was serious, serious. He was – I don't know how to say it. He didn't talk. Him and me never talked. I don't think so. I'm not sure, but I don't think so. Maybe one or two words when I got mad at 'im.

That man had a bad temper. Aagh! The dog? If it just barked because a car passed, there he goes. Bam! Bam! Bam! Oh, he beat that dog so bad!

And he was really hard with the boys. I felt so sorry for them. He hit 'em for nothing. Bam! Bam!

My dad also hit my brothers. Yeah, he did. He said, *"Frega'o muchacho carajo.* I'm gonna . . .". Wham! But my dad just kick at 'im, and there goes the boy running, and my dad didn't go after 'im. He just got mad quick and then got over it. That was it.

But, you think the boys would run away from *don Juan?* I think he could'a killed 'em! One time we was all eating. I already had *Elvira.*[7] Mike was sitting down and *Cesáreo* and *Moisés* were next to him. Johnny was already married, and they lived downstairs. Then, *Moisés* and *Cesáreo* started to argue about a plate that was broken. It had a little chip on the side.

"This ain't my plate. You got mine."

"No, that one's broken. That's yours. I didn't get nothin'."

Don Juan was just quiet. He just said, "*Cállense.*"

They didn't pay attention, or maybe they didn't hear, and they kept on arguing. Then *Moisés* pushed 'is plate and tried to get the one from *Cesáreo.*

So, *don Juan* gets up, and he takes off his belt. "You don't throw your plate like that. ¡Here! ¡Let me show you!" *¡Shúpale!* He beat both of 'em with that belt. Right there at supper time. He hit 'em so hard, I couldn't eat!

And he looked at Mike and he told 'im, "*¡Y tú!* You don't get up from there. Eat! Just 'cause you're married, I'm not afraid of you. I'll take care of you, too."

Dije, "¡I am going to get up from here!" I pushed my plate and grabbed my baby and ran out. Anyway, what was he gonna do? He wasn't gonna hit me! I wasn't afraid of him.

Mike just put his head down and didn't say one word. Mike never told me nothing about anything I said to them. I got mad at them. I did.

That's why one time *Chole* went and told my mom, "*Ay, Jacinta*," *dice*. "You should see how grouchy Elvira is. ¡She even talks back to *Papá Yoni!*"

Oh, *don Juan* was terrible. He was so mean with his kids. I don't know why, but that's the way he was. *Que Dios lo perdone.* It's not that I'm talking about him. I am not saying anything that it's wrong, *pero* that's the way he was. It's the truth.

---

[7] Her first child, also named '*Elvira*'.

That's why one day, the last time *Moisés* came here to see me, may God help him. We was visiting and we mentioned *don Juan. Dice Moisés,* "I hate my dad."

Le dije, "*Moisés,* don't hate your dad. He's gone. ¿Why do you have to hate him?" I said, "My dad was mean, too, but we never hated 'im."

"¡I don't even want to remember him!"

Le dije, "Then, ¿why are you talking about 'im?" *Dije,* "Look, he's dead now. Forgive everything he did, whatever it was. He's not from here anymore. ¿Why do you still have that hate for him?"

Dijo, "The hate I have is to remember what he did to us."

I said, "Forget it. He didn't know any better. Like our Lord said, 'Forgive them Father, they don't know what they're doing.' He forgave the ones that crucified him."

"No," dijo. "I don't forgive him. I don't know where he is, and I don't care." He said, "I don't even want to think about my dad."

Well, that was his business. But *don Juan* really was horrible.

One day that we was having breakfast, I got so mad he even made me cry. Oh! I didn't know what to do. Because I already gave *Elvira* her breakfast so we could eat by ourselves. She was real little. She wasn't even two years old yet, but she already was walking and she talked real nice. She only talked in Spanish – all of my children only spoke Spanish when we lived there with my in-laws. 'Cause *Chole* and *don Juan* didn't know English, so nobody talked to them in English. Nothing.

Pero mijita[8] she was so cute. *Maique* made her a pretty little toilet. When she wanted to go do something, we gave her the funnies to look at. Then she stood up and looked down to see if she did something. If there wasn't anything, she would sit down again. She minded real good, and ever since she was a baby, she was real quiet. She never cried.

---

[8] 'my little daughter', an affectionate shortening of *mi hijita.*

The boys really loved her. They called her *"La Beibe"*,[9] and for a long time that was her name – *"Beibe"* instead of *Elvira*. Sometimes they even got together to play ball with her. They would throw her from one to the other one. Real soft. And she laughed so hard. Oh! I just closed my eyes.

Digo, "¡The baby's gonna fall!"

"No, she won't fall."

Yeah. When *don Juan* wasn't there, the boys liked to play around. I remember one day *Moisés* and *Pánfilo Quijas,* a guy from around there, was climbing up a tree. Father McDade just was passing by and saw them up there.

He told 'em, "You boys get down from there. You're gonna fall."

Pánfilo pretended he didn't understand, and he told *Moisés,* *"Dile que no sabemos inglés."*

But the priest, he knew Spanish, and he told him, *"¿Y por qué no saben?"*

Pánfilo didn't even know what to say 'cause he was so surprised that Father understood him. He just said, *"¡Porque no nos han enseña'o!"*[10]

If *don Juan* caught 'em up there, I don't know what he would do. I don't think he would'a hit *Pánfilo,* but *Moisés* he would have, for sure. He hit 'em for nothing. And hard!

Anyway, the day I was talking about, I gave *Elvira* her breakfast first so the rest of us could eat. Because we all had to sit down at the same time, and that was it! So, when she finished eating, we all sat down to eat breakfast.

But the baby really liked *'agüita'* – *la yemita del huevo.*[11] She was walking around the table and she went up to one of the boys – *Cesáreo* or I don't know which one – to ask for *'agüita'.*

---

[9] Spanish rendering of 'the baby'.
[10] 'Because nobody taught us!'
[11] *'agüita* – the liquid yolk of the egg'; *agüita* is the diminutive form of *agua,* 'water'.

"Nomach agüita, nomach agüita," she told him. She wanted 'just a little *agüita'* from his plate. We was all eating eggs sunny side up.

Then, *don Juan* looks at him and said, "¡Don't give her any! Don't none of you give that bribona[12] anything else. ¿You hear me? She already ate her breakfast. These kids," *dijo,* "if you let 'em do what they want, they just take advantage. You have to make 'em listen and respect you. ¡Don't give her any! She's just a spoiled kid."

But there she goes, asking everyone. Then the baby went with Mike and said, *"Agüita,* Daddy. *Nomach agüita."*

"No, mija. Your mom already gave you *agüita,"* he told her. *"Go on to your mom."* Mike was afraid of *don Juan.* Even if he was married, he was afraid of him.

So then she came with me. I gave her a little taste. *"Váyase, mija,"* I told her. "Go on." But I didn't pick her up so I wouldn't make no more commotion.

Then *Elvira* passed by her grandpa. She just looked at 'im. She didn't ask him 'cause she already knew how he was. She didn't ask 'im, but went over to her grandma. She was sitting right next to *don Juan. "Mema, nomach agüita, Mema. Nomach agüita."*

"No, no, hijita," she said. "Go on now. You already had breakfast. No more. Go on."

Then, the baby began to cry because not even her grandma gave her any. There she is cryin' and cryin'.

So, *don Juan* gets up. Boy! He grabbed her and spanked her two times real hard and sat her down on the floor! *Dijo,* "And I don't want nobody to pick up that stubborn girl!"

Nobody? Ha! Well, he can go to the dickens! I pushed my plate and my chair, and I picked up my baby. Oh! I felt like he tore out my heart from my body.

---

[12] 'cheater, trouble maker'.

Dijo, "Well, now. I thought I just said nobody to pick up that spoiled girl." Then he looked at Mike, *"¡Y tú!* ¡You don't say a thing!" Like he wanted 'im to scold me or something.

I was the one that said something. "¡Yes, she's spoiled!" I felt like my head was on fire. *Le dije,* "But at least I don't hit her like some people like to hit their kids. They're really good for hitting." I was so mad, I wanted to die. I didn't know what to do. Well, he hit her so hard and he sat her down on the floor without nothing. Just the bare floor, of wood. *¡Pum!*

I went out with my baby, and I went down the street crying because I was so mad.

Then, *don Juan les dijo a los muchachos,* "You eat." He got up and hit each one of 'em on the head with a spoon – *Cesáreo* and *Moisés* – and he told Mike, "And don't think because you're married I can't do the same to you."

They kept eating breakfast, but Mike couldn't eat no more. He just stayed quiet. He didn't say a word.

Chole

Chole, she never told 'im anything, either. But one day, he was drinking his coffee, and she said something to him. Just some little word that he didn't like, I can't remember what. *¡Shuun!* He throws his cup of coffee at her. But it hit the stove and broke. No, she never said nothing to him. Not even a chance!

She was very good with me, though, but once in a while we fought like two cats. Both of us argued about this and that. Mike never said nothing. Oh, Mike was really good with me. He just put on his hat and went out. He never butt in with us. Or that he would say something to me – that 'Why do you get mad at Mom?' or this or that. No. "Anyway," *decía,* "anyway, you always make up."

Oh, and with the kids *Chole* was so loving. I remember one time she took *Elvira* to the toilet. It was one of those outside toilets with two holes for the seat. Nobody thought anything bad for two people to go in there together.

So, her grandma said to *Elvira,* "*Mijita,* I love you a lot. ¿Do you love me?"

"*Sí, Mema. Yo te quero.*"

"¿How much? ¿As much as this big board?" She point at one of the boards on the toilet.

"*Sí, Mema.*"

"¿As much as two boards?"

"*Sí.*"

"¿As much as how many boards do you love me?"

Then Elvira told her real loud, "¡As much as the WHOLE toilet!"

Chole came in the house laughing so hard. "Look," *me dijo.* "Look at what Beibe told me." That she told her she loved her like the WHOLE toilet. Oh! Both of us laughed so hard!

That's how *Chole* was, very funny. Like when we used to make *empanaditas*[13] to sell after Mass. There's *Chole* selling outside the church, saying, "¡Come on, gentlemen! ¡Come and get a nice, warm *empinadita!*[14] ¡Come and get your *empinadita!*" Oh, she was such a joker.

She was never afraid of sayin' something. One time, we was walking on Broadway and there was some Russian ladies talkin' by the sidewalk. We was passing, and they was talkin' in German. And then we heard 'em say "*Mexikander*". They said something about *Mexikander.* "There go some *Mexikanders,*" or something like that.

Dijo Chole, "Look at those darn women. They're saying 'Here come some Mexicans'. So then we passed by, and *Chole* turned around real fast and said, "Teka gud luk! Teka gud luk!"[15] Oh, they was so surprised, they left right away. That's how she was, a joker.

---

[13] 'a fruit filled pastry'

[14] 'a girl bending over'. Of course, playing suggestively with the word '*empanadita*'.

[15] Chole's pronunciation of "Take a good look!"

FIGURE 5. THE FAMILY OF JUAN HERNANDEZ
AND SOLEDAD FONSECA

Juan Hernández + Soledad Fonseca
(don Juan)   (Chole)

       |

—Miguel (Maique) + Elvira Chávez (Vera)
—Johnny Mack + Ramona Rico (Monchi)
—Cesáreo + Teresa Chávez (Tere)
—Moisés + Carmen Torres (Carmela)

ELVIRA'S WEDDING

<u>Back Row</u>: Maid of Honor Ramona Rico; Best Man Estevan Rico; Groomsman Manuel Chávez; Bridesmaid Luz de la Rosa.

<u>Front Row</u>: Flower Girl Teresa Chávez, Maique, Elvira.

The Newlyweds

Elvira in the latest style and Maique also in his finest: *"de pipa y guante"*.

don Juan Hernández

In front of the Juan Hernández house in Scottsbluff.

Left to Right: Moisés, Cesáreo, Johnny Mack, Tere Chávez, Elvira and Maique, Chole's sister Mercedes (Meche) Fonseca, Chole, don Juan.

Photo taken February 1929

155

Elvira, Jr. "La Beibe" at one and a half.

The wedding of Teresa Chávez and Cesáreo Hernández.

Chapter Eleven

CHITO

I was always afraid – all of us was in my family.
Papá Lolo and my mom and my dad always told stories.
Dead people came and talked to us, and we saw ghosts.

Chito's Death

In nineteen thirty-one, after we finished topping, Mike and I went to Kansas City because he wanted to get his electricity certificate to work on the cars. He already had his mechanic certificate 'cause before we got married, *la familia Hernández* used to pass the winter in Kansas, so Mike went to school there, but he didn't have the electricity. Then, afterwards, he could get work in any place as a mechanic. I still have his diploma. Mary Lou put it in a frame for me.

I was expecting my second baby that was gonna be born in Kansas. We stayed over there with *Coni, Chole's* sister. She came to Kansas with them when *Chole* and *don Juan* came from *León.* There in Kansas is where she met *Chente – Vicente Velásquez.* They had three children – little *Chente, Pedro,* and *Conchita.* They was all still little when we stayed with them. Afterwards, *Chente* came to visit us in Scottsbluff when he was in the army.[1]

---

[1] See *Figure 6. The Family of Concepción Fonseca and Vicente Velásquez,* page 166 at the end of this chapter.

Chito

We stayed with *Coni* in a house that I think was on Third Street, there in Armourdale in Kansas City. That place was ugly. Really ugly. It was one of those big old houses, kinda old fashion that had rooms on top, like the ones that are in the cowboy shows. *Coni* and *Chente* lived downstairs, and we had the upstairs. It had a long dark, dark hall, and it had steps to go down and some more to go to the yard. It had three other rooms and one great big one in the front that was for us. That's where we had our bedroom and the kitchen. In that room, the wall was all windows from one corner to the other one. Nothing but windows.

Chito lived in the next room to us, and there was two more rooms on the other side. He was a nephew of *Coni* and *Chole,* the son of one of the *Fonsecas,* one of their brothers. They had two or three brothers in Mexico. They was all tall, but one of 'em, *Chole* said that that brother, if they went to the depot to wait for the train, or where there was a lotta people, he was so tall that his hat stuck up over everybody. *Eduardo's* son Michael probably has *Fonseca* blood, too. He's like his grandpa because *Maique* was tall, too, maybe six foot tall.

Chole decía, "I was the shortest one of all my family."

Anyway, that's where *Chito* lived, in the next room to us. They called 'im *'Chito'* or *'Muchito',*[2] but I think his name was Ezequiel, I'm not sure. He looked a lot like Chente, junior. I got a picture of him here somewhere. His head was white, white, like all the *Fonsecas.* My daughter Terry and *Eduardo's* daughter Michelle have hair like that. Johnny Mack, too. That's where they get their white hair, from the *Fonsecas.* That family has real strong blood.

When they killed *Chito,* he was about thirty or so. And I saw that from our bedroom. Mike slept on one side of the bed, and I slept on the side so I could watch *Elvira* in her little bed. So I could get down right away.

Then I heard talking and talking. 'What's that?' So I got up to look. It was dark inside, but I could see outside because the windows were big, and there was lights in the street.

---

[2] A shortened form of *'muchachito', little boy.*

158

There was two men coming up to the house, and I'm looking out the window, when bang! bang! bang! The shots. I even saw the fire come out of the gun. *¡Pum!* He fell down right in front of the door. Oh, I got so scared. 'Who could it be?'

Oh! I run. *"¡Maique! ¡Maique!"* Oh, Mike was such a sleepy head. He was hard to wake up. No matter what, he didn't wake up.

Finally, he asked me, *"¿*What are you doing awake at this hour?"

Le dije, "They just killed somebody right outside."

Then he got up in a big hurry. There he goes without pants on, without nothing. He just had his shorts. He thought it was outside the bedroom, in the hallway.

Le dije, "No, not inside. Downstairs, outside. I saw the gun, and then I saw the man run."

*"¿*Well, what can we do? Go to bed."

Oh. I laid down, but I was more scared than anything. I stayed awake, listening. Mike went back to sleep.

Then, the other man knocked on the door for *Chente* and *Coni*, the one that was with *Chito*. *Chito* was the one they killed, but I didn't know that yet. The man knocked hard so they could hear. *¡Tras, tras, tras!* They didn't hear, or they just didn't get up. Okay. So, the man ran to get the police.

But the man and the policeman went first to get the killer because the guy who was with *Chito* knew who he was, 'cause he was a friend of them. They was all out drinking on a street like Ninth Street here, and they was fighting with the one who killed 'im – both of 'em, this guy and *Chito*. All three of 'em was drunk. They fought over there and they beat up the killer. So, *Chito* and his friend came over here to *Coni's* house, and the other one went home. But he went to get his gun.

Coni's house had a porch with a roof that made kind of a hallway to the front door. The windows on the upstairs came out to the sidewalk, and the door was back. It made a little dark hall. That's where the killer was hiding. Well, who could see him? The other two was coming on the sidewalk when he shot at 'em, and right away he ran home.

So, yeah, they caught 'im at home. They found 'im drunk on his bed with his shoes on. He was already asleep, but he still had his shoes on. Then, they went to take the prisoner to jail. But they didn't come and take *Chito* to the hospital. Nothing. They just left 'im there. Oh! I even heard 'im groaning from up there. I heard him breathing! He wasn't dead yet.

No, they went to take the prisoner first. They caught him, but they didn't do nothin' to 'im. Anyway, if a Mexican killed a Mexican, that's okay.

After a while, I heard somebody coming, talkin' and talkin'. I was still really scared, but I got up to see who it was. It was the policeman and the other one that was comin' again. The policeman came and knocked on the door real hard so they would wake up. No, they didn't answer.

Then, they put a light on 'im, the one that was laying there. And I saw it was *Chito!*

"*¡Maique, Maique! ¡Get up! ¡It's Chito!*"

"*¡No!*"

Dije, "Yeah. It's Chito. They put 'im the light. Come on."

By now, *Chente* heard 'em and he got up. *Dijo,* "¡Darn kids! They sure bother. It's the ones that are looking for trouble."

They already heard the knocking, but they didn't want to get up. Nobody said anything, so they thought it was just anybody.

Chente said, "Okay. If they knock on the door again, I'm gonna beat 'em." He got a stick and went out the back door to go around to the front.

Mike already got up and put his clothes on, so we went downstairs. *Coni* was in bed shaking and shaking 'cause she was so scared, but she still didn't know who it was. I was the only one, and I didn't tell her it was *Chito* until they told her. I only told Mike.

Dijo Coni, "I don't know who wants to break the door." She said, "They been pounding on it."

They heard 'em, but they didn't want to get up to see who it was. They didn't hear the gun. I was the only one. I even saw the fire.

So then, *Chente* went to the front door and saw *Chito*. He said, "¡Ay! *Chito,* doggone it. This dang guy gets drunk, then he can't even get home."

So he went and picked 'im up. *¡Iiiy!* He saw the blood and saw that he was dead. Boy! He got so scared, and that's when *Chente* started to lose his head.

Anyway, they brought the *mortoria* – the ambulance – and they took 'im away.

Coni was just shaking and shaking because *Chente* came in and told her. He was white like a sheet. Well, he never thought he was gonna see him shot dead. Both of 'em didn't know what to do. They was just shaking.

One time before I got married, I saw something similar in Scottsbluff. Right there on Seventh Street. We got so scared. Somebody was fighting. We didn't know who it was or nothin'. They was running. One of 'em was comin', and the other one was behind. We was all outside in the yard, and the man comes in! The one that was in front, and the other one in back. He came in running in the yard. He was running, and we was scared that they was gonna fight. The man in back kneeled down, and he shot at the other man, but he ran over to the tracks. *¡Tras, tras!* But he didn't hit 'im. And then, this one ran over there. I think he wanted to catch him on the other side, but he didn't.

My dad wasn't there. *Dijo mi mamá*, "¡Ay! ¡Lock the doors! Lock them all, *¡por Dios!*"

It's a good thing he didn't shoot any of the kids that was outside playin' 'cause it wasn't dark yet. That was the only time I see anything like that.

The Scaredy Cat

The night they killed *Chito*, I didn't go outta my room no more because I was so scared, and I couldn't sleep or nothing. Then upstairs, *Chito's* room was right next to my kitchen. *¡Ay, Dios de mi vida!* I was so afraid. I was really a scaredy cat. Too much. And then the hall was dark, dark, dark, all the way back. ¡Ooh! There was his room and then two more rooms that was empty. *¡Ay, Dios!* I was so scared.

The next day at night, Mike told me, "I'm gonna go meet my friends. I won't be long." He was gonna go see some ballplayers that played with him before in Kansas City when he was young.

He said, "They're gonna get together, and they invited me."

I said, *"¡Ay!* I'm gonna stay by myself."

Me dijo, "Go downstairs with my aunt. Anyway, you can leave the baby asleep." So, Okay. He went. ¡Eee! I was so scared I was shaking because Chito's room was right next to us.

'No', *dije*. 'As soon as I put Elvira to sleep, I am going downstairs. ¡Oh! I'm not gonna stay here.' So, I put the baby to bed. '¿But, how can I go?' There was three rooms alone over there, and me over here, and the hallway so dark without lights or anything, and the steps was so big. '¿How can I go?' I was dying!

But I got brave. '¡Yes! I'm going.' I went out real quiet. But as soon as I went out, I heard somebody coming behind me. I started to run, and they threw rocks at me! The rocks was following me on the steps, and I went running and yelling.

Coni opened the door, "¿What's the matter?"

The rocks were hitting my feet, but she didn't believe me. She went to look, and sure enough there was some little rocks. *Dijo*, "I think those little rocks fell from over there." Oh, I got so scared.

I was always afraid. All of us was in my family because *Papá Lolo* and my mom and my dad always told stories about things that happened. Dead people came and talked to us, and we saw ghosts. Oh, we didn't go out at night by ourselves. *¡Ni qué esperanzas!* We was afraid of the dark. No, no, no! We was too afraid. Sometimes we got so scared that we got bumps on our skin.

Well, when Mike got back from his meeting, I told 'im, "We gotta get outta here. Dead people come, or I don't know what. I can't stay here no more." Because they just killed *Chito* there. Oh, it was scary! And then, I was expecting my baby in two or three weeks.

Coni and *Chente* didn't want to stay, either, because that's where they killed *Chito*. No. Right away the next day they started to look for a house. They found one on Sixth Street close to John J. Ingalls. Behind it, was Fifth Street, and John J. Ingalls was on Sixth. We was across. We moved in about a week, a little bit after we buried *Chito*. I just couldn't take it. I couldn't.

And I didn't let Mike leave me alone for nothing. Uh-uh. Not until after we moved. Then, two weeks later, Eduardo was born in the other house. I think I got so scared that the baby was born sick. He was the only one that was born sick.

And *Chente* didn't feel good either. He got a nervous breakdown also from that, from the shock he got with *Chito*. The poor guy went crazy. He lost his mind. It was pretty bad for him to lose his head so much. They had to put 'im in the insane asylum – *en el manicomio*.

He stayed a lotta years, and then they let 'im come out. But he did some real bad things there with *Coni* – he even chased her with a knife. So, they put him in again. But the last time he came out, he was much better.

Oh, Robert[3] liked him so much. We went to see the *Velásquez* family when *Coni* died. I think it was in nineteen sixty-three. Robert was little, about three or four years old.

He told *Vicente,* "Uncle, can we go get some candy?"

Chente dijo, "Say, Mike, ¿can I take Bobby to the store?"

I told 'im, "No, he better stay here." I was afraid for him to take 'im.

---

[3] Elvira's grandson and adopted son.

Maique said, "Yes, take him." *¡Ay!* I don't know what I felt like. Well, he had already been in the insane asylum two times. But he got better.

Las Bilis

They tell me that it was because I got so scared when they killed *Chito* that Eduardo was born crying. But really, he was born sick. He never stopped crying. That's why Mike built 'im a little *cuna*. It was just a wood frame that we nailed some canvas on it really good, and we put a little mattress in the middle. On the corners, Mike put four little ropes that I tied together, and then a long one that I tied on a hook over the bed. Because he wouldn't let us sleep unless we rocked 'im.

Oh! He would wake up cryin' and cryin' and cryin'! *¡Pum!* I swung the *cuna*. He was quiet for a little while. Then it stopped, and there he is cryin' again, and I had to push the *cuna*. All night long.

And then he threw up everything – breast milk, cow milk, *leche de águila,*[4] can milk, powder milk. The doctor even gave us a prescription so we can give 'im special milk for a medicine. Everything, but nothing was any good. Sick and sick and sick.

When he was born, the doctor went to our house to take care of me because in those times, they was born at home. But he never registered the birth certificate. Oh, Kansas City was terrible. A Mexican was born, like he was an animal. He didn't register him. And then his baptism certificate got lost because there was a fire in the church and all the papers got burned.

That's why when Eddie was older and he needed a birth certificate to play baseball, we had to go to the school and to the priest to sign papers that they knew him and that he was born on a certain day and on a certain place.

When we baptized him, *Chole* and *don Juan* went to Kansas City. They stayed there with *Coni* and with us for a few days.

---

[4] a brand of sweetened milk.

Chole helped me a lot with Eduardo, but she didn't know why he was so sick, either. *Coni* and *Vicente* was going to be the *padrinos.* They all went to the baptism, and I stayed at home 'cause I was still pretty sick. I didn't feel good. Mike stayed with me.

I said that his name was gonna be *'Miguel'.* But *don Juan* wanted them to put *'Eduardo',* I don't know why. Maybe that was an uncle of *don Juan,* or who knows? I told 'em, "No, I want *'Miguel'".* Because I wanted to name him after his dad.

So, they all went to baptize him. But, because I couldn't go, *don Juan* was stubborn and they put him *'Eduardo',* but with *'Miguel'* in the middle only because I wanted it – because he wanted *'Eduardo',* and I didn't. That's how *don Juan* was. He always wanted things his own way.

That's why when they finally gave him his birth certificate, they put him 'Edward Michael'. Afterwards, when he was in college in California, he made 'em change it back to *'Eduardo'.* But since he did that, he should'a changed it to *'Miguel Eduardo'.* That's what I wanted, but he didn't know it, I guess.

The baby stayed real sick until a Mexican woman – *una curandera* – told Mike, "*¿Sabe qué?* He has *bilis,* and he's sick in his stomach."

I gave him *bilis. Bilis* is when you're sick on account of an upset or something like that. I don't know. They say that *bilis* affects your system.

She said, "And look, in Texas there's this Dr. So-and-So that's really good to cure *bilis* in little babies. A Mexican. A Mexican doctor."

So *Maique* wrote down the address to send for the medicine. It was some real little pills. *Y luego,* the woman told us, "After you give him the pills, you have to give him *leche de chiva.*" Okay. We gave him the pills, and we got some goat milk there in Kansas City.

When we got back to Scottsbluff, *Eduardo* was skinny, skinny. You could even see his ribs. Right away we bought a *chiva.*

Before Mike went to work, I told him, "You have to milk the goat. *Yo no la ordeño." El la ordeñaba.* Then, I let the milk cool off, and I strained it with a cheesecloth to clean it. *¡Uuy!* It smelled so bad. Even by cooking it, it smelled. *¡Ay!* I didn't taste that milk. But Mike really liked it. I made his oatmeal *con leche de chiva.* And the kids were all brought up with that milk. With that and with the pills, little by little *Eduardo* got well, but we worked hard with him for two years.

¡Pobrecita de la chiva! Later on, when we worked over there with Baltes, one day we went to town. We had her tied up, and some dogs came and killed her. Well, she had no place to run. *Pobre chiva.*

FIGURE 6. THE FAMILY OF CONCEPCION FONSECA AND VICENTE VELASQUEZ

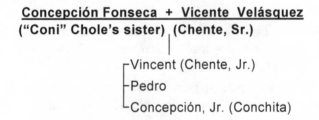

Concepción Fonseca + Vicente Velásquez
("Coni" Chole's sister) (Chente, Sr.)

┌Vincent (Chente, Jr.)
├Pedro
└Concepción, Jr. (Conchita)

Young <u>Chito</u>: Ezequiel Fonseca

Maique's first cousin, the son of one of Chole's brothers.

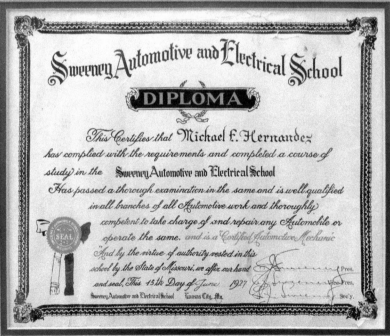

Maique's diploma from Sweeny Automotive School in Kansas City, Missouri in 1927.

Chapter Twelve

MAIQUE'S EMANCIPATION

Don Juan was sitting there. He was like a king, you know.
Le dijo Maique, "You! ¿How have you treated my mother?
You keep my mother down.
I'm not going to treat my wife like you do."

Her Own Kitchen

I was with them in the same kitchen for three years. 'Twenty-nine, 'thirty, and 'thirty-one. Until we got back from Kansas in nineteen thirty-two. I didn't wanna be together with them no more. I just didn't want to be. So then, they gave us two rooms 'cause Eddie was a little baby. I made one of 'em a little kitchen and the other one our bedroom. The other kitchen was theirs, and the living room was for everybody. Now I was happier. At least I had my own kitchen, and we didn't have to be eating with them.

So, when we got back from Kansas City, right away Mike got work in a garage. But he couldn't go on with that work. It wasn't good for him to be shut up in a garage with all the smoke, the gas, and everything, so he got real sick. He even threw up. They brought him home one day all passed out. So, he had to leave that work. But he still worked for a while, especially because the field work didn't start yet.

One time he went to fix his car there in *don Juan's* garage, and he didn't come in to eat. Chole said, *"Y Miguelito, ¿Why isn't he here? The supper's ready."*

Yo le dije, "I don't think he's gonna be long."

But still, I thought it was strange, and I went out to look for him. There he was, passed out on the hood of the car. From the gas. That's why he couldn't work as a mechanic. Otherwise, he would've, and we wouldn't have to stay working on the farms. But the farm was all there was.

We stayed living there with *don Juan* for two more years until nineteen thirty-four. But he didn't give us any money for everything we worked because we was all there like one family. He never gave us a penny. So we didn't save when we were there with them.

That's why, after topping was finished, Mike right away went to look for work at the factory because that's when they needed people to make the sugar. They didn't pay very much, about a dollar a day. *Pero, peor es chile y l'agua lejos.*[1] He worked there until we started to thin beets.

Every year about in April, *don Juan* was the one that found the work for all of us. But in 'thirty-four, the Depression was pretty strong. Really bad. And they didn't give him the job where we worked every year.

Work was real scarce, and people came from everywhere to work in the beets. Everybody was grabbing what they could, *peor me digan los rusos.*[2] Right away, they got the best fields. The fields were full of Germans, and they didn't leave any for the Mexicans, or they left the worse ones.

When there wasn't any workers, the Mexican people, we was important. But not in that time. It was so hard to find a job. We were right in the middle of the Depression. You had run hard to see where you could find a farm to work.

And *don Juan* didn't go out to look. He expected the *revisador* to come and get 'im. He just stayed there in the house, waiting. But he was not that important anymore.

---

[1] 'It's better than nothing.' Literally, *'It's worse eating chile and not having any water.'*

[2] 'especially the Russians.' Literally, 'worse, they tell me, the Russians'.

Entons' le dije a Mike, "Look, your dad won't go out to find work, and your job at the factory is gonna be over. ¿What are we gonna do?"

I was anxious to get out of there. I'd get so mad 'cause *don Juan* would catch *Eduardo* and hit 'im because he used to run around a lot. He was just two years old then, but he went everywhere. He even got on top of the garage!

Don Juan yelled at him, "Boy, ¡you get down from there! ¡You're like a *chivo!*" And wham! He'd give 'im a spanking. *¡Ay!* I got so mad. I was insisting for us to get out of there.

I even scared Mike. I told 'im, "If we don't get outta here, we're not gonna have nothin' to eat. Your dad don't get a job. Don't wait for him. ¿Why don't you go out and look for a farm?"

He said, "But I have to tell my dad." He was afraid to tell him. But finally he did. He asked him if he found a farm yet.

Don Juan said, "Well, I haven't heard from the *revisador* yet."

"Well," Mike told 'im, "we have to go look, to see where we can find something."

So, *don Juan* stayed without work, and Mike went out to look. Right away, he found a little acreage of beets there with Baltes in Scottsbluff, right across from the cemetery. So then he told *don Juan* that he'd found a small place and that we was gonna move.

We moved in May. Oh! After five years, I was so happy that I was gonna have my own house with my children! *¡Ay! Dije, 'Gracias a Dios* for giving us this work.'

It was twenty-five acres just for me and Mike. The house was in the middle of a field. There was beets all around it. I liked that because I could go out of the house in a hurry to thin beets a little bit while the kids were asleep.

Sometimes, I would take them out there to play close to me while I worked because I didn't have nobody to watch 'em. Well, the kids were all little. *Elvira* was four and a half, and Eddie was two. Bobby was just born, and he was about ten months.

But I was happy.

Los Huesos³

At Baltes, the front room was the bedroom of all of us. *Elvira* slept in a little cot that we bought for her, and I had the *cuna* that Mike made for *Eduardo* hanging up for Bobby. Afterwards, when Terry was born, I put her in the *cuna*, and that's how I changed 'em around.

But *Eduardo* was in the baby bed, the one that *Elvira* used to have. I had 'im close to my bed because he was the one that cried at night. The other ones didn't. *Elvira* hardly didn't wake up, and Bobby, I just gave 'im his bottle, and he went to sleep right away.

I don't know what it was with *Eduardo*. He didn't stop cryin' until about two and a half years. When we started working there at Baltes farm, he still was getting afraid. He was two years old in February.

Anyway, one night he woke me up, *"¡Ma! ¡Ma!"* Cryin' and cryin'.

"What's the matter?" I got up right away.

He was yelling, *"¡Huesos! ¡There's huesos here!"*

So I turned on the light. We didn't have no electricity. I had a lamp by my side, one of those little kerosene lamps that I had to light with a match.

"¿Cuáles huesos?

"¡Here! ¡On my bed!"

So, I calmed 'im down and everything, and I put 'im back to bed.

No, after a little while, he starts yellin', *"¡Aquí! ¡Los huesos!*

¡Válgame Dios!

Mike said, "Bring him over here in the middle." So I got 'im and laid 'im down between us to see if he didn't see the *huesos* no more.

All of a sudden, *"¡Los huesos! ¡Aquí andan! ¡Aquí andan!"*

---

³ 'The bones'.

*¡Ay, Dios santo! ¿*What *huesos?* No, well we didn't see nothing. So finally, we calmed him down and everything.

"Say," Mike said. "¿What does this boy see?"

"Well, that there's *huesos."* What *huesos?* Who knows? I think it was the scare of when *Papá Lolo* was dying. He lived close to my mom, just across a ditch. All of us lived at Neil's farm since before I got married, and Dad and Mom still lived there. *Mi tío José* and *Papá Lolo* were right across, on Charley Barbour's farm.

Well, we went to see him. And we took *Elvira* and *Eduardo* because *Papá Lolo* wanted to tell them goodbye. Bobby was too little. But *Papá Lolo* couldn't talk no more, so he made signs for them to get close to him.

I told the kids, "Go on. Talk to *Papá Lolo.* He's sick, and he can't talk."

Elvira went, and *Papá Lolo* got her hand and gave her a kiss. But *Eduardo* stayed back. *Papá Lolo* looked real old, and his hair wasn't combed. And he moved his mouth, but he didn't talk.

Then, *Papá Lolo* lifted 'imself. He put his hand out and tried to reach *Eduardo*, but he grabbed 'im by his hair. He loved 'im a lot and just wanted to say goodbye. Oh! *Eduardo* got so scared, and he started to cry.

I think that's why, after we buried *Papá Lolo*, *Eduardo* cried and cried all night long because he was seeing *huesos* that was trying to grab 'im.

Mike said, "Well, ¿what's the matter with this boy? Bring him over here to our bed." Okay. We put him in the middle and he quieted down.

I told Mike, "He got scared with *Papá Lolo.* And then, he watched when we buried him." That was the year we lived with Baltes, right in front of the cemetery. I think that made the baby more scared, and that's why he saw *huesos.*

Free at Last!

With Johnny, my in-laws, and us, the three families bought a washing machine together. Well, the depression was really bad then, and we didn't have enough money. Because when we lived with them, *don Juan* took it all. He had money, but he didn't spend it.

Before that, we all washed by hand, with a washboard. But now with the washing machine, we got it one day every week for each one to wash. *Chole* stayed with the machine in her house, and I went over there from Baltes to wash 'cause we didn't have no electricity.

Anyway, one day we was gonna go there to wash, *y me dijo* Mike, "Say, when you finish washing and you dry all the clothes, we'll come home before supper."

I didn't have a clothesline at home, so we couldn't leave until the clothes dried and everything. We went early to go wash, but Mike didn't want us to stay and eat supper no more.

Don Juan got fed up with the kids. *Decía*, "You just leave those kids running around."

Well, we had 'em. What'd he want us to do with 'em? For us to be telling 'em, 'No, don't run' or 'Sit down'? *Válgame*, we hardly let 'em go inside the house!

So then Mike said, "Dad always looks mad. We're not gonna stay for supper." He was tired of his dad's attitude.

So, Mike told me, "But you take the blame. When you finish everything, you tell me, 'Let's go.' ¿Okay?"

He didn't wanna be the one to say 'cause he was still afraid of *don Juan*.

"You're the one to say for us to go."

"Okay."

Anyway, I finished washing and drying the clothes, *y le dije a Teresa, mi hermana,* "Go find Eddie and Bobby, and all of you go get in the car."

At that time, *Teresa* was staying with me. Mom sent her to help me with the kids. She was about thirteen years old. She was thirteen in October, and all of this was after topping.

"I'm just gonna take down the clothes, put 'em in a sheet, and put it in the car. We're not gonna fold 'em until we get home." *Elvira* was with me, and the boys were running around outside.

I went in to tell Mike that all the clothes were done. I went in the living room, and I told 'im, "I'm finished."

He didn't say nothing. Not 'yes', not 'no'. Nothing.

Don Juan was sitting there. He looked like a king, you know. He was like a king. He had his chair close to the door, and he was always there, like an owl. Owls don't talk, they just think.

Chole was in the kitchen, and as soon as she heard me tell Mike, she got up in a hurry to get some food, and she said, *"Ay, you're not leaving yet."* She was so good, and she wanted us to stay for supper.

I told her, "Chole, no. We're not gonna stay." Le dije, "Because the children are tired now. I have to go feed 'em supper and put 'em to bed. I already have the clothes in the car."

"No, no, no. I'll fix some . . . ".

Le dije, "Don't worry about making supper." I told her, "We're going now."

Don Juan was just listening.

I went back to the living room. "Mike," I said, *"Vámonos."*

Quiet.

Before we came, he was the one that said, "You tell me that we have to go. I won't tell you. You tell me."

He didn't answer, so after a while, I called 'im again, "Mike!" This time, I said it more loud. "Mike, the kids are already in the car. I have to go give them supper. Are we going, or not?"

Okay. Then, he stood up in the door of the kitchen, and put his hands on the frame.

Chole said, *"Ay, hijo. 'Horita hago unos frijoles."*

"No," he said. "Don't make anything, Mom. Elvira has to give the kids supper and put them to bed. We better go."

I gave her a hug – she was so good – and I told her, "No, *Chole*. We're going."

So, we started to leave, and I told Mike, "Okay. Come on." That's all I said.

¡Ay! Don Juan I think he was ready to choke me.

Mike said to them, "We'll see you here next week."

Right away, his dad answered him. *Le dijo,* "Yes, that's fine. But if you come, come by yourself so I can show you how to wear pants."

Then, Mike answered 'im, "¿What did you tell me, Dad?"

"What you heard. You're bossed by a woman. You don't wear pants, that's the matter with you." Oh, he told 'im so much.

Then they got into it. Mike turned to me and told me, "Go on."

I went out to the kitchen, but I could still hear 'em.

Entons' Maique le dijo, "No, Dad. I'm going to tell you something. I'm not bossed by any woman. She does what I tell her."

"Oh, yeah," he said. "I can see she's got you right here, look." That I held on to him tight.

That's when Mike started to tell 'im. "Don't you tell me that she bosses me." *Dijo,* "Like I love her, that's how she loves me, and we don't fight." He said, "¿You know what, Dad?" *Dijo,* "I'm not like you. I'm not the only one who says what we do. She tells me, too. A marriage," *dijo,* "a marriage is fifty percent. But not you." *Le dijo,* "You. ¿How have you treated my mother? You keep my mother down. I'm not going to treat my wife like you do. You have bossed all of us. Well, I live alone now, and I'm married, and I'm in another place."

I said, 'Oh, my gosh!' He never talked back to him a single word. When we lived with them, Mike couldn't talk back because that was *don Juan's* house.

I said, 'He's gonna get up and beat 'im up. But if he does, he won't be a son of him no more. I'll call the police.' I would have. *¡Uj!* I never thought that he would talk back to his dad. I don't know how he did it. I don't know. He was just so filled up of him.

They argued like that, but Mike was telling the truth to him. *Don Juan* was a very mean man. *Don Juan* just stayed there and didn't say one more word he was so shocked. And *Chole* didn't say nothing. She was so scared, she just listened.

That's all I heard. I went out to the car. After a while he came out, but we didn't say any more. Mike and I, we didn't comment on anything. He was just really hurt. His heart was very sad. *Sea por Dios.*

Moving Back with don Juan

We worked in the beets all that year for Baltes. But he didn't pay us until March of next year. We worked almost a year without nothing, and we ran out of money. We hardly had anything. We was eating only beans, almost. Or potatoes. The farmer told us that he didn't get what the sugar factory owed 'im until March. But he had his cows, so he had money! I don't know why he didn't pay us. I guess he said, 'Let 'em suffer!'

Well, Baltes came over and told Mike that he would find 'im work at I don't know what farm, but he wanted Mike to take his own truck. Mike told 'im that he didn't wanna do that because he would spend more on gas than what he would earn. He told 'im, "But you're going over there, too. I'll go with you."

Baltes said 'okay'. But one day that doggone guy went and didn't wait for 'im. So, Mike got his truck and told me, "We're leaving from here." He said, "I'm not gonna work no more for this darn man." He said, "¿What does he think? ¿That we're beggars? No, we did his beets for 'im. I'm not gonna work for free no more." He said, "I'm not gonna use my gas all the way to Morrill or Mitchell." I don't know where they was going. He said, "No."

Right away he found work at Woodruff's farm. Woodruff was Summerville's father-in-law, the one that had the filling station that we went to. But we only worked there less than one year. Yeah, half a year. We only did the thinning and the cleaning.[4] I was expecting Terry, so Mike got work at the factory because he didn't want to top beets for Woodruff by himself.

So, in September, we moved back to town with *don Juan* and *Chole* until the baby was born. *Chole* wanted me to go have her there and get well. I didn't want to live with them, but who else could stay with my children?

My mom could barely take care of her kids. *Teresa, Consuelo,* and *Arturo* was already pretty big, but they had to help pick potatoes and top beets. So did Ruth. But *Hermelinda, Ramiro,* and *María* was still little. So my mom couldn't help me.

And then, Jobita was married, but she had to take care of her own little ones and also work in the field. So, we had to go stay with *Chole*. She didn't let me get out of bed for ten days.

The Repatriation(i)

And then around that time, my mom was getting the family ready and cleaning up the *chante* to go back to Mexico. Because in nineteen thirty-five, 'thirty-six, they was sending a lotta people outta here. The Depression was still really bad and there was hardly any work, so they wanted to send back as many Mexicans as wanted to go. They was letting 'em take anything they wanted free. No charge. They didn't even charge 'em at the customs. Nothing. Anybody that wanna go, they could take what they wanted. They was taking trucks, cars, furniture, anything they wanted to.

A lot of 'em went because they just wanna go back to Mexico. So, after topping in nineteen thirty-five my mom and dad went back 'cause they wanted to spend Christmas in Mexico.

My mom didn't want to go at all. *Decía,* "¿What are we going for?" She cried so much because she was going and was leaving me and Jobita here, the ones that was already married. *Altagracia, Cuca* and all the other kids went with 'em.

---

[4] 'weeding the grown beets', i.e. "cleaning" the field of weeds. Translation of the Spanish *limpia* with the same meanings.

On the way, they got in a wreck, I don't know where. *Mi tío José* wrecked my dad's car, or something, and my mom, she got hurt. I think they stayed two days in *Juárez*.

They stayed many years over there, but afterwards they all came back again. The only ones that didn't were *Teresa* and *Consuelo* because they got married in Mexico. *Altagracia* also got married in *Durango*, but Bise was from here in Colorado, so right away they came over there.

Poor Bise! He loved Alta so much, and when my dad and mom went back, he followed her on the bus. But he fell asleep on the way, and they stole all his money. When my parents got to *Durango*, there was Bise, standing by a light post, waiting for them. Well, what could he do without money?

My dad didn't let 'im get married to Alta, but he gave 'im money for 'im to come back. Bise came back to Nebraska to work all summer to make enough money to get married. And he followed her to *Durango* again. That's how much in love he was! This time, my dad let 'em get married.

I don't know if it's true, but the story is that my dad put Alta in a convent and *Basilio* went in and kidnapped her.[5] They got married in September, nineteen thirty-six. Poor Bise. He suffered so much to get Alta. I guess he really loved her, didn't he?

After my dad and mom went to Mexico, then *don Juan* said they were gonna go, too. Because the government was telling all the Mexicans to go back. There wasn't very many jobs, and the ones they had, right away they gave to the *rusos* because *don Juan* wouldn't get out of his chair to go look for a farm.

Don Juan insisted for us to go with 'em. He just wanted to have all the family together, to keep us under him, I think.

I told Mike, "I'm not going."

So, Mike told *don Juan*, "We don't have the money." We were saving, and we only had $100.

---

[5] This anecdote was related by Alta's daughter, Ruth Duran Flaherty.

Don Juan said, "It won't cost you so much. You just take everything you want, and we'll go."

Mike told me, "Look. Your dad and mom already left. If you want to . . .".

I said, "¡No! ¡I won't go! If you want to go with them, why don't you go? I'll stay here with the kids."

He said, "You're crazy."

"No, I'm not crazy. But they're insisting that you go, and I don't wanna go." I didn't want to go with them. *Yo no quería ir con ellos.* That was the main thing. I didn't want to go with <u>them</u>. 'Cause we was gonna go and live with them, and I was up to here!

I told 'im, "No, I'll stay here with my kids. How can we go, anyway, with four children and no money?"

What were we gonna do over there? How were we gonna live? I don't know. Living with *don Juan*? No way! Uh-uh.

Then, we asked 'im to sell us the house. We wanted a home, and we wanted that home because that was where we lived for five years after we got married. Mike told 'im that we would buy the house from 'im. Baltes already paid us what he owed us, and Mike was working at the factory, so we had a little bit of money put away.

Mike told 'im, "We'll pay you." He said, "First, I'll give you what we have, and then after we get paid by Woodruff, we'll give you the rest."

He wouldn't. He wouldn't sell it and he wouldn't sell it. He said, "I need my money to make a shoe shop in Mexico."

He sold it for five hundred dollars.

Oh, *don Juan* got so mad at us because we didn't want to go with them. He even went and talked about us in Kansas. Right away, he told *Coni* that I had ahold of Mike. He said, "She wasn't gonna let 'im. She bosses 'im."

Don Juan went with the whole family – *Cesáreo, Moisés,* Johnny Mack and Ramona and their kids. Johnny and Ramona had Freddy and Rocky[6] and the oldest one, Reuben, but he was adopted. His parents were *Hernández,* too, but from a different family. I knew 'em. They died real young, I don't know from what. Some sickness. First the mother, then afterward, the father.

Rubén was Johnny Mack and *Ramona's ahijado*[7] because they took 'im to get baptized. So, they adopted 'im, and he went to live with them. He was still little. I think he was maybe six or seven years old. So he stayed *'Hernández'*. He didn't have the same blood as *don Juan,* but he kept his name anyway and is part of our family. He lives in Lincoln. Reuben had some other brothers and a sister, but I don't remember them. They went to other families there in Scottsbluff. I think they were their *padrinos.*

Johnny Mack didn't stay in Mexico too long. They came back right away. Ramona told me that *don Juan* had 'em there like slaves. Reuben told me, too, that when they got to *León,* right away he put 'em to work in a factory where they cleaned the animal skins for making shoes. Cow skins or horse skins or I don't know what. 'Cause they was gonna be shoemakers. *Cesáreo* and *Moisés* were already big, but Reuben was only nine years old.

Don Juan didn't wanna sell us the house, but he still had a lotta nerve to write and ask Mike for two hundred dollars worth of equipment from Sears to put a shoemaker shop. He said *Cesáreo* was gonna learn to be a shoemaker. Mike sent 'im $200 worth, plus how much it cost to send it. We even had to borrow the money. Did he ever pay it back? Nothing. Never. Never even mentioned it ever again. No, we stayed with that debt.

---

[6] Their two first-born children, Frederick John and Ramona Rochelle.
[7] 'godson'. For the special relationship between godchildren and godparents, refer to Comment (iii) of Chapter Seven, p. 111.

Soledad and don Juan Hernández.
"*He looked like a King*".

The funeral of Papá Lolo in Our Lady of Guadalupe church, Scottsbluff, Nebraska, *April 24, 1934.*

Maique, front left, and don Juan, rear right, are pallbearers.

The wedding of Altagracia Chávez and Basilio Durán in Durango, Dgo.

Comments on Language and Culture

i   During the Great Depression of the 1930's, and as a consequence of the long period of xenophopia and racism following the war against Mexico as well as the First World War and the Mexican Revolution, a policy of 'repatriation' was established which was to return as many Mexicans as possible to Mexico. Mexicans were accused of taking 'American' jobs. They persuaded many to leave 'voluntarily', offering the incentive of taking with them whatever possessions they wanted, tax free. The Chávez and Hernández families, and many others, left Nebraska in this way. Others, especially in Texas and California, were taken by force in trainloads of repatriates, many of whom were U.S. citizens.

Chapter Thirteen

NEIL'S FARM

*My children were never hungry. We had our garden
and everything I canned. All we had to do was work hard.
We had everything – everthing but money.*

The *Chante*

When my dad and mom was leaving, Terry was already born, so Mike went with Neil Barbour to ask for work and for him to let us have the little *chante* where Mom and Dad lived that we could have for our house. I wanted to get out from *don Juan* as soon as we could. Neil already knew us because before I got married, we lived in that *chante* and I worked there with my dad.

But Neil already told *Chencho Hernández* that he could live there for the winter. He was already living there. So, Neil told us, "But I'll tell him to get out as soon as he can."

That's what he did. He told *Chencho,* "I already hired Mike, and he's gonna come live here."

Then, he told Mike that he would give us two of the rooms until *Chencho* found another place. He said the back one wasn't too good and it needed fixing. It had cracks where the snow and the wind came in a lot. It was about December or January. Cold!

The *chante* was long and at first Mike put a divider to separate *Chencho's* part from our part. We put a kitchen and a bedroom, and one of those coal heaters. Then we moved there.

A few weeks later, after *Chencho* moved out of the *chante*, then we had more room. We put the kitchen and the bedroom for the kids in front, and me and Mike was in back. That was our bedroom. But afterward, we changed the kitchen to the back and put the front for the bedrooms and the living room. We had a bed in the living room, too.

We wasn't gonna begin thinning until June, and that's why Mike had to look for work with the government. The factory job was done, but the county hired people to pick up the trash from the ditches before they started to irrigate. When they didn't have no work in the county, he worked on the government farm that they called the experimental farm. They paid 'em a dollar a day. One dollar. That's why I think they said, 'Another day, another dollar'.

The experimental farm used to give 'im jars like this full of pure cream. *Pura crema.* Because they had a lotta cows and a lotta milk. So, every day he brought home a quart of cream. *Pura crema.* Eee! It was so good! I made butter with it. And *jocoque.*[1] Oh, we all liked *jocoque,* especially with a toasted *tortilla.* ¡Mmm. Good!

En marzo Neil *le dio el trabajo.* He gave 'im the job in March so they could get the fields ready to plant. That's when Mike fixed up the whole *chante.* He put tin *láminas* on the roof and covered all the outside with tar paper – that tar paper that looks like bricks – so the snow and the dirt wouldn't come in so much. That was the time when there was a lotta dust storms that filled me up all with dirt – the stove, the table, all the furniture. Terrible!

The toilet was outside. We always had it outside until after we moved to town when Bobby died. We never had a bathroom on the farm. Never. Imagine! In the middle of winter, we had to go outside to the toilet in the snow, and sometime you could hardly

---

[1] 'a dish made of fermented milk or cream', similar to yoghurt or buttermilk; from Náhuatl *xococ*. It is generally eaten chilled, and for this reason there is the saying, *"El que con leche se quema, hasta al jocoque le sopla,"* (He who burns himself with milk even blows on the *jocoque.*)

pass. And it made really strong wind. Ooh! Just by thinking about it, I get cold.

But, what could we do? I couldn't stand it even one more day with *don Juan,* and we didn't have no place else to go.

Our pump was about from here to my mailbox. Less. About thirty or forty feet. We carried pails of water from over there to drink and to wash. For everything.

In winter, the pump sometimes froze, but we took out *patos*[2] full of boiling water so it would prime and we could get water out. I always had two or three pails of clean water inside so we didn't have to go out too often.

A few years later, Mike dug a deep hole right outside the kitchen, and he put a new pump in there. Then he put a cement border around it with some boards so we didn't have to step in the mud. I remember he put his initials in the cement and the date when he made it – May 18, 1944.

Anyway, when we first moved to the *chante,* they had a whole bunch of old boards, tires, and I don't know what kind of junk behind the toilet. That was just a *criadero*[3] for rats and mice. Ooh! I really worked hard to get rid of all that garbage! I lasted more than a year to clean all that so that at least there wouldn't be any more rats. If I saw one, I hit it with a shovel or a broom – whatever I had in my hands. Sometimes I'd even throw a piece of coal at 'em.

When we moved there, you ought'a see the snakes there was. Oof! Rattlesnakes! I remember my mom said, "Don't say 'rattlesnake'. They scare me."

"No," le digo. "If it goes straight, it won't bite you." *Le digo,* "But if it's curled up, that's when it bites – ¡poom! Then you have to run." I learned that from my dad because I was always with him.

Me decía, "No, when you see a rattlesnake that stands up and tries to curl up, that means it's trying to bite. Get away. But if you

---

[2] 'teakettles', metaphor on the word meaning "ducks".
[3] 'breeding ground'.

see it going straight, you can go behind it until it goes in the weeds and hides, and it won't do anything. Then, we don't do nothing to it. We just get away."

My dad also showed me how to kill rattlesnakes. One time, I came home and I went out to the trees where Alta, Jobita, and *Cuca* were in the back. They were still little. That was before I got married. There was a rattlesnake close by a tree. It was curled up and was looking at them like this. They had a stick and was trying to hit it. Oh, my gosh!

I told 'em, "Get off of there! Get away! Let me kill 'er!" Right away, I took the stick away from 'em so I could kill 'er.

That's when my dad came over. *Dice, "¿Qué estás haciendo?*

"I'm gonna kill this rattlesnake."

"You can't kill nothing," he said. "Let me show you."

He went and got a shovel, and he said, "A rattlesnake like this one is gonna jump at you and kill you. You have to find another way to kill it." The snake was still curled up. He just put the shovel real slow until it jumped, trying to bite the shovel. Right away quick, before it could curl up again, my dad runs with the shovel and chops off its head! He was so good for that.

That's how I learned. And when I saw a rattlesnake close to the house, I just got my shovel and cut off its head. I killed a bunch of 'em until they didn't come close to the house no more.

Bob

I remember our dog Bob so much. He belonged to *Cesáreo* and *Moisés,* but they was gonna go to Mexico, so we stayed with it. That dog minded so good! And he was so pretty. His fur was reddish-brown and his feet and collar were all white. I think he was part collie. No matter what we told 'im, he always minded.

One day, I was outside cutting some weeds and I saw a little animal, about this big, drinking water from Bob's plate. I looked, and it looked like a little bunny. Then, all of a sudden, the dog jumped on it.

'Oh!' I said. 'He's gonna kill the bunny.' I yelled at 'im, "Bob! *¡Déjalo!* Leave 'im alone!" He understood both languages. Right away he let it go. But then, I noticed it wasn't a bunny. It was a rat, this big!

I yelled at 'im again, "Get 'im, Bob! Kill 'im!" Then he did. Bob got the rat in his mouth and bit it. He shook it up and down until he killed it. That dog helped me a lot to get rid of all the rats.

No. Bob was really, really good. He took good care of my kids. When *Elvira* was a baby, she laid down on top of 'im and went to sleep. Bob just turned around and looked at 'er, but he didn't move for nothing until *Elvira* woke up.

One time – we were still with *don Juan* before they went – we was all living on a farm, and we had the dog there. Anyway, one day *Elvira* went outside. I didn't see her because Edward was still little, or I don't know what. She was already bigger, about two years and a half 'cause it was in the summer.

After a while, I noticed that she wasn't there. 'Oh!' I said. 'I hope she's not getting in the water tanks.' The farmer had big water tanks for the animals to drink, and *Elvira* always liked to play in the water. 'Oh! She might drown!'

I ran outside right away. *Eduardo* was asleep, so I left 'im there with *Chole*. But, do you think I could find *Elvira*? I couldn't find 'er. Or the dog. 'Well, where could she be? Where could they be?'

I ran to the water tank. They wasn't there. I ran to the dump. Not there, either. *¡Válgame Dios!* I got so worried, I hollered at Bob, "Bob! Bob!"

Then I saw him stick up his head from the ditch. Oh! My heart pounded! The irrigation ditch was across the road, and it had a *compuerta*[4] where the water could fall. And *Elvira* liked water so much!

---

[4] 'dam' or 'weir', used to regulate the flow of water.

Dije, '¡God help me! *Elvira* is over there with Bob.' And I run to the ditch. Well, *Elvira* was getting into the water, and the waterfall was right there!

I barely caught 'er, but Bob was the one that saved her. Oh! I got so scared! But he saved 'er 'cause he followed her and followed her. *Elvira* crossed the road, there he goes, too. He didn't leave 'er alone. *Elvira* tried to get in the ditch, the dog goes right there with 'er. I called 'im, "Bob!" but he wouldn't come. He just put his head up, but he didn't leave her.

Oh, that dog protected my children so much. One time, Edward and me was out in the yard, and Bob was there, too. I don't remember *qué travesura hizo Eduardo.*[5] He threw a rock at a car that was passing, or I don't know. So, I picked up a little stick and told him, "Okay. I'm going to spank you for that."

Oh! Then he start to yell, "Mom, no! No! Mom, Mom!" You think I was beating 'im up, like *don Juan* beat everybody up! But I didn't even touch 'im yet. That's how Edward was. *Escandaloso.*[6]

And then, the dog came after me! He got in the middle of the two of us, he growled, and he showed his teeth. "Get away from here," *le dije.* He scared me. "You darn dog! Get outta here!" But not until I threw the stick and Edward stopped yelling. Then he did.

Well, when the kids all started going to school, Bob was always waiting for the bus to bring 'em home. Every day, a little bit before four o'clock, the bus turned from the highway over there by where the Sievers farm was. About two miles away. That was the farm where *Aniseto Rico* lived. The bus stopped for the tracks, and then it went all the way around the curve to where our house was.

Mike made me a cellar outside. A cellar to keep all my canning and some of the vegetables from the garden. He covered it with some big branches and some straw, and then with dirt on top. It was like a little hill. It had steps to go down and a door.

---

[5] 'what mischief *Eduardo* did'.
[6] 'extremely excitable or emotional'.

So, every day about three thirty, Bob got on top of the cellar and he laid down there to wait for the kids to come. When it was time for the bus, he knew and he started to look. Oh! He was so happy when the bus came! There he goes running to meet it, wagging his tail.

But, how did that dog know it was time for them to come? I never knew a dog that knows how to tell time, but Bob did. Maybe he could hear the bus, but I don't think so. It was too far away.

Bob really loved the kids. And they did, too. They never had another dog they loved so much. They always had a dog, but not the same.

When Neil poisoned him, oh, how they cried! They didn't stop crying all night long, and the next day, too. Neil had sheep, and he didn't like dogs to be around them. So, he got a big piece of meat, and he put some of that strychnine poison. Terrible poison. He put it over there on the pasture by the sheep.

The dog hardly ever went over there, but that time he did and he ate some of that. He saw the meat and he ate it, because he was a dog. But he didn't attack the sheep. Oh, no! There's no way Bob would do anything to the sheep. Why? Collies are sheep dogs. They watch the sheep.

So, when I saw him coming home, he was walking like he was drunk. I told Mike, "Hey, look how the dog is walking."

They say that when somebody would get poison, they cure 'em by turning 'em around and around so they would get sick and throw up. So right away, we got some eggs and lard that we had, and we gave 'im what we could. And there's Mike, doing *malacanchoncha* with 'im. Oh, how Mike tried to bring 'im alive, but he couldn't. Bob died.

We put 'im in the weeds over there by the garden so the kids wouldn't see 'im. Then, we had to go to town to buy something, I don't know what, and when we got back, Mike was gonna bury him. The kids were all in school, except Bill and Terry because they was too little, so we took them with us. Mary Lou wasn't even born yet.

We were almost back from town when the kids got home from school. Bob didn't go meet them when the bus got there, so Eddie went outside to look for him.

He looked for 'im and called 'im. Then, he looked over by the garden and that's when he saw the dog in the weeds. He began to call 'im, "Bob. Bob." But he wouldn't come, so he went to where he was and saw that he was dead. *¡Ay!* He went running to the house crying.

When the other ones found out, they all started cryin' and cryin' so much we couldn't get 'em to stop. I was cryin' with 'em, too. Well, when you love something or someone, and all of a sudden something happens to it, you can't stand the suffering. The next day, all of us went and buried him on the other side of the garden, in the bar pit[7](i) of the tracks.

The Garden

I canned a lotta things that I got from my garden, and I put 'em in the cellar that Mike made for me. 'Cause Neil gave us a little piece of land there behind the house by the ditch so we could plant whatever we wanted. I planted *chiles, tomates, melones.* Everything – corn, cucumbers. And dill to make pickles. Everything. We got the irrigation water from the ditch, so it didn't cost nothing to grow all of that.

The beet greens didn't cost us nothing either – the little tender leaves of the beets. When we were thinning, I took a big pan and put it on the end. When I went home to go make dinner, I told the boys to fill it up with all the little beets we thinned. They were so tender! I took 'em home, I washed 'em, and cooked 'em in a *guiso*[8] with *chile,* onion and tomato for dinner. They were kinda like spinach, but better. No. On the farm we used everything we could, so we could have enough.

I remember Bobby one time when he was little. Mike and I was in the garden planting tomatoes. We had some manure to put in

---

[7] 'ditch alongside a road or track'.
[8] 'a sautéed dish', pronounced [GEESE-oh].

the dirt, but it was still in big *cacas* from the cows. They was dry, and we were breaking 'em in pieces to put a little bit of fertilizer on each plant.

I think Bobby was about six or seven years old. He saw what we was doing, and he said, "What are you doing, Dad?" He already knew English because he was already in school.

Mike told 'im, "We're planting tomatoes to eat."

"To eat?" He said, "Is that gonna go in there?" He pointed to the manure.

"Sure."

"*¡A mí no me gustan cacas!*" He didn't wanna eat no *cacas*. I think he thought we were planting *cacas* to eat. So, he said, "*¡A mí no me gustan cacas!*"

I canned a lotta things from the garden in July and August when there wasn't so much work in the fields. Especially tomatoes, *chiles,* and *pepinos.* What I didn't can was corn or green beans because those were dangerous. You could get food poison. But I did can peaches when they were in season. I bought bushel baskets full of peaches. Ooh! The kids loved the fresh peaches. Then, I made peach jam and canned peaches.

When the corn started to get ripe, we did some really good *elotadas.*[9] I would send the boys out to the garden to pick *elotes,* and they would bring me a basket full. We peeled 'em right away, and I cooked 'em for dinner. They was so good they hardly ate anything else, and they filled up just with corn.

One day we went to an *elotada* out on the farm with *Piedad* and *Crescencio,* some friends that were also from Mexico. Ack! What *elotes!* She brought *elotes* from the field that was big and too old. She left some of the leaves on 'em and cooked 'em without water, just steamed 'em. Ack, what *elotes!* They turned out so dry.

Another time, they came to visit us, and I cooked a big *olla de elotes.* I pick 'em real tender, then I cook 'em in water and salt.

---

[9] 'corn feast'. Derived from *elote,* 'fresh corn'; from Náhuatl *elotl.*

That's all. Oh! What *elotes*! Well, yeah! Tender, picked right out of the garden and cooked right away? Delicious. You just lick your lips.

Dice Piedad, "Oh. ¿Did you put sugar in the elotes?"

Le dije, "No, you don't put sugar in 'em. Just salt."

Dice, "Well, ¿why are they so sweet?"

Le dije, "Because they're tender and I cook them in water."

"*Say,* ¿but why do you cook them in so much water?"

Le dije, "That way they have more juice. They taste better than if they're dry. Dry, they don't have much taste."

Dijo, "Well, maybe I'll try to see if I can cook them like that."

They liked 'em, and we finished the whole *olla* because all the kids were there.

My *elotes* always came out really sweet. That's why one day Mike and I went out to the garden to pick some for supper. He told me, "You're just as sweet as that corn." And he kissed me on my forehead.

Then he said, "Let's go in the house now." So we went in. Yeah![10]

Mike and I was always together in the garden – planting, watering, or whatever. That was our happiness.

In the Fall, Mike always dug some holes in the floor of the cellar. We put carrots, pumpkins, and watermelons from the garden in there, and potatoes from the field. Then we covered them with straw so they last a long time without going bad.

All of that was for the winter, 'cause then there wasn't any fresh fruits and vegetables. That way we saved a little bit of money because I didn't have to buy so much. We didn't have it like they do now. Now they bring everything from Texas or from Mexico or from other places.

---

[10] Elvira related this anecdote to her caregiver, Anna Saldivar.

Chickens

That's why I always had chickens on the farm. I never bought eggs or chicken from the store. Every morning I just sent one of the kids to the chicken coop to bring some fresh eggs so I could make 'em their scrambled eggs or whatever they wanted.

When the fryers were pretty big, I told Eddie or Bobby, "See there, catch me those two chickens." I pointed them which ones I wanted for dinner. There they go running after them while I sharpened my knife. I was the one that killed 'em. They caught 'em for me, but do you think they would kill any of 'em? They was more chicken than the chickens!

You know, it was so easy. I brought my bucket, then I just got the chicken by the legs, I held its wings, and then cut off its neck. I never let 'em jump around and get full of dirt. Afterward, I put 'em in a pail of boiling water so I could peel 'em. Then right away I fried 'em up real tender for a chicken dinner.

One day, I was sitting outside. I had brought some vegetables from the garden and I was shelling some peas for dinner. The car was parked in the driveway when I saw a chicken coming behind the car. It had something behind her. I thought it was some rags or some weeds that had stuck on her. Then she went under the car, and I kept on lookin' at 'er. There she comes pecking – walking and walking and pecking and pecking, with the rags behind her.

Pretty soon, she came out from underneath the car, and then I saw! They weren't rags. No! She was so fat that she broke open and all her insides fell out and she was dragging them. Poor thing.

Well, I picked her up and right away I cut off 'er head. I cooked it in soup for dinner because it was too fatty to fry. But it was good.

During that same time, I used to help a lady who had a lotta chickens to sell. They were leghorns, real small chickens. White. I helped her kill 'em.

We got about twenty-five or thirty at one time. We tied their legs and hung 'em on a clothesline. Then, we got a real thin knife – curved. We opened up their mouth and cut their throat. They didn't even move. We let 'em hangin' for a while until all their blood drained, then we put 'em in a big tub full of water and real quick we peeled baskets full of chickens.

Another time I remember, we were at *Cuca's* house in town after Mass. She was already married. We was gonna stay for dinner to eat chicken. But before we cooked the dinner, *Cuca* and I went to the store, and the kids all stayed there at *Cuca's* house. Mary Lou came with us because she was still little.

Well, I don't know why Vera[11] got it in her head to kill a rooster that Ruth had there and get it ready for dinner. That wasn't even the chicken that Ruth was gonna cook. But okay, Elvira told Eddie and Bobby to catch it for her and she went in the house to get the knife. But she didn't even think about sharpening it. I don't think she knew how to do that.

So she started to cut off its head, and she cut and she cut, and nothing. So, she dropped the knife and went to the kitchen to get another one. Poor rooster! He was there outside just squawking, "Kwa! Kwa!", with it neck cut in half. She finally brought another knife and finished killing it. But she didn't even think that to kill a chicken, the knife has to be real, real sharp.

I always had a lotta chickens that I raised since they was little chicks. So, when the pullets were big enough to eat, I killed a bunch of 'em and canned 'em. That way, the chickens didn't get old and we had real tender meat to eat in the winter. We didn't have no freezer like they do now.

I just put the pieces of chicken in a big pressure cooker that I had with some water and a little bit of onion, garlic, and salt. Then, when the meat was nice and tender, I put it in jars and canned it. Oh! That chicken soup was so delicious!

Well, one time I was cooking a bunch of chicken for Elvira's birth'ay. She was sixteen years old, and I was gonna make some sandwiches and some other things for the party. She invited some friends to come over. We was already living in the big house.

---

[11] The nickname used in English by friends and family for both Elviras.

I had the chicken in the pressure cooker on the stove, and when it started to make steam, I went over to look. Boom! It exploded in my face! I think I didn't close the lid very good and it blew off. It covered me all up with boiling water.

Oh, my gosh! It burned my neck, my shoulders, and my chest down to here. *¡Ay, Madre Santísima!* I almost fainted. I didn't know what to do! *Me arranqué toda la blusa y el corpiño que tenía puesto.*[12] I dried myself and put on another blouse. It burned like if I was inside a fire!

Mike was over at Neil's taking care of the animals. So, how was I gonna let 'im know? Elvira wasn't there because she was at the store, but the boys were big enough. I told 'em what happened and to watch Bill and Mary Lou and to run and tell their dad.

So, I got in the car, *y yo misma me fui a sesenta hasta el* St. Mary's Hospital.[13](ii) They took me in right away. They put me I don't know what — some kinda cream — and some bandages. I think they gave me a shot for the pain 'cause I couldn't stand the burning.

Mike right away went home. He tore off the pressure valve from the lid so I couldn't use it anymore like a pressure cooker. Well, what for? I wasn't ever gonna use it for that no more. How could I?

No. They treated me at the hospital, and I went back home. Vera was already back and was making the sandwiches. I couldn't help because for a long time I couldn't do nothing, until my burns got better. Mike and Elvira were the ones that had to do all the housework. I still have the scars here on my arms and my shoulders.

The Kids

The same thing happened to Terry one time, but not exactly. We all took a bath in the kitchen with the door closed, right by the

---

[12] 'I tore off my blouse and the camisole I had on'.
[13] 'I went by myself at sixty miles an hour to St. Mary's Hospital.'

stove. Bill and Mary Lou, I gave 'em their bath because they was little.

I heated up the water in a boiler, and I put it on the floor to pour water in the tub. And I had two pails of water from the pump to cool the hot water. It was in the summer time, and the kids were all outside running around. The kitchen door to the outside was open, just with the spring.[14]

I was in the other room getting out the clean clothes for when they got done with their bath. And then I heard Terry yelling, "Mom! Mom!"

'Well, what's the matter with her?' So I went to the kitchen to see. When I got there, here comes Terry runnin' in through the spring door, "Mom! Mom!"

She turned around to look outside 'cause Bill was chasing her with a stick like he was gonna hit 'er. They were just running and playing. So, there comes Bill. Terry backed up *y no vio el hervidor.* Bam! She tripped and fell sitting down in the hot water.

Oh! It's a good thing that some friends came to take Mike to a baseball game. Because he left me the car. So, I pulled Terry out as fast as I could, and there I go running in a hurry to take 'er to the hospital. She didn't get burned a lot, a lot because the water wasn't boiling.

But it's funny that Terry didn't even cry. Nothing. Not even when she fell in the water or afterward. *¡Y ahora tan chillona!*[15] It had to hurt her because the water was real hot, and she sat all the way down. But I was just comin' in when that happened, so I pulled 'er out right away.

Cuca came over to help me with her. Somewhere here I have a picture of *Cuca* outside rocking Terry in the baby basket. I ask God that I still have that picture, but I don't think so because there's people who sneak around and take everything.

---

[14] 'screen door'; see Chapter Three, Comment (vii), p. 43, for the complex borrowing and re-borrowing of *screen* and *spring*.

[15] 'and now she's such a crybaby!'

A lotta things like that happened when we lived on that farm. 'Cause the Depression was still hard when we moved to the *chante*.

That's where Bill and Mary Lou were born. First, Bill in nineteen thirty-seven. His name is *César Basilio* 'cause that's how we named him after *Cesáreo* and Bise.

We thought Terry was gonna be the last one, but she wasn't because Bill came next. That's why we called 'im *el pilón*.[16](iii) Afterward, the kids all started to call 'im *'Pili'* and then 'Billy' in English. We still call 'im 'Bill'.

When he was a little baby, he got used to sleeping in our bed with us. Then afterward, when he was about one year, we bought him a baby basket. I had a little rocking chair that was brand new. That chair is so cute. I still have it there in the other room.

Well, I used to put his baby basket across the arms of the rocking chair so I could rock him to sleep. But, do you think he would stay there? I put 'im in there and rocked 'im, but there he comes. He wouldn't go to sleep and he wouldn't go.

"Daddy, Daddy." He wanted to sleep close to Mike.

"Let him come," Mike said. "Otherwise he's not gonna let us sleep, either."

But when Mary Lou was born, I put her in the baby basket from the very beginning, on top of the rocking chair. She got used to sleeping in there. If she cried a little bit at night, I just pushed 'er a little bit and she quieted down. That's why she wants me to give 'er that chair, and I'm gonna give it to her.

When Bill started in kindergarten, the teacher asked 'im 'is name. And, of course, he told her 'Billy' – that that was his name. Well, when they gave 'im his first report card, it had his name on it – 'William Hernandez'. When we registered him in the office, we put 'im *'César'*, but the teacher didn't notice it. We had to go to the school to explain and to tell 'em to put down his real name on the records.

---

[16] 'the extra, unexpected, one'.

But Bill wasn't the *pilón,* and Mary Lou wasn't either.[17] We put her name in English – Mary Louise – because Elvira wanted it. Vera was eleven years old in nineteen forty-one when Mary Lou was born, and she liked that name. I think it was because she had one of her friends that was named like that.

All the rest of 'em had their names in Spanish and in English because in school they couldn't say them in Spanish. They changed all the Mexicans' names, anyway. And then, the kids didn't wanna be different from the *güeros,* anyway.

That's why, when they went to school, none of the kids wanted to take *tacos* in their lunches because the rest of the kids was gonna see that they ate *tortillas.* I used to be the same, too. When a *güero* came to the house, right away we put the *tortillas* away. I don't know why 'cause all it was, was Mexican food. No. Now the *güeros* like Mexican food even more than the Mexicans.

¡Ay Dios de mi vida! We had such a large family! We should'a had more education. At least reading. But we were not readers. A little more education to know what to do. How you do it. Knowing other things.

For me now, I was born too early. I was born ignorant with my parents being the way they were. But we didn't know anything except what they told us – if we had children, we had to support them. That was it. That's how we were brought up, so we believe that we have to a'cept what God gives us.

But a lot of 'em don't want to have kids, and that's why they kill them before they're born or even afterward. But there's a lot of 'em who really treat 'em bad after they have them.

We didn't treat our children bad at all. Oh, I used to hit 'em with a little stick when they didn't behave, or with my broom. But they would run away.

But then I told 'em, "Okay. You're gonna get it when your dad gets home." Then, Mike would spank them because they didn't mind me, sometimes even with the razor strap. But not like *don*

---

[17] See *Figure 7. The Family of Elvira Chávez and Maique Hernández,* page 207 at the end of this chapter.

Juan did with the boys. No way! Mike just punished 'em what they deserved.

To say the truth, we were not very loving with the kids. We never said, *"Ay, mijito. Men aquí y name un bechito."*[18] Not even with *Elvira*, who was the first one. The only one was Mary Lou. She was her dad's favorite. I won't say the 'spoiled one'. I think it was because she was the baby and the other ones were bigger.

Mike used to play 'little horsie' with her on his knee. Then, he lifted 'er up over his head, and the baby laughed so hard. Mike called her his *"Táquiris"*. I don't know where he got that name, but that's what he called her. In English, he called her "Honeybun", too.

He didn't have nicknames for none of the other ones except Vera. But everybody called *Elvira "Beibe"*, not just Mike. He loved Vera a lot because she was a little girl and him and his brothers never had a sister.

When Mary Lou was about two years old, she wouldn't let go of her bottle. I wanted to take it away from 'er, but she wouldn't let me. She wanted her "baboo", and that was it! She cried if I didn't give it to her.

One day, there she is, whining and whining for me to give 'er her baboo. I hadn't warmed up her milk, and I was busy tryin' to make supper. So, I gave her the bottle, empty like that just so she'd quit bothering. Darn her! She threw it. It hit the stove, and it broke.

Then I told 'er. I said, "See what you did? You broke the bottle."

She just looked at me and said, "Coke a baboo?"

I told her, "Yes. You coke a baboo. Who coke a baboo?" I scolded 'er.

She didn't say anything. I swept up the glass. Because in those times, the bottles were all glass. There wasn't any plastic or

---

[18] Spanish baby-talk pronunciation for something like, 'Oh, honey. Come 'ere an' gimme a witto kiss.'

things like that. I showed it to her, and she asked me, "Coke a baboo?"

I told her, "*Sí.* You coke a baboo, so now you have to drink your milk out of a glass."

So, I warmed up her milk, and I gave her a nice and warm glass of milk. She drank it. And from there on, when she wanted milk, I gave it to her in a glass. Then she said, "Coke a baboo?"

I just told her, "You coke a baboo. Now drink your milk." No. She quit asking for her bottle real quick.

I think she was really spoiled by her dad. He never said anything to her like, "*¡Malcriada!*" or "*¡Quítate!*"[19] He was always so loving with her.

But one time he did. Mike came home real tired from irrigating, and me and Mary Lou were in the kitchen. She must have been about four, and was just playing around. The other kids were outside, so I told 'er, "Mary Lou, go call the kids. Tell 'em supper's ready."

She didn't pay attention. I told 'er again. "Mary Lou, go call the kids."

But this time, she said, "I don't wanna." Mike was just listening.

I said, "Mary Lou! Right now!"

She said, "No!" She just got stubborn.

Okay, then. Now her dad got up, and he told her, "You can't talk to your mom like that." And he gave 'er a little spank. Almost nothing. "Now go do what she told you."

You think he took her heart out! She cried so loud and so hurt, and then she started to sob so much I thought she was gonna choke. Her dad never scolded her, and much less did he ever spank her.

I went out to call the kids, and when I came back in, Mary Lou was still sobbing but not so hard. Mike sat down with her and told

---

[19] "Bad girl!" or "Get away!"

her why he scolded her. No. Everything was okay, and we all sat down to eat supper.

Another time, Mary Lou was a little bit bigger. I was getting ready to go visit one of my friends, *Micaelita Huerta*.

"Where you goin', Mom?" she asked me.

"Nowhere," *le dije*. "I'm just goin' to see *Micaelita*. I'll be right back."

I finished dressing. Then, I went to see what I was gonna make for dinner afterward. And there's Mary Lou, watching me. Then she asks, "Aren't you gonna go see your *Caelita*?"

"My what?"

"Your *Caelita*. You said you was gonna go visit your *Caelita*."

Golly! She thought I told her I was gonna go see *'mi caelita"* instead of *"Micaelita".* 'Aren't you gonna go see "your *Caelita"*?' I start to laugh so hard. Well, yeah. I think she hadn't ever heard the name *'Micaelita'*.

We lived pretty good there on Neil's farm. Poor, but happy. Most of the time. All we had to do was work hard. I canned a lot. My children were never hungry. Never. We had the garden, and then everything that I canned. We always had potatoes and beans. A sack of potatoes or beans lasted all winter. We had everything − everything but money.

I had to take off the roots from the potatoes once in a while because in the cellar they got soft when the roots grew out. One time after we moved to the big house, I put Bill out in the yard with a full sack to take off the roots. I think he was about nine or ten because Eddie and Bobby, they didn't graduated yet.

So, there's Bill crying and crying because he didn't want to and he didn't want to. He said, "Why don't Eddie and Bobby have to do this?"

Le digo, "Look. They do a lotta work, because they always have to work in the field and help clean the weeds and irrigate the garden. And they have a lot of other things to do. Now you can do something. You do that."

Le dije, "Now, you sit there and take off all the roots from those potatoes. One sack of potatoes isn't gonna hurt you. Now stop crying." How was that gonna hurt 'im? But he didn't want to.

Then, Eddie and Bobby were watching, and Bobby goes in the house so I don't see 'im to get the camera. Eddie had one of those Brownie cameras that Vera gave 'im. Because she owed him I don't know how much money, so instead of payin' 'im, she gave 'im the camera.

I was over on the corner sweeping the trash, *y le dije a* Bill, "Look, if you keep crying, I'm going to hit you with this broom so you'll cry more." I lifted up the broom, pretending to hit 'im.

That's when Bill turned around and saw they were gonna take his picture, and he laughed. And me with the broom up in the air! I have that picture somewhere. I saw the boys, and I went after them with the broom, but they went running and laughing because they took my picture.

We always had potatoes. So, once in a while, I cooked a round steak with potatoes, tomato, and onion, or else some pork chops and mash potatoes. But not too often because that meat is too expensive. More often I bought liver or kidney that was a lot cheaper and that Mike really liked. The kids didn't like it at all, but they had to eat it.

Sometimes they saw I was cooking liver, and they said, "Oh, we don't like that!"

I just turned around and told 'em, "Okay, then. *Coman caca!*"[20]

They complained about it, but when it was supper time, they ate it.

In the winter, I made soup with beef and with soup bones that was really good. I put in carrots, potatoes, and cabbage. And to make *pozol,*[21] I bought neck bones of pork, and I put in that Gebhart's chili powder. At the store, they didn't charge me for the neck bones and the soup bones because they didn't have too

---

[20] Not nearly as strong a word as in English. *¡Ni qué esperanzas!*

[21] 'soup made with hominy (*pozol*), pork meat, and red chile'.

much meat on 'em. But they had enough to make soup if I put in *bastantes huesos.*

Besides that, the chickens. No. There was always enough food for everybody.

Sometimes, even some tramps(iv) came by hungry and dirty. I told 'em to wash their hands over by the pump and I warmed up a plate for them of whatever I had, even if only a taco of beans. Poor people. They went from one town to another one on top of the trains looking for little jobs or for someone to give 'em something to eat. Well, our house was right next to the tracks. I never ran 'em off.

In the summer, I worked all the time out in the field. In the winter, I would do sewing. Because when the kids were little, I made their clothes. Not all of 'em, just the ones that cost too much to buy 'em.

I washed the flour sacks. They were big sacks because I made a lotta tortillas and I bought fifty pounds at a time. I also cut up old dresses and coats and used all that material to sew the clothes. I had a real good Singer sewing machine. It was one of those that you used with a pedal on the bottom, not like the ones they have now that are all electric.

For the girls, I made them some pretty skirts. With flowers and pleats that moved from one side to the other one when they walked. They looked real pretty.

And for the boys, I patched their pants and shirts. I remember one time I made 'em some jackets out of a big, old overcoat. It was a double coat. I tore it so I could make the Eisenhower jackets. That was during the war, and those were in style, but we didn't have the money to buy 'em, so I made 'em. They fit down to their waist. Ooh! They were so happy with their Eisenhower jackets.

I used to go to town every Saturday to buy everything I needed for the week. The groceries and other little things I needed. Because on Saturday, we just worked in the field until noon. Then we went home to eat dinner, we got all ready, and we went to town. Not Mike. He never went out for nothing, especially shopping. I was the one that bought everything.

I took all the kids because they liked to see the movies that they was showing and the serials. They called 'em 'the chapters'. Oh, no way did they stay home!

I told 'em, "Hurry. Clean up and get ready." Because it was five cents before two o'clock. Afterwards, it was a dime. Ooh! Right away they washed up and got ready. I gave each one their ten cents – five cents for the show and then five cents for their popcorn or a candy or what each one wanted. They were so happy to go see their show. Then, I was happy to go do my shopping by myself.

I let 'em off at the Bluffs Theater because that's where they showed the serials and the cowboy shows. They hardly ever went to the Egyptian because they had to sit on one side in the back, until after it burned down. Afterwards, they made another one where that one was, and in that one they let 'em go in front. By that time there wasn't as much discrimination.

But when they got big, they went to the Otoe Theater instead, the one they called 'El Piojo'.[22] I don't know why they called it like that. I think because that's the one that all the Mexicans went to. That's where they went to see all their friends from town.

---

[22] 'The Louse', ironic self-deprecating word for 'the Mexican Theater'.

FIGURE 7. THE FAMILY OF ELVIRA CHAVEZ
AND MAIQUE HERNANDEZ

Elvira Chavez + Michael Hernández

┌─Elvira (Vera, junior)
├─Eduardo (Edward, Eddie)
├─Roberto (Robert, Bobby)
├─Theresa (Terry)
├─César (Bill)
├─Mary Louise (Mary Lou)
├─Leonard
└─Robert (Roberto; adopted)

ELVIRA'S OLDER CHILDREN (LEONARD WASN'T BORN YET)
Back Row: Terry, Bobby, Eddie, Elvira.
Front Row: Mary Lou, Bill.

"El chante", now abandoned, where Jacobo Chávez lived with his family and, later, where Elvira and her family lived for many years.

The dog Bob in don Juan's back yard. With the dog are Eddie, *Beibe*, Freddy, and a neighbor child. Behind them is the goat they milked for *Eduardo* when he was a baby.

Photo taken in 1936.

Bill unwillingly removing roots from potatoes

The razor strop used by Maique from time to time to discipline the boys.

Elvira's sister Ruth, comforting Terry after she got burned.

Photo taken in 1939.

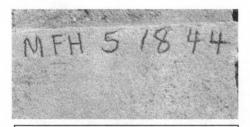

A block of the cement border that Maique placed around the pump at the *chante*.

Shown are his initials and the date, May 18, 1944.

A hand pump.

Micaelita Huerta, center, with Altagracia and Elvira.

Comments on Language and Culture

i The 'bar pit' runs alongside a railroad track or roads. The pit is dug to 'borrow' the dirt to construct the foundation of the tracks or roads. So, the pit is technically referred to as a 'borrow pit'. In colloquial usage, the phrase is abbreviated to 'bar pit' and, for all intents and purposes, the original sense is lost in this usage.

ii In those years, sixty miles per hour (*a sesenta*) was the highest speed limit on the highways. So, going *a sesenta* meant going as fast as possible either in a vehicle or on foot. In English, a similar phrase was used: 'going like sixty'.

iii In Mexican shops, when selling a dozen eggs or a certain number of items of bread or produce, the shopkeeper customarily adds an additional free piece, called *el pilón*.

iv During the Great Depression, many unemployed men – "tramps" – traveled from town to town looking for work or asking for help. They would look for an empty railroad car and ride until the train stopped at the next town. During nice weather, if they couldn't find an empty car, they got on top of the cars and traveled in that way.

Chapter Fourteen

FARMWORKERS

And that dang farmer didn't give him even one cent.
No. If something happened to one of the workers,
that was their business.
The farmers didn't a'cept no responsibility. Nothing.

Working in the Field

Neil had a great big farm, like about two hundred acres. Because he also had cows and sheep in a big pasture. Where he didn't plant beets, he had a lotta potatoes, beans, and other crops. We mainly worked the beets and the potatoes, and in the summer we also had work in cleaning the weeds and in shocking the barley and oats.(i)

And when we weren't doing that work, they hired Mike as a *peón*.[1](ii) That's why he was almost never outta work. And then, Neil right away put him in charge of the other *peones* when they worked together. I think it's because he was the one who did the best work for Neil, and that's why. Oh, Mike learned to farm real good.

Sometimes, when there wasn't enough work there with Neil, we found little jobs on other farms. I remember when Mike got hurt. *¡Ay, pobrecito!* That was so hard. That year, we finished the

---

[1] 'hired hand'.

potatoes at Neil, but it wasn't time yet for the topping. I think the farmers were waiting for a frost to start the beets. They needed a heavy frost because that way the beets made more sugar and they got more money.

While we were waiting for the topping to start at Neil, we went to a farm in Gering to help them finish picking potatoes. They hired Mike to run the potato digger, and I was picking. The boys were helping me take the vines off the rows.(iii) They used to come after school to help me. I think this was in nineteen forty-three. Edward was eleven, and Bobby just was ten in July.

And that's when Mike got hurt, in September. Me and the boys were working in the potatoes. Mike was working on the digger, and it grabbed his pants. He fell under the machine, and it tore the meat off of his legs. It almost killed 'im.

I heard the yelling, and I took off running. When I got there, he was stuck under the machine, all bloody with his pants torn. *¡Ay, Dios santísimo!* When they ran to get the car, somehow I finished tearing his pants to get 'im out from under the digger.

We put 'im in the car, and we went as fast as we could to take him to the hospital. There wasn't any other way. Way out there on the farm, we couldn't call an ambulance. I think the farmer called the hospital from his house because they were waiting when I got there. He's the one who took my kids home, too. You can imagine how I was! Praying and praying to God and the Holy Virgin to help us.

And they did. They helped us. In the hospital they operated him and sewed up everything. He didn't break none of his bones, *gracias a Dios.* But that dang machine ran over him and cut open his whole leg.

But thank God it wasn't worse. He was in the hospital more than a week, and then I took 'im home. *¡Ay, pobrecito!* He could hardly even get up to use the *bacinilla.*[2]

---

[2] 'chamber pot'.

The same thing happened to *Ramiro*. Worse. And that dang farmer where that happened didn't give him even one cent. No. If something happened to one of the workers, that was their business. The farmers didn't a'cept no responsibility. Nothing. Mom had to ask for a loan from all the brothers and sisters to pay the hospital. And us, we were all barely making it, too. But, well, we had to pay it.

Ramiro and the farmer were cutting alfalfa when the mower grabbed 'is foot. It almost cut it all the way off, but *Ramiro* was stuck there in the machine. The farmer – I don't remember his name, but he was a German – almost all of 'em were – he ran to get his truck. But *Ramiro* didn't even faint. I don't know why not!

The farmer came back, but neither one of 'em could pull his foot out from the mower, and *Ramiro* saw he was gonna bleed to death. Well, believe it or not! He took out his knife that he always had in his pocket, and he finished cutting off his own foot!

In the hospital, they had to cut off all his leg up to his knee. But, you know? Until the day he died, he walked really good on his artificial leg.

I remember Eddie there in the hospital. He was always a chicken to see blood. That's why he wouldn't ever kill a chicken for me. Anyway, in the room where they put *Ramiro*, the nurse started to tell us everything what they did, and all of a sudden Edward turned real white, and poom! He passed out. Then the nurses were taking care of him instead of *Ramiro*. Waking him up. Afterward, we all laughed so much.

Edward was like the guy that went to the hospital with his wife who was gonna have a baby. That was when they didn't let the man go in. But the man could hear his wife crying and yelling inside. He just went poom! He fell down and hit his head on some iron. Then he's the one who stayed in the hospital, and she came out.

Another one like that was here at Our Lady for a wedding. I wish I could remember who it was, but I can't. The *novio* was in the sacristy waiting for the bride. Then, the *novia* came in and the *novio* came out to meet 'er. But as soon as he saw 'er, he fell down. He fainted. Right away, they put 'im in the sacristy again.

All the people, we were just sayin', 'I wonder what happened to the *novio*.' She waited for 'im and after a while, he came out, and they went on with the wedding. It was funny, though. But nobody laughed or anything until after they got out of Mass. It was really funny.

Another time, a girl did the same thing when she was gonna get married. 'Cause she was expecting a baby. There she goes, all in white, trying not to show it, but she did. She fainted in her chair and couldn't get up.

Anyway, when Mike got hurt, I didn't faint. I don't know why, but I always had my dad's strength. I took 'im to the hospital all by myself, and I stayed there until they sewed 'im up and I saw he was gonna be all right.

But then I remembered that we were gonna start the topping at Neil. ¡*Caramba!* What was I gonna do all by myself? We had about forty acres of beets to top. That was our contract. If we didn't do it, how were we gonna make it in the winter?

At least, the farmer in Gering helped us pay the hospital. It was from the money he owed us for our work, anyway. But that's all. He didn't give us nothing for all the work we lost. Because there wasn't no help from the government. Nothing. There wasn't no worker compensation, either. None of that, like there is now.

So, I started to think. 'I have to take the boys out of school so we can do the topping.' But the government wouldn't let 'em work 'cause they were too young. But the farmers looked the other way because there wasn't enough people to work. It was during the war. But Neil knew we didn't have much money, so when I told 'im, he let 'em work.

Right away, *don Másimo* came over to tell me that they would do our contract. Well, of course! With the forty acres, or whatever it was, they would earn a lot more. And us? We would stay without nothing.

I told *don Másimo,* "Thank you, but no. Me and my boys will do it."

They didn't believe me. How was I gonna top forty acres with one woman by herself and two little kids? But when we did it, they saw.

No. *Petra* and *don Másimo* wanted to get as many acres as they could. Them and us were the ones that worked there at Neil. When we started a field on the thinning, each family took out a claim of rows – *una clema*. Then at the end of the field, the rows that was left didn't belong to anybody. The ones that finished first their last piece could get those rows, too. We all worked as fast as we could to claim more rows. Then, those were your rows for the *tapeo*, too.

There was always a lotta competition with *Petra*. We sat down to eat lunch, and we said, "Come on. Hurry. They did another round already." I don't think they rested or they rested very little.

One time I remember, we still had six or seven rows to do, but they finished first. We were eating lunch on the end of the row when *don Másimo* passed by. He was gonna get the last piece of about fifteen or sixteen rows.

He passed by and kinda shook his head. He said, *"¡Pos ya no quería!"*[3] Telling us that *Petra* made 'im go get those last rows. I think he was a little bit embarrassed because they worked so fast to finish before we did. But if he really didn't want no more, well why didn't he just leave 'em for us?

That's why afterward, anytime one of us got the last piece of something – a piece of meat or a cookie – we said, *"¡Pos ya no quería!"* But we took it, anyway.

Those were hard, hard times in the field. That's why we always told 'em, "Look, the reason we're all working so hard is so there'll be a little bit of money to send you to college, if any of you want to."

But I remember that we were the happiest when we were together, working. *Pobrecitos mis hijos.* They worked on the row

---

[3] "Well, I really didn't want any more."

real fast because they wanted to beat me, and they laughed, "We're ahead of Mom!"

Because, in the topping, we put the beets in two piles – four rows on one pile and four rows on the other one. I topped by myself on one pile and both of them on the other one. Eddie was left handed and Bobby was right handed, so Bobby ran ahead and worked toward Eddie. After they met, they got another piece, and so on. But they worked fast so they could beat me.

No. They learned right away. If they finished their row first, they helped me with mine. Oh, we got so tired! But when we got to the end, we laid down a little while in the weeds before we started to pile some more rows. Then, about every two, three hours, we sat down in the shade to eat some *taquitos*.[4]

I always got up early to make *tortillas* and the food for all day. Because working so hard, we had to eat a lotta lunches. I woke *Elvira* up to help me fold the *tacos*. But I let the boys sleep a little bit more until everything was ready. Then I woke 'em up so they could eat a *taquito* and a cup of cream-a-wheat before they went out to work.

For dinner, I used to run home to make it about eleven thirty. Because at noon we went home to eat a hot dinner. We never had a watch, but the boys learned real quick to tell the time by the sun. They stood up straight, straight and looked at their shadow. When it was almost getting close to north, they told me, "Mom. It's eleven thirty." They were anxious for me to go make dinner.

In the afternoon it was harder to tell time by the shadow. So, one day I told Bobby to go ask *don Másimo* what time it was. 'Cause he had a watch. They were working close by where we were.

"Tell 'im I want to know." So, there goes Bobby.

He told *don Másimo*, "*Tío,*" he said – in Spanish because *don Másimo* didn't know English. "*Tío,* Mom wants to know, *¿qué horas son trais?*"

---

[4] 'little tacos', pron. [ta-KEE-toes].

I don't even know if he told 'im the time because they all started laughing – *don Másimo, Petra,* and *Luz* – all three of 'em because they all heard.

I didn't know why they were laughing so much. Well, here comes *don Másimo* to tell me what Bobby asked 'im. Then I started laughing, too. He mixed up the two languages. Instead of saying, *"¿Qué horas son?"* – What hour is it? He put in *"trais".* *"Tío,* what time is it do you have?" We thought it was really funny. Bobby didn't care. He just wanted to know if it was time to quit to go eat supper."

None of the other kids helped us in the beets and the potatoes. Just Terry, she did. After she started high school, then she came out to help us in the thinning. But by that time we didn't need it so much. I think she liked that more than staying home with the rest of 'em doing the housework.

Well, after getting out of the hospital, Mike went out to the field with his cane. He went out and sat on the end of the row to help out a little bit. He told us, "I'll sit down here, and you put a big pile of beets around me." We left him part of a row and we made his pile, so there he is sitting, topping. It was so sad to see him!

So after that, the boys came out of school every year to do the potatoes and the beets, from September until November, sometimes all the way to Thanksgiving. And when they got out of school in May, right away they started thinning and then the *limpias.*[5] No, they learned real quick to work the same as a man.

¡Ay, Dios! It's terrible to be so poor. And that was the time when people didn't earn hardly anything. This was in nineteen forty-three, 'forty-four. At that time, the thinning and the *limpias* were all by the acre. We got, I think, thirteen dollars an acre which was nothing for so much work. If a strong worker thinned all day, they could thin three-fourths of an acre or maybe one acre if the dirt was nice and soft and didn't have too much weeds.

In the potatoes, they paid us by the bushel, and by the ton for topping. So, if we worked real hard we could earn *al menos para*

---

[5] "cleaning", i.e. weeding the field.

la sal, como dicen.[6] But they should'a paid us all the same, but by the hour, so we didn't have to work always in a rush. But the farmers didn't like that. But in the *limpias* where we could do three or four acres a day, then they paid us by the hour!

The Big House

In Spring of nineteen forty-five, Carl Schmidt, who was one of the *peones,* quit at Neil to go work I don't know where. Him and Tyra lived in a big house over there in the middle of the fields, a long ways from the road. Neil gave us that house because Mike did everything for Neil, so after so many years we didn't have to live in a *chante* no more.

Oh! When we went to see that house, what a dump they left us. The cupboards and the stove in the kitchen was all full of *cagarruchas de ratón.*[7] I told Mike to throw all that out, and we bought other ones at the second-hand store. In the bedrooms, the wallpaper and the cracks in the windows were all full of *chinches!*[8] We had to fumigate the house before we moved, and we washed everything from the ceiling to the floor.

When we moved to that house in nineteen forty-five, it didn't have electricity because it was the time of the war and they didn't have no copper for the wires. At night we used kerosene lamps, and in the kitchen we had a real good one of gasoline that we pumped up to light it. The kids all did their school work with those lamps. And we had a radio that worked with a car battery.

We never had a refrigerator, anyway. Just a little icebox. I sent the boys to the icehouse in town to bring big blocks of ice so that the meat and the milk didn't spoil. Finally, around nineteen forty-seven, they put us electricity, and then we bought an electric refrigerator.

But that was a nice house. It was a two-story house, and it wasn't too old. It had two rooms upstairs and one, two, three, four

---

[6] 'at least to buy some salt, like they say'.
[7] 'mouse droppings'.
[8] 'bedbugs'.

downstairs – the living room, our bedroom, the dining room, and the kitchen. The dining room was a great big one.

We put Elvira's piano in the dining room. It looked pretty nice. She used to go to Ethel Barbour[9] to give her lessons, and she learned to play real good. When she got bigger, she started playing the organ in church. She still knows how to play.

In the big house, the girls all slept upstairs in one room and the boys in the other. Billy and Bobby on one bed, and Edward on the other one. He slept alone because he fought with the other ones.

Mike bought a big heater for the living room, really pretty with porcelain all on the outside. In the winter we threw in big blocks of coal so they lasted all night. In the morning, *nomás les atisábamos,*[10] and they lit right away. Right on top of it in the ceiling, it had a register so that the warm air could go up to the bedrooms of the kids.

I was very happy in the big house because the kids never bothered nobody – just me. I enjoyed it there because they didn't go out to the road or nothing. It was about a half a mile to the road, by the trees. That's where the bus came to take 'em to school. When they saw it comin', there they all go running so it wouldn't leave 'em.

But when they got bigger, Eddie and Bobby bought a motor scooter. *¡Ay!* I was so scared 'cause they was everywhere on that scooter. They went to town where there was a lotta traffic. *Gracias a Dios* they never wrecked. But at least I didn't have to take them to the swimming pool or the baseball games no more. They went together on their motor scooter, happy as can be.

One time, Elvira and Mary Lou went for a ride on the motor scooter – I don't know where to. Some dogs came out and they grabbed Mary Lou and bit her real bad. The motor scooter was a little one and it didn't go very fast, so they couldn't run away from

---

[9] Charley Barbour's wife who lived close by on the neighboring farm.
[10] 'we just stoked them'.

the dogs. When they got home, ¡*Válgame Dios!* She was all
bloody and scared. But, well, what could we do?

The kids always had something happen. If it wasn't one thing,
it was another. They came home all scraped on their knees or
their legs. But I was happy because we were on the farm. Alone
by ourselves. They didn't bother anybody, and nobody bothered
them.

We had a big yard with a little garage for the car and another
building where we put the coal. And we had a big chicken coop for
all my chickens.

Out there behind the garage close to the ditch, we planted the
garden. The ditch was right there. It was a state irrigation ditch. A
great big one, 'cause it had a bridge to cross to the pasture. I was
so scared of the kids because they went swimming there. Before I
knew it, they came home all wet.

"We went to the ditch."

I said, 'Oh, my gosh! They're gonna drown.' But their dad
showed 'em all how to swim when they was real little. Everyone
but Vera.

The Blizzard of 'Forty-Nine

Oh! When the blizzard came. It was in January of nineteen
forty-nine. It covered the garage with snow. All of it up to the top.
The chicken house, too. And so many chickens! *Pobrecitas.* We
couldn't even go in to give 'em food and water. They didn't die, but
the snow and the wind lasted for three days. We couldn't even get
outta the house.

A lotta animals died in that blizzard, and some people, too. On
account of the cold. There was some days it got to thirty degrees
below zero! If people ran out of wood or coal for their heaters,
they froze in their house because they had no way to go get some.
Some of 'em, the army threw sacks of coal and alfalfa for the cows
out of aeroplanes.

Ahh, the kids! Oh, after the blizzard, they were having fun in
the snow. But when they had to shovel the snow, then they didn't

have fun. Right away after it stopped snowing, they had to take the snow off the chicken coop and the shed where we had the coal because the snow melted during the day, and at night it would freeze again and make ice.

That's why the drifts got so hard. They could even get on top of 'em with their sleds. Afterwards, to go to the big road, we walked on the driveway about a half a mile. It was a private driveway, so the county wouldn't clean it. We couldn't get the car out for about three months, I think, until everything melted.

Mike's ears froze real bad one night when we were coming back from Mass. Paul used to come get us at the mailbox, at the main road. That night, Mike forgot his earmuffs, and the wind was blowing real hard. When Paul brought us back after Mass, we all had to walk from there to the house. Oh, Mike covered his ears with his gloves, but when we got home, you could almost see through 'em! I heated water all night long to put warm towels on his ears. He was like that, hurting so much for two or three days until they finally unfroze.

The kids had to go walking to school because the bus couldn't pass. I sent 'em with their sleds to the store to get groceries. The snow plows came to take the snow from the big road, but right away the snow drifts covered it up because of those winds that came. The wind lasted a lotta days after the snow stopped. Nebraska people suffered a lot with that blizzard.

They knocked that big house down now and they closed the driveway to make it all fields.

Farmworkers

Eddie and Bobby shoveling snow after the great blizzard of 1949. Bill is sliding down the snowdrift on his sled.

Plowing snow after the great blizzard.

Bill and Leonard digging potatoes with the potato digger. Dangerous!

Terry takes a break from thinning beets in front of the big house.

Mary Lou with her kitty among the chickens at the big house.
Photo taken in 1945.

Farmworkers

Bobby on his motor scooter
outside the big house.

Mike (right) with the
farmhand Carl Schmidt.

Comments on Language and Culture

i   "Shocking" consisted of stacking upright in "shocks" four or five bundles of barley or oats that the mower had cut and left to dry. Once they completely dried, the shocks were loaded on wagons with pitchforks and taken to the threshing machine that separated the grain from the straw.

ii   'Peones' were hired hands – as opposed to seasonal workers, who thinned and topped beets and picked potatoes. The *peones* performed those jobs that were tied to the general operation of the farm such as plowing, planting, irrigating, etc. They operated all the machinery required for that and for the harvest, driving trucks, wagons, teams of horses or mules (or, later, after the nineteen thirties, tractors). They also took care of the cattle and sheep, if the farmer had any.

    These jobs were not as hard as those performed by the beet workers. On the other hand, they were paid by the hour, but they couldn't earn the same as farmworkers who were paid by the acre or by the ton even though their work season was relatively short. The *peones* had more stable jobs on any given farm and, in general lived in better houses than the beet workers.

iii   The potato digger dug the potatoes, which grew under the soil. The potatoes – tubers attached to the root of the plant – passed over a continuous chain made of metal rods. This chain screened the dirt and deposited the potatoes, still attached to the plant which was called a "vine", on the surface of the row. Underage workers shook the potatoes loose and discarded the vine so that the picker did not have to perform that operation and could devote all her energies to picking the potatoes.

Chapter Fifteen

BROKEN SPANISH, PROFANITIES
AND OTHER ANECDOTES

When you're losing the language,
you use one word for another.
Ya no saben hablar español.
No. Muchos ya quieren olvidar de que son mexicanos.

Don Juan's Death

In nineteen forty-five, *don Juan* died, *que Dios lo tenga en su santo descanso.*[1] It was in February, I think. February, 1945. We didn't move to the big house until Mike got back from Mexico.

Mike and Johnny both went on the bus – the Continental Trailways bus. They didn't make it to the funeral because over there, they buried them on the next day or in two days. They didn't embalm 'em, so before they started to smell, they buried them right away. Then, by the time Mike and Johnny got ready and found their papers and got tickets and everything, well it was already one or two days.

No. They had to go anyway to be with the family *y a consolar a Chole.* Even if *don Juan* treated them bad when they were little, he was their father and *Chole* was their mother. And she was so good.

Mike wanted me to go with 'im.

---

[1] 'may God keep him in his holy rest'.

229

"No," le dije. "I'm not going. I'll stay here alone with my children."

"¿What do you mean you'll stay here alone?" He told me we could find somebody to stay here with the kids.

"I'm not leaving my kids with nobody. Anybody could stay here and not take care of my children like I take care of 'em. Take *Elvira* instead."

When I told *Elvira*, boy! She was so happy she was goin' with her dad! *Contenta de la vida.* She was fifteen years old. Over there she made some good friends – boys that wrote to her for a long time after they got back.

Well, *en la garita* the Border Patrol didn't let Mike pass. Johnny had to go first. They told Mike that if he went over, he couldn't come back. Because when the *Hernández* crossed over here the last time in nineteen twenty-three, they gave Mike back his old passport that was supposed to stay *en la garita*. Yes, Mike had a passport, but when they passed the last time, they gave 'im the wrong one.

They asked 'im why he had that passport. They thought somebody had given it to 'im *de contrabando* or something. So, they didn't let 'im cross until he talked to Neil on the telephone and he talked with the sugar factory to prove that he had been here for so many years. Finally, they made him a new passport so they could go on to *León.*

They were there a few days visiting with the family. The four brothers went and took a picture where they all look so serious. I have that picture here someplace. And that's the time when *Elvira* met some boys that lived close by, and they became friends.

Ohh! My kids really missed 'em! The Continental bus that came and went from Cheyenne passed by the highway every day at the same time. And every day at that time, there go the kids running to look, to see if they were comin' back that day.

And the day they got back, the bus let 'em off right by the house, over there on the highway close to the tracks. Oh, how they were all so happy! Well, we had never been separated before.

Bad Words

When they got back, Mike started to plow and disc the fields because it was already March. Vera went back to school, excited 'cause she was gonna tell her friends all about her trip.

I remember one time me and her was over there in Gering at the house of people that we knew. We were talkin' about a lotta things, and they were sayin' they was gonna make a barbecue.

Then *Elvira* said, "Oh, in Mexico they cooked some really good meat that they called *'barbacoa'*. I wonder if that's the same as 'barbecue'. It was a small animal. It was so good, but they made it in a dirt oven."

Le dije, "That was *cabrito,* a little goat."

She started thinking, and then she looked up and said, "¡Oh! Around here I hear 'em say, 'You *cabrón'* and 'Hey, *cabrón'.*[2] ¿Does that mean they're calling each other a 'big goat'?"

See, at home they never heard a word like that. She never heard a bad word, especially from her dad. But she did hear those *pela'os*[3] at school talk like that. And the people where we were, they knew all those words. When they heard Elvira say she thought a *cabrón* was a big goat, they ran out because they couldn't stop laughing.

But Terry came out a little bit different. When I came home from the hospital one time that I wrecked – one time out of all of my wrecks – a lotta people came over to see me. Ruth Chávez and her daughter Becky was there, and *Luz de la Rosa,* Terry, and another friend of mine. I don't know who else. The house was full. Then, Father Jenovec came over, too.

I told him, "Sit down and eat with us, Father."

He sat down, but he said, "I'm not hungry."

---

[2] A harsh and insulting swear word, equivalent perhaps to English 's.o.b.'. It is derived from the word *cabra,* 'goat'.
[3] 'bums'.

I told him, "I don't care if you're not hungry.You go ahead and eat something." No, he served himself, and he's talkin' and laughin' with everybody.

Terry was back and forth, serving and getting people the things they want. The Broncos[4] was playing, and she ran back and forth to the living room to watch television to see what was happening in the game.

¡Caramba! She always makes a big *escándalo* with those Broncos. Then, something happened one time. I don't know what the Broncos did wrong. A mistake.

Terry yells loud, "Goddammit!" It was so loud that we heard it all the way to the kitchen.

Father just laughed.

Oh, boy, her poor mother! *¡Dios Santísimo!* My face got real red. They probably say, 'This is the way she raised them.' I didn't raise them like that! At home, they didn't hear anyone talk about the 'big goat' or any other bad word.

I just said, "Father, I need to wash that girl's mouth with soap."

But even the priests, sometimes they say the wrong word. I remember Father Dowd. He knew Spanish and he liked talking it with us. One day after Mass, he went to the hall downstairs where we served the food. The women from the church, we always made food so that all the people could eat breakfast. That was to make money to pay for building the church. We made *enchiladas o tacos* or whatever. Mexican food.

Then, after Father ate, he came to the kitchen. He wanted to tell us a compliment, and he said, *"Ustedes son buenas cochineras."*

We all started laughing. Not too loud because we knew what he wanna say, that we were good *cocineras.* But we thought it was funny when he said it.

He said, "What did I say? Did I say something wrong?"

---

[4] A professional football team from Denver, where Terry lived.

I told him, "No, Father. Thank you for the compliment. But the way you said it is that we are 'good pig tenders'."

Oh, he got so embarrassed! But, no. It was okay. We all laughed a little bit, and that's all.

But then,Terry, another time. *Cuca* was here combing her hair because she was going out, I don't know where. She had her hair long, and she was making it into a *chongo*.[5]

Terry comes in and said, "Oh, Auntie. Your hair is so pretty."

I told her, "Terry, your hair is too long, now. Why don't you cut it?"

"No, I don't like it short. I like it long. Ruth, you gotta show me how to do that. I never learned how to make a *chingón*."[6]

Oh, how *Cuca* laughed! She almost choked. Because she was really a joker, and every now and then she put in her bad words, too.

I didn't laugh. I just told her, "Terry!!"

She said, "What? What did I say?" She didn't know how to say 'chongo'. And she didn't even know what came out of her mouth.

You know, when you're losing the language, you use one word for another. They don't know how to speak Spanish anymore.

They Don't Want to Be Mexicans Anymore

And there's a lot of 'em that don't even want to speak it. You talk to them, and they say, "What?" Acting like dummies.

It's like the story of the *bracero* who was here for a lotta years. He went to Mexico to visit his mother. And before he came over here, he liked *atole* a lot.

So, his mother made him a cup of *atole*, and she told him, "Here, son. Have some *atole* that you used to like so much."

He said, "*¿'Tol? ¿'Tol?*"

---

[5] 'a bun'.
[6] An extremely harsh epithet, source unknown.

But he sat down, and he started to turn the cup around and 'round, the way everybody stirs *atole* without a spoon.

His mother said, "Oh, ¿how did you like the *atole?*"

"It's good. The *'tol* is good."

"¿You see, son? his mother said. You forgot how *atole* is called. But you didn't forget how to stir it."

No. A lot of 'em now wanna forget that they're Mexicans.

There was one guy here, his name was *Daniel Ramírez*. He put himself 'Dan Rames' by the court because he didn't wanna be a Mexican. Everybody called him *'el judío'*. They called him *'ese judío chaquetero'*[7] (i) because he turned his jacket around to be from another country. He had a little rundown store there next to the Ace Body Shop.

Here, a lotta people changed their name. Like the Joseph brothers. They used to be 'Masid'. They had the Masid Chevrolet. But here, they put themselves 'Joseph'. People called them Jews, but they weren't Jews, they were Arabs. Here, anybody that's from the Middle East, they call 'em Jews, but I knew they wasn't Jews.

They made 'em take off the name 'Joseph' by law because it was not their name. They were not registered with that name. You have to go to court to get it.

The *Castañedas*, too. They were 'Kennedy's'. That's how they put their name, 'Kennedy'. One of 'em, his mom was a *güera*, the mother of the Kennedy's. So, they all came out *güeritos* and they didn't wanna be Mexicans no more. But they couldn't keep it. They made 'em take their name off by law.

The 'Castinados' took off *Castañeda*, too. They're *Castañeda*, but they put the name 'Castinado' so the name doesn't sound like Spanish. Italian, maybe, or French. They still live here.

---

[7] 'that turncoat Jew'. From *chaqueta*, an adaptation of English *jacket*.

Mean Woman

María, one of the other *Castañedas* – the ones that didn't take off their name – she didn't like my cousin *Chuy.* But, when *Chuy's* dad – my uncle – when he was still healthy, she still would go over to his house.

"Ay, don José. Make me a little bit of bread," *or "Ay, don José* make me some *polvorones."*

My uncle learned to be a good baker in Mexico, and over here he made a lotta different kinds for the family.

Yeah, *María* asked my uncle to make her bread, but she treated his son real bad. Because *Chuy* was kinda slow in his head – a little bit retarded. But he went walking everywhere. And, you oughtta see what a worker he was! He did what any other man did – no, more. Because he was a strong man. And he was so good. He never did anybody anything. Nobody. He was always laughing, and he did anything you told 'im. He didn't know how to read, but if you told 'im a phone number, he learned it right away, and he wouldn't forget it.

Anyway, one day he passed in front of *María's* house right there on Eleventh. She just came out of the hospital and was sitting on the porch with a hose watering her grass. Because she had a stroke and was all paralyzed on one side. But with her good hand, she sat there to water the lawn.

Well, *Chuy* passed by and told her, "¿How are you, *María?* ¿So you're out of the hospital?"

She told 'im, "Don't be talking to me. Get outta here. Don't talk to me."

María always thought she was such an important person, so she told him, "¡Don't talk to me any more!"

Chuy told 'er, "No. You know I just wanna say hello and to see how you are. To see if you are better now. I'm not comin' to tell you nothing."

Then she said, "I'll show you how I am. ¡Here!" And she wet him all over. She threw water at 'im with the hose.

I got so angry when I found out. It made me so mad. I didn't know until one time I went to visit him and my uncle. That's when he told me what happened.

So then I went to *María* and I talked to her. "Hey," I told her. "I need to talk to you." I told her, "I could put a claim there, you know. I'm not gonna do it, but I want you to know what happened. Because he's a little bit retarded," I told her.

She said, "And if he keeps coming by this sidewalk, I'm gonna call the police to take him away."

I said, "We'll see. We'll see if they take him. *Chuy's* been here seventy years. ¿Have you ever heard of *Chuy* doing something bad?"

When *Chuy* found out that I talked with *María,* he told me, *"Ay, tía. ¡Caramba!"* He knew how I was because I always got involved when I saw they treated somebody bad, especially somebody in the family.

I went with the lawyers. Yes, I did. I was mad. What made me more mad was that she told him she didn't want him to pass on the sidewalk, and if he did it again, she was gonna call the police. I went two times to the legal aides – the lawyers. He was entitled to have a legal aide.

I said, "I'm telling you so that it's on the record. I want you to put it in your record because she could tell the police to take 'im – 'That guy is retarded.' Well, they believe her, not him."

I went and told Father because, *¡Válgame Dios!* I told 'im, "Mary is just getting into trouble." So, they put it on the record.

No. I'm just like my dad. I don't let 'em do nothing. I don't know why, but that's the way I am.

THE FOUR BROTHERS AT THE FUNERAL
OF DON JUAN HERNANDEZ, **1945**

Cesáreo, Miguel, Moisés, Juan, Jr.

Comments on Language and Culture

[i]   There were virtually no Jews in Scottsbluff in Elvira's time. Yet, there was an antipathy toward Jews in the Mexican community that was evident in such expressions as *"ese judío chaquetero"* and other expressions heard publicly from time to time. These attitudes in Scottsbluff were undoubtedly Catholic anti-semitic baggage imported from Mexico. Because of this religious underpinning, this discrimination is different, I believe, from discrimination based on skin color which is endemic in Mexican society, as it is in the U.S.

Chapter Sixteen

THE BOYS LEAVE HOME

One superintendent in Kansas told 'im straight,
"Mr. Hernandez, we like your qualifications,
but we can't hire you. Our parents
would never allow a Mexican to teach their children."

De Pipa y Guante[1]

When we lived in the big house, the kids started to leave home, one by one. The girls stayed longer, but the boys left right away after they graduated from high school. They worked in the field really hard, and they didn't want to stay here no more. When we was workin', we told 'em, "The reason we're working so hard is so you can all go to college if you want to."

Eddie was the first one. He went to college in nineteen forty-nine.[2] He was pretty young because he graduated when he was seventeen. That's why me and Mike took 'im to Lincoln.

When he went to sign up for his classes, we went around looking for someplace where he was gonna stay. I wanted him to stay with a Mexican family, but we didn't know if there was any Mexicans in that big city.

No, we drove around the streets for about two or three hours when I saw a woman sitting on a porch who looked like a Mexican.

---

[1] 'wearing fancy clothes'. Literally, *'(smoking) a pipe and (wearing white) gloves'*.
[2] The University of Nebraska.

Le dije a Maique, "Stop here. I'm gonna go talk to her."

*"¿*Right here?*"* It was a big street with a lotta trees. It was less than two miles from the college.

"Sí, aquí. I'll cross walking."

I asked the woman, *"¿Habla español?"*

Me dijo, "Sí, señora."

¡Ay! I was so happy that the first one we found was a Mexican! So I told 'er, *"Señora,* we're tryin' to find a family that has a room for a boy who is gonna go to college here."

Right away she said, *"No, señora. Yo no tengo bordantes,* but the lady that lives over there on the corner. . .".

She pointed to a big house about a block away on the other side of the street.

"That lady had a boarder that just left. I think she might be looking for someone that could stay there. Her name is *Mercedes Villanueva. ¿*Why don't you go talk with her?"

I thanked her, and we went over to talk to Mrs. *Villanueva.* She was an old lady, about sixty-five years old. She didn't know English – she only spoke Spanish. She had two daughters that lived there with her. One was about twenty-two, and the other one was a little bit older.

No. They invited us in and were very polite with us. They had an empty bedroom and, yes, they was lookin' for a nice person to live there. They would give 'im his room and his meals.

I explained a litte bit about *Eduardo* and what he was like and what he was comin' for, and everything. So, right away we settled everything, and I was glad that he was gonna live with a good family and one that spoke Spanish. That way, he wouldn't forget it.

But Eddie had a lotta trouble with his classes, and after two years he couldn't do it, so he quit college.

But, see who I went to leave 'im with in Lincoln! Right at the door of the one he was gonna get married to. *La señora Villanueva* was the grandmother of some girls that lived there not too far away – *las Gándara.* So, *Eduardo* met them there because they used to go visit their grandma. Good girls. Their father worked in the county.

Eddie was after one of 'em that he liked, then after another one. In nineteen fifty-one, in the summer after we finished work in the beets, he told us that he wanna get married to Eleanor. He was like his dad. He was afraid to tell us, but he finally did.

So, before we started to work in the potatoes, we went to Lincoln to ask for her, and they got married in November of nineteen fifty-one, right after topping. So young! Well, *sea por Dios*.

The next year, we rented the Summerville farm and became farmers. Just before Michael was born – their first little baby – Eddie came to help us with our first year of topping. When we finished, before he went back to Lincoln, he went to Gering to help my dad who still didn't finish his beets.

I remember that so much, and it makes me laugh. One day, they was working together, and my dad was getting more ahead and more ahead. *Eduardo* got too tired and had to top the beets kneeling down. Well, he got even farther back of my dad! When they got done, his grandpa scolded 'im.

"No. You guys go to college, and you come back *de pipa y guante*, and you forget how to work."

Oh, how that made me laugh! Yeah, well my dad was seventy-four and Eddie was twenty-one. A man so young and strong should last longer than an old man. But Edward had two years that he didn't top beets, so it was a lot harder for him, and my dad was used to it.

Jacobo's Death

No. My dad was still real strong, especially now that he didn't get drunk no more. Because after they came back from Mexico in nineteen forty, I used to tell 'im, "Look, Dad. Don't drink any more. Remember that all us girls are big now, and we don't like you to be drunk."

I think my dad listened. He did, because I told 'im, "Dad, you just come in drunk and you hit my mom. ¿Is that how you love Mom so much? You hug 'er, but there you go, slapping 'er. ¿Why?"

Dijo, "Because I feel like slapping 'er. That's how I'm used to it."

"Well, get un-used to it," I told him. By that time, I learned to be a little bit more brave with him. Before, I didn't tell 'im nothing.

"Get un-used to it," I told 'im, and he just laughed.

I prayed to God for him to get well. And he did. He wasn't the same *Papá.* He changed. He didn't drink no more. Until he died.

I was the last one to see my dad before he died. That day, I felt like goin' to Jobita. My dad was living with them while he was working with another farmer.

When I got there, my dad was by himself. Alone. Nobody. Jobita? I think she took 'em all to church, 'Let's go play the organ.' Well, my dad was still out topping. Manuel and Joe was working someplace else, and they probably went to eat supper somewhere.

So, when I got there, Dad was just sitting there. I asked 'im, "¿Are you here by yourself?"

"Eiy," dijo. "¡I'm tired! Look at my hands how tired they are." He said, "Look, *hija.* This is gonna be my last year that I work. I'm done."

I told 'im, "You should'a been done a long time ago."

"Eiy. But I just have tomorrow to work, then I'm leaving to Mexico. I just came back here to make a few *pesos* because in Mexico it's worth double."

Le dije, "Well, right now, wash up. ¿You haven't had supper yet, have you?"

"No." Well, how could he? He was there alone.

I told 'im, "Okay. You'll see." *Le dije,* "Lemme see what Jobita has. She has tortillas here, she has beans, she has eggs. She has everything. I'll get you something right away." So, I gave him some supper.

Afterward, I told 'im, "Look. It's late now. You go to bed now, so you can rest."

The next day, when he finished the little piece of beets that he had left, *Ramiro* came over. He told my dad, "I'm gonna go to Alliance. ¿Do you want to go with me?"

Yeah. He went with him. On the way back, almost getting home, the car slid and turned over. My dad fell on the cement, and *Ramiro* fell out and landed in the weeds. Neither one of 'em had a seat belt on because in those years the cars didn't have that. I think that *Ramiro* was driving too fast, and he couldn't turn on Jobita's road.

My dad died instantly, right there.

That was in 'fifty-two. November second, nineteen fifty-two.

Everybody came to the funeral. From Denver, from *Durango,* from Mexico City. My kids were all there, and Eddie, too. I was real happy that he came back from Lincoln. He just left because he was helping my dad who told 'im he came back from college *'de pipa y guante'.*

Graduating from College

But Edward always wanted to finish college. I think he was the first Mexican from here to go to college, and everybody looked up to him. I think he was ashamed because he didn't finish. But he didn't wanna stay working in the field. So, in nineteen fifty-four, he got a job at night with the railroad there in Lincoln, and he went back in to study his classes.

Then, when he graduated, him and Eleanor already had three kids. He wanted to get a job as a teacher, but nobody wanna hire him anywhere.

One superintendent in Kansas told 'im straight, "Mr. Hernandez, we like your qualifications, but we can't hire you."

Edward asked 'im, "Why?"

"Well, you're qualified, but our parents would never allow a Mexican to teach their children." They didn't want a Mexican for a teacher. Can you imagine?

243

So, he applied in California, and over there they gave him a job. In California, there was discrimination, too, but not as much as here. I guess because there was a lot more Mexicans than in Nebraska. So, he went to live over there, and afterward, the rest of 'em moved, one by one, and everybody became Californians.

The Champ

Bobby was the next one. He graduated from high school, too, but he didn't go to college. Instead, after thinning, he got work here at S&T Oldsmobile selling car parts. It was easier for Bobby to get a job because by that time there was more Mexicans that graduated from high school. Eddie was one of the first ones. So, how long did they help us on the farm? Just a few years.

And then, Bobby was real white, like the *Fonsecas*. His cheeks were red, red. *Don Másimo* even called him *'el Colora'o'* – *'¿Where's el Colora'o'* or *'Here comes el Colora'o'*.

Even Bobby said, "I'm like an egg."

"What do you mean 'like an egg'?"

"Soy muy blanquillo."[3]

Everybody in Scottsbluff liked Bobby. He had a real good personality, and he got along good with everybody – with Mexicans and with *güeros*. With everybody. And then he was one of the best boxers from here in Scottsbluff. He always won his fights in the Golden Gloves, and his name and his picture came out in the *Star Herald*. Everybody liked Bobby Hernandez, the Champ.

When he was fifteen years old, he won the championship the first time. A guy came from New York to tell 'im to go be a professional boxer, and he would pay 'im a hundred dollars a fight. Over here, you had to work two whole weeks to earn that much money.

---

[3] 'I'm very white.' *Blanquillo,* 'a little white person or thing' is used as a euphemism for 'egg' to avoid saying the word *huevo,* which also references certain male body parts.

But right away his dad said 'no', and he told the man to get out. We didn't want a fifteen-year-old boy to fight with professionals just so they would have somebody to practice with. *¡Ni lo mande Dios!* They would beat 'im up real bad, no matter how good a boxer Bobby was.

Yeah, Bobby was really good. He won in Omaha and then in Chicago. One time, he went to a national tournament and he almost won over there.

When he went in the army, right away they sent 'im to Germany. I have pictures of 'im there. Over there, he won first place in a tournament of all the army.

But he liked to go out with his friends to the bars. I think that over there in Germany they got drunk and they fought each other. He wrote one time that one of 'em hit 'im over the head with a beer bottle. They almost killed 'im. They knocked 'im out, and they had to take him to the hospital of the army camp. All that boxing and the fighting affected 'is head. Well, sure!

The first thing when he got out of the army, in February, 1957, he got married with Betty, one of the *Montañeses* from over here in Hunt's Acres.[4] Right away, they decided to go to Corning where Edward was in California. It didn't take long and he got a job with the Chevrolet dealer selling parts. Rhonda, their first little baby, was born over there in October.

Brain Cancer

Over there is when he started to get real bad headaches. They couldn't find anything, and they couldn't find anything. Finally they had to take him to San Francisco to the army hospital. *¡Ay, pobrecito!* They found a tumor in his head. They never told 'im it was cancer, they just said it was 'a tumor'. I think they didn't want to scare 'im or I don't know what. No. They had to open up his head to operate on 'im.

---

[4] A trailer park and low-income housing on the west side of Scottsbluff.

Ohh! I went flying over there, even if I was so afraid of aeroplanes. I stayed there with my brother Jimmy and Onie. At that time, Jimmy was working as a baker in San Francisco.

I used to go in the bus from their apartment to the hospital that was on top of a big hill close to the ocean. I went and I came back by myself because, well, *Joaquín* and Onie was both working. Sometimes I didn't come back until it was dark.

I remember one time I came back really late, about ten o'clock at night. To go where they lived, I had to get off of one bus and wait on the corner to catch another one that took me to the street where Jimmy lived.

I got outta the first bus, and the driver showed me where I was supposed to cross to get the other one. So, I crossed the street, but there wasn't no place to sit, so I stood right on the corner, close to a light post. On that same corner but a little off to one side, a man was standing there. A Negro. Tall.

¡Ay! I felt like I don't know what. Scared, I guess. Because in Scottsbluff there wasn't no Negroes, and the ones that there was lived over there by Ninth Street. We never saw 'em. One of the men from our church – I don't remember which one – was married to a Negro woman. She was very Catholic. She came to Mass every Sunday. A real good lady, but she's the only Negro I knew.

But in San Franciso, there was a lot of 'em everywhere, and I was really afraid of 'em. I think that was from when they told us bad things and hit us at John J. Ingalls in Kansas City. But, then, we also have the fault of putting somebody down all the time.

Like I remember my *comadre Dorador.* Oh, I was so embarrassed! One time, she came over and we was talking about the workers who came in the summer from Texas – *mexicanos.* We didn't like 'em because they wasn't too clean and the men was always drinking and fighting.

I said, *"¡Mugrosos tejanos!"*[5]

---

[5] 'Dirty Tejanos.' Scottsbluff Mexicans always referred to the Mexicans from Texas as *tejanos*. White people from Texas were called *Texans*.

My *comadre* just looked at me and said, *"Comadre, ¡yo soy tejana!"*

Oh, my gosh! I was so embarrassed. My face got all red. But what could I say? Nothing. That's why I say we shouldn't be talkin' bad about any other people.

Okay, then. When that man in San Francisco was standing there, I didn't know what to do. '¿What will I do if that man comes to grab me?' Well, what could I do? So, I started to pray to my guardian angel. That angel is always with me, taking care of me. So there I am, prayin' and prayin'.

Then, the man starts to come close! *¡Ay, Dios de mi vida!*

He tells me, "Ma'am, are you waiting for the bus?" He told me the number of the bus that I had to catch. How did that man know that? I even got more scared.

I told 'im, "Yes, are you?" Well, I didn't know what else to say.

"No," he said. "I'm waiting for another one. Yours should be here in about five minutes." How did he know the schedule for my bus?

"You know," he said, "you shouldn't be out here at this time of night. This is not a very safe neighborhood. I'll stand here and wait with you. Do you mind?"

I told 'im, "No, I don't mind. Thank you very much." Well, even if I mind, what was I gonna do? No. He stood waiting there on the corner until my bus came. I thanked him and I got on.

Now, I think that man was my guardian angel that was watching over me. Well, what was he doing there at that time? How did he know the number of my bus? And why did he come over to help me? I think my guardian angel appeared to me as a Negro on purpose.

And you know what? Since that time, I started to have a different idea about Negroes. There's good ones, and there's bad ones, but they are all people like everybody else. We don't have to discriminate against nobody just because they're Negroes or Mexicans or whatever.

After the operation, Bobby got better and they let 'im out of the hospital. He thought they cured him, but I think the doctors just didn't want to tell 'im the truth. I have a picture of 'im when he went back to Corning.

No, before a month, he got real sick and he had to go back to the hospital. Mike and I went to stay with 'im in San Francisco again. We just finished thinning the beets. Bill stayed there to watch the farm.

We already knew that Bobby wasn't gonna live. At first, he still talked to us, always joking around, I remember, and laughing. That's the way Bobby was, always happy. But then at the end, he was always just sleeping. He just held my hand, and then his eyes got full of tears. We begged the Virgin Mary to pray for him, and to God, too, to let 'im live. We wanted Him to grant us another miracle.

But, no. God doesn't give you everything you ask for. He has His own plan, and we have to a'cept it. Oh, that was so hard! *Taba tan* young. He died on the fourteenth of June of nineteen fifty-eight. He was just gonna be twenty-five years old in July. If only he hadn't been a boxer, and if only he didn't fight so much in Germany!

The day he left us, me and Mike went to rest a little bit over with Onie. Edward stayed at the hospital and Johnny Mack did, too, because he came all the way to San Francisco from Merced to be with us.[6] Then Bobby started to breathe real hard. The doctor came in, and he said for them to call us, that for them to let us know because he didn't have much time.

Johnny called us right away, and there we go in a hurry. We were goin' like sixty on those high streets in San Francisco. Sometimes, Mike didn't even stop for the lights. If there was a red light, he would slow down just to see if a car was comin', and he'd take off again. If a policeman stopped us, we would just say, "Drive ahead of us to the hospital! It's a matter of life or death!" No, nobody stopped us.

---

[6] Merced is about 150 miles east of San Francisco.

But we didn't get there to Bobby. He died before we got there. That's the way it happened when Mike died, too. I didn't get to be with any of 'em, to be with 'em at the "hour of their death".[7] Well, *sea por Dios.*

The House on West Overland

Betty was expecting her second baby, and she came back to Scottsbluff. When the baby was born, she asked Elvira what name she should put her. Elvira suggested for her to put her 'Roberta', in memory of her dad. We all still call her 'Bobbie'.

And that's when Betty asked us to buy these two houses together here on West Overland. She wanted to be close to us because of the girls.

That was good because Rhonda and Bobbie were always over here at my house. Those girls are so good. They always brought me something that they knew I liked, or even to come over and say hello. And when I was making tortillas and I saw 'em outside, I told 'em to come in and have a nice and warm *tortilla* with butter and salt. Ohh! How they liked my tortillas.

Now that they don't live here, when they come to visit their mom, they never leave unless they come over to see me. Rhonda and Bobbie are very close with me. My other grandchildren, too, but not like them. *Eduardo's* kids, especially. When they go to vacation, they always come over here to pass one or two days with their grandma. The bigger ones of Bill, too. The other ones, I don't see 'em so much.

Anyway, we bought the houses – we bought this one and Betty the other one that was newer. The one who owned this house built the other one that Betty bought. They rented this one, but they left it without nothing. It didn't have anything. I don't know why we let 'em sell us this house. *¡No sé por qué!* It was so ugly! Oh, it was terrible!

---

[7] A phrase from the 'Hail Mary' prayer.

We bought it cheap, that's why. But it was worthless. Look. It didn't have water. Just water from the pump that you couldn't drink because of all the septic tanks that there was. We had to go buy city water to drink and wash the dishes. Until we had them put city water ourselves. And it didn't have electricity. We used candles and lamps here until we put the electricity.

Oh, what ugly cupboards. Dirty drawers *llenos de cagarruchas de ratones.* I told Mike, "Take everything out! Sink and everything. We'll buy a new sink and you can make me new cupboards."

Right away he started to make 'em. He made all these cupboards. He made me such good cupboards! Then, he tore down two walls to make the living room and dining room bigger. Everything was so closed up. Dark. If he had lived, he would'a fixed this house up really good.

He told me, "Oh, we'll make it better. The way you want it." We would'a put a double bathroom, and he would'a done a lot to this little house.

He wasn't a carpenter. He was a mechanic, that's all he was. But he learned to do everything. He even made me a little room for my sewing machine with a closet, right here where there wasn't nothing. He made it so good! And it's lasted a long time! Over forty-five years.

And I lived here since then, and here is where I'm gonna die.

Bill

When we rented the farm in nineteen fifty-two, Eddie and Bobby was already gone, and they didn't help us in the field anymore. They're the ones that had been our hardest workers. Bill and Terry helped us to thin or to top just a little bit after school. We never took them out.

Sometimes in the topping, when there was a moon, we all worked after the sun went down. Because it used to get dark real early, and we had to take advantage of the moonlight.

I remember one time that we was finishing the last row – in the dark, before we went home. We couldn't hardly see. Bill and Terry was topping fast, fast so they could finish quick. They got to the last beet of the row, and both of 'em tried to get it at the same time. Terry picked[8] it first. But Bill couldn't stop his . He picked Terry real good on her hand. It wasn't too hard, but I think she still has the scar there.

In the summer, Bill had to learn to drive the tractor to help Mike cultivate the beans and the beets.(i) He thought that was a lot harder than thinning beets. But he hardly ever thinned. There's no comparison of work on a tractor and working all day bending over and cutting, cutting, cutting with a hoe.

That's why in nineteen fifty-five, right away after he graduated, Bill went to the army, and they sent him to Germany, too. He sent me some pretty things from over there – one of those clocks that run with little balls that turn, and a set of china, and other things. That's one thing about Bill. He recognized nice things, and he still does.

When he got back, he went to college in Chicago. He was there for one year, and then he went to California to see what there was over there. But he came back right away and he met *Hortensia*, here from Alliance. *Se volaron*[9], both of 'em, and they went together to California. After two years, they got married. I think that was in nineteen sixty because Delfina was born on November 10 of that year.

Hortensia was one of those mean women. Really nasty. She would get mad at Bill for no reason and told him ugly things. She yelled at the kids and hit 'em for nothing, too.

One time when Delfina was little – she was just one year old – we were all visiting over there at *Eduardo*. The baby was crying that she wanted something. We didn't know what she wanted, but she was bothering and bothering. Then, *Hortensia* gets up! She spanked her so hard! And not just one or two times. A lot. And hard. The baby almost choked from cryin' so hard.

---

[8] 'modeled on Spanish *picó*, 'punctured', in this case with the sharp hook at the end of the knife.
[9] 'they got carried away'. Literally, *'they flew away'*.

Mike told *Hortensia*, "*Hortensia!* That's a terrible way to discipline a child!"

Hortensia turned and showed her teeth to Mike, "Mr. Hernandez, she's my child, and I'll discipline her the way I want. It's none of your business, anyway."

Mike just told 'er, "You know what? You are nothing but a rattlesnake."

Mike didn't say any more to her because he wasn't in his own house, and Bill didn't say anything, either. Mike didn't say one more word to that woman, ever.

After a lotta years, Bill got a divorce from her. I don't know what took 'im so long.

> "No. You guys go to college, and you come back *de pipa y guante*, and you forget how to work."
> — *Jacobo Chávez to his grandson Eduardo*

Six Scottsbluff Fighters Enter Class A at Terrytown

Six Scottsbluff fighters will enter in the Class A division of the Western Nebraska Golden Gloves at Terrytown. The matches get underway next Monday night. The boxers have been working out at SERC under the management of Charles Blalock. Heading the list is Bobby Hernandez, a former Midwest AAU lightweight titlist and middle weight champ at Terrytown last winter. The fighters are (left to right): Tommy Quijas, Josie Ramirez, Valentine Phillips, Tommy Hogan, Bobby Hernandez and Eddie Guzman. (Star-Herald photo by Vern Marek)

THE CHAMP

<u>Left</u>: Bobby, champion boxer

<u>Below Left</u>: Bobby in Germany, partying with a friend

<u>Below Right</u>: Bobby mowing weeds in his yard in Corning, CA a few days before being hospitalized for the last time.

The house on *West Overland* that Elvira and Maique bought after Bobby died and where Elvira was to live for the rest of her life.

Comments on Language and Culture

i   'Cultivating' involved cutting the weeds along a row of crops. This was done with a special implement called a 'cultivator', equipped with blades that sliced the dirt and weeds away from either side of the row of plants. This could be done only when the plants were small so that the blades could come as close as possible without cutting the plants themselves. This required the tractor driver to rivet his attention on guiding the cultivator along the rows in a very precise manner.

Chapter Seventeen

A TRUE MIRACLE

This was a miracle – a real miracle of God. Why?
Because I was praying all the time for her,
and I asked our blessed mother to pray for me
to our Lord Jesus Christ. That's why.

Elvira Runs away from Home

When she was seventeen years old, *Elvira* ran away from home – *se nos jue juida*. She didn't even graduated from high school yet. I think she ran away because we didn't let her go out alone. Especially with a boy! Sometimes her friends came over to see her, and I let her go with them to town or to ride on their bicycles.

But I always told 'er, to come back before it gets late. *"No se dilaten."* I never wanted 'er to be out at night.

No. I used to be real strict then, especially with the girls. With the boys, too, but not so much. The only thing with them is I didn't want 'em to go to the pool hall(i) or to go out and drink beer. The girls, I was always watching to see that they didn't go crazy with a boy. But I couldn't always do that. Well, anyway.

So, one Sunday I let Elvira go to the show with some friends. It was a matinee. They always came home from the show by five or six at the latest because the show was over about four, and afterward, all the friends could walk around town for a while.

That day, she didn't come and she didn't come. It was already dark a long time ago, and she still didn't come. No. Finally I saw a car comin', and then she came in by herself. The other ones just dropped 'er off and went. I don't know if they had some boys with 'em.

Le dije, "Say, ¿where were you?"

She said, "Oh, we was just riding around town."

"Around town!? ¿At this hour? ¿Can't you see what time it is? ¡I told you not to come home late!" I really scolded 'er.

Then, she answered me back, "Well, what difference does it make? I'm here now. I'm old enough to know what I'm doing."

Old enough!? Not at seventeen years old. She made me so mad! And I slapped 'er. Not too hard, but hard enough so she wouldn't talk back to me.

But then, her dad came in. He was in the living room, and he heard us. "¿What's going on in here? Vera, you can't talk to your mom like that. You know you were supposed to be here early. You go on up to your room."

Elvira didn't say anything. She didn't cry or nothing. She just turned and ran upstairs to her room. That was it.

The next day, she came down real quiet. She didn't say nothing. She washed up, ate breakfast, swept the kitchen and did her other work, and then she went outside. I saw her walking real slow over in the trees, and then she crossed the bridge and went walking by the ditch. Slow, slow.

I could tell she was upset by something, probably because I slapped 'er. Maybe. I never hit 'er since she was a baby when I gave her a little spanking one time. But, no. I never hit the girls. Just the boys if I could catch 'em. Because they ran.

After a while, she came back and started to play the piano. She was learning to play real good because Ethel was giving 'er lessons. She went to her lesson one time every week. And a lotta times she went to the church to play the organ because they needed somebody to play for the high Mass.

So, the next day she said, "I'm going to the church to practice the organ. Is that all right?"

Well, yes, of course. She liked to do that all the time, anyway, so I didn't think anything about it. It was about one o'clock in the afternoon.

So, after about four or five, when she didn't come, I start to think, 'Well, ¿Why is Elvira so late? I hope she comes home soon.'

But she didn't come and she didn't come. Then I got mad because this was the second time she did that. '¡That darn girl! I wonder where she is. ¡She better not be with a boy because then she's gonna find out!' I wasn't gonna let 'er go no place no more!

After a while, Mike came home from work. He was out irrigating, and it got late for 'im. *Le dije,* "Look. Elvira hasn't come back yet. It's too late for her to be out there alone. We have to go look for her."

"¿But where?"

Le dije, "She was goin' to the church. Let's go there first."

We went, but nothing. Everything was dark. Then we went to ask the father because the rectory was right there close.

He said, "No, I haven't seen her. She usually comes here to get the key." Darn her! She told me she was goin' to the church.

We thanked Father, and then we drove by the houses of some of her friends to see if we saw her bicycle. No, we didn't. We didn't stop and ask because we didn't wanna let everybody know about it.

I said, "Well, let's go home to see if she's there yet."

No, she wasn't. So, there we are, waiting and waiting. Well, we waited all night, and nothing.

'¡Ay, Dios de mi vida! Where is she? What could have happened to her?' Then I really got scared.

In the morning, Mike went to work, and I went in the car to look for her. I just told the kids not to leave the yard, and I went. I didn't know where, but I wanted to see if I could find 'er. Oh! I was so worried I didn't know what to do.

I even went to the house of one of her friends that lived close by the river on the way to Mitchell. They were *güeros* of a different religion. No, there was nothing. They told me they hadn't seen Elvira.

Lies! Because afterward we found out they hid 'er and helped 'er go to Denver.

So, one day passed, and then another one, and she didn't come back. I went out every day to look for her, but where else was I gonna look?

Then, Terry got a letter that Elvira sent, but she didn't put an address or nothing. She said, "I'm going to send you the little things that I have. It's not much, but where I'm going, I won't need them." She told 'er she wasn't going to need anything she had! *¡Ay, virgen santa!*

I think she wanted to go in a convent or something like that because she always liked the religion. But I got so scared when Terry showed me that letter.

I said, 'Ohh! I bet she wanna commit suicide because she was so depressed.'

'Oh, no! Oh, no! Was she so sad because we scolded her or because we didn't let 'er go out?' I started to cry.

The Miracle

I told Mike, "No. We have to go." Because on the letter it had the mark from Denver.

Mike said, "And what are we gonna do over there? We don't know Denver. We don't know anything about Colorado. ¿Where are we gonna go?"

I told 'im, "¿What do you mean, '¿Where are we gonna go?' We're going."

He said, "No, we can't go because ¿what are we gonna do?"

I told 'im, "Look. The police will help us to find her. We have to go." I said, "Okay. ¿You say 'no'? Then I'm going by myself."

"What? Are you that brave?"

"Yes, I am."

I cried and I prayed. Every day. Until I told 'im, "¿Well, are we going or aren't we?"

"Okay. Let's go." I took Mary Lou with me. She was about six years old.

When we got to Denver, we drove around downtown Denver until we got to the President's House, a big building where all the bigshots are. "There," I told 'im. "Let's stop here."

Dijo, "¿What are we gonna do here?"

Dije, "We have to look for her in a restaurant. At home, that's all she worked in after school."

So, we stopped there. There wasn't any people goin' in or goin' out. It was up high, and the street was down below.

I told 'im, "Look. Down there, you go in one restaurant. Then you go in another one. You just ask if Elvira is working there. If they ask you who you are, you just tell 'em you're her father and you're looking for her."

There was about three or four restaurants. Mary Lou and me, we stayed sitting there on the lawn of the building, and he went down.

He went in the first one. It was the Brown Palace, a hotel that had a restaurant. That's what it was called. After about a half an hour or more, *dije,* '¿What time is he going to come out of that restaurant?' He wasn't coming out.

Then, 'Oh!' I saw them coming. I couldn't believe it. I just couldn't believe it. The first one! There come both of them. Her dad has his arm around Elvira. She was embarrassed, but happy. Oh! How happy I was when I saw her coming!

This was a miracle, a real miracle of God. Why? Because I was praying all the time for her, and I asked our blessed mother to pray for me to our Lord Jesus Christ. That's why. Every day, crying for her. I was so sad when she went. Then, when Terry got that letter, I almost died because I was afraid I wasn't gonna see Elvira no more. Oh! I have cried more with her than with the rest of 'em. The other ones, I got mad at.

That was the first one of my miracles that our Lord God gave me for all the supplications that I made to His holy mother. In the first restaurant! And in such a big city that we didn't know at all! That was a miracle!

Afterward, I asked Elvira that when did she came to Denver and why. I didn't scold her or anything, I just asked. She told us that the parents of her friend had friends there in Denver, and they're the ones who helped her find the job in that restaurant.

But, how dumb! Instead of saying to her to go back home, they helped 'er run away. But, well. Those people have other ways.

But Elvira was never happy here after that. That's when she start to help the church a little bit more. She always was interested in the religion and the church and all that. After a while, she decided to leave Scottsbluff and she went to Omaha and Lincoln to keep on with that work.

Afterwards, she went to California to help Mary Lou with her baby, but she didn't like it there at all, so right away she left and went to Vermont, and over there, she worked for a lotta years helping the priests. She did everything in the rectory.

Many years later, she went to Texas to work with the migrants. Afterward, she went to Alaska, lookin' for something, I don't know what. Then, she even went to live in New Mexico for a while where Edward was. Now, she came back to Nebraska, and she's still doing work for the church.

Comments on Language and Culture

i   Pool halls were seen as places that had bars and were frequented by rough-talking men who smoked and drank beer. So, parents of "nice" boys did not allow them to go in there. This was true for Lawlor's Pool hall, a hangout for Mexican men, although it illegally allowed teenagers of sixteen or seventeen to enter and play and, sometimes, even to drink beer. The Midwest Pool Hall, patronized mostly by Anglos, allowed smoking but did not sell beer.

Chapter Eighteen

AN ADOPTED SON

Mike said, "This child has a bad temper,
and that man doesn't want 'im.
He's gonna mistreat him, and if we make 'im go back,
there he goes – he's gonna be a bum and a drunkard."

Out!

When Mary Lou found out she was expecting, the dang guy that put 'er like that wanted to get married, and he came with his parents to ask for her. They didn't even bring the priest that's the one that always goes with the parents. The boy came, too, but he wasn't supposed to be there.

When they came, we still didn't know she was expecting. So, when they came to ask for her, *les dijo Maique,* "Well, let's talk about it, but this is a surprise. She's too young yet to get married."

She was only seventeen. That was in nineteen fifty-eight. She didn't even finish high school yet. She graduated afterward, but she didn't go to the ceremony.

When Mike told 'em that, the mother and father just stayed quiet. The boy didn't say nothing, either.

Then, the father said, "Well, they HAVE to get married."

Mike said, "What!?"

"They have to." That they was gonna have a baby.

Mike said, "Oh." That's all.

His heart must'a really been hurting. Mine too. It hit us like a lightning because that was the last thing we expected.

But Mike didn't show them how he was feeling. *Nomás dijo,* "Well, that's another story. I will see. But first, I'm going to talk to the priest."

Then, the man just tells the priest a really bad thing. "The priest can go to hell!!"

You think they put a fire on top of Mike's head! He didn't say nothing. Not one word. He got up from his chair. He opened the door. And with his hand, he told 'em to get out. He didn't even tell 'em nothing. Oh! He must'a been so mad! Not one word. He opened the door, and 'Out'!

You should'a seen 'em. There they go, the three of 'em, with their tail between their legs. Mary Lou didn't know what to say. She was just. . . .

That hurt both of us so much, especially her dad. We never expected that from Mary Lou. We were so sad when we found out why they came to ask for her.

But we wasn't gonna let her get married with that man. Because the more we found out, the more we saw *que era un borrachales y un sinvergüenza.*[1]

I told Mary Lou, "Look, if you get married to that one, he's gonna go out drinking all the time and goin' with other women. And I know he's gonna hit you a lot."

I know she thought about it because she didn't wanna see him no more.

So then, she went to live in Omaha with Elvira. Elvira found her a really good residence in Lincoln for girls like her that wasn't married. So, she went to stay in a special section of St. Elizabeth Hospital until the baby was born.

He was born on the 28th of June, one day after my fiftieth birth'ay in nineteen fifty-nine. She put 'im the name 'Robert' so he could have the same name like Bobby, the one who just died a year ago.

---

[1] 'he was a drunkard and a cheat'.

That's when Mary Lou went to California to stay with Bill and *Hortensia*. She right away got a job in San Francisco. She thought *Hortensia* was gonna help 'er take care of the baby. But how was that woman gonna help? They was still living together before they got married. They didn't get married until nineteen sixty.

So, she went to live with my brother Jim and his wife, Onie. By that time, they lived close by there. Mary Lou says that they treated her real good and Onie took good care of the baby when Mary Lou went to work. She lived there with them, and they didn't charge her nothing. Not a penny. Onie was really good.

Terry

That's when Vera and Terry, both of 'em went to California to see how they could help Mary Lou. But Elvira didn't like it over there at all. For her especially, California was a pagan state! So right away she took off as far away from California that she could.

Terry stayed in California for a while, and her and Mary Lou got an apartment together. Terry started to take care of the baby, but after a while, she didn't like it there, either. I think she was lonely after Vera left because Mary Lou was always workin'. Besides, she was anxious to go to Colorado because there was a guy there from Scottsbluff, and they liked each other, but he went to live in Denver. His name was Richard Chavez.

No. He wanted her to come from over there because he was insisting on her to get married. So, he went to California to get 'er, and right away she came with 'im. They got married in Denver.

At first, I didn't like that matrimony because he was a lot older than her. *Pero, bueno, sea por Dios.*They had two children, and they were okay for a lotta years. But not too long ago, Richard died, and then one year later, so did their daughter Beth. Both of 'em died from cancer, so she stayed alone with Rollie.

Rollie's such a good boy, and always laughing. He does everything Terry asks 'im to do. What's he gonna do alone if she dies? He didn't have too much education. No. I tell Terry I hope that God gives her more life.

263

I hope she doesn't get sick because she got cancer, too. When I used to go to Denver to see her – I went a lotta times to visit – she was sick with a bump about this big, right there on her breast. She went to the doctor.

"Oh," he said. "It'll go away."

Three years she had that bump, and all the time it got bigger and a little bit bigger.

I said, "Don't you let that doctor get away with it. Tell 'im to examine you real good. Make 'im examine you."

She did. Cancer. They had to operate on 'er. She was in the hospital for a month.

Le dije, "¿See? That's why I told you, you have to be rude sometimes with the doctor and make 'im. If he doesn't, get another one."

Bad Baby Care

So, when Terry went to Denver, Mary Lou went to live by herself, and she had to hire a baby sitter. But that woman didn't take care of 'im. She didn't clean 'im. She didn't even change his diaper in the whole day. And that's how he stayed, all wet and dirty until Mary Lou got home from work.

No. The baby got real sick, and Mary Lou didn't know what to do. That's why she called me, and asked me to take care of him.

"Mom, can you take care of Robert for a while? Just until I get a better job and I can get a better baby sitter."

I told Mary Lou, "Okay. I'll take care of him until he gets better and you find a better job. And then, you can take 'im back."

She told me 'Okay', and she brought 'im to Scottsbluff. He was a little more than a year. It was in the summer. About a year and a couple of months when she told me to take care of 'im.

Mira, tenía unas ronchas y llagas así,[2] from here to here. All between his legs. From the front all the way back. No wonder he

---

[2] 'Look, he had some bumps on his skin and open sores this big'.

screamed and he yelled, and he turned and he jumped until, poom! He would fall down. I think he was hurting from all the *ronchas* that burned 'im. And he had so many!

Right away, I took 'im to the doctor. He said, "My goodness. This baby hasn't been taken care of at all. He could'a died of infection with all this." That's all he said.

He gave me an ointment, and he told me to give 'im a bath every day and to put that on. Then I bought a roll of gauze, and I wrapped 'im with that under his diaper so he would be dry. Then when he did the bathroom, I took it off and put a clean one. I gave 'im a bath every day. Oh, how I worked with that child. For a month, he was so bad.

No. Two months later, he was already laughing and playing. He really looked better, and he wasn't cryin' the way he used to.

To Adopt or Not.

Then, when Mary Lou told me she was gonna get married to Weldon, I thought 'Okay, then. Now maybe she'll take 'im back.'

Robert was going on three years. I had 'im for over a year.

At the wedding, she told us, "No, not right now. Let him grow up a little bit more, then I'll bring 'im. Let's wait until after we make our house."

So, we took 'im back to Scottsbluff with us. But afterward, her dad called Mary Lou to find out when we could take 'er the baby.

She said, "No, Dad. We just got married. We have to fix 'im a home, and then we'll take him."

I think she wanted to have another baby with her husband. But he didn't want to take Robert.

Mike told her, "You should take 'im, Mary Lou, because he's yours. He's not ours. He's just our grandson."

"Well, he loves you and you love him."

By that time he was more than three years old, and Mike took 'im out to the field. Robert loved to go over there with him. He would say, "Daddy, daddy! Daddy, daddy!" For Mike to take 'im.

Mike told her, "Yes, we love him, but it's your boy. You should take 'im. *No tiene nombre.* He's gotta have a name. You can give 'im a name."

Then, Mary Lou told him, "But he's a Hernandez. If you keep 'im, he can still have that name."

¡Válgame Dios! What are we gonna do?

Mike told me, "Come 'ere. Let's talk." That's when he proposed for us to adopt Robert.

Dice, "This child *es muy renegado,* and that man doesn't want 'im. If we force him to go, pretty soon there he goes – on the streets, a drunkard."

Ever since he was a baby, he was real stubborn. He's still that way, but not as much.

When he did something, I told 'im, "Robert! You stop it! We're gonna take you to your mom!"

"No! You're my mom. I don't wanna go no place."

He always called me 'Mom' and he called Mike 'Dad'. Even now he does. He calls her 'Mary Lou' even if he already knows that she's his mother.

Mike and I, we were always in agreement. But if I thought one way, and he thought another way, we had to do what he said – naturally. Because he was the husband. Especially when it had to do with Mary Lou!

Bueno. Lo adoptamos. And he stayed *Hernández.* Until the day that Mike died, Robert was out in the field with 'im.

Oh! There goes Robert. He was five years old and he already put the water on the beets. Gee manee! He got a sack of tubes and he start to put 'em in the ditch until he couldn't do it no more. And he learned how to put the tubes on every row and start the water.

Every time he saw his dad goin' to the farm, "Daddy, daddy! I'm goin' with you!" Because when we adopted him, we had our farm there with Summerville, but we had our house here in town. Mike used to go to the farm and then come back home. It wasn't too far, about four or five miles on the way to Mitchell.

Mike said, "Well, what am I gonna do? He wants to go." Because Robert wouldn't stay and he wouldn't stay. Mike said, "I'll watch him over there. I'll see what he does." Yeah, there he goes to bring the water jug or a shovel or whatever else. He learned to help his dad real quick.

One time they were goin' on the tractor on the road. Because Mike went to the farm and went back on that big red tractor he had. Robert was on top, sitting with his dad on the tractor. Well, a policeman stopped 'em. Oh! He told 'im 'no', but he didn't give 'im a ticket. He just said, "He can't go up there."

"What?"

"No. It's against the law to give a ride on a tractor."

So, from then on, both of 'em went to the farm in the pickup.

Mike takes his Farmall out of the garage,
getting ready to go out to the farm.

Robert, who just turned three, 'helping' his dad with the irrigation

Elvira's brother Jim and his wife Onie Price who helped Mary Lou take care of Robert.

Chapter Nineteen

ALLÁ EN EL RANCHO GRANDE[1]

Mike had to get the operation. Ohh!
I don't know how I was gonna do the topping by myself.
¡Ay Dios de mi vida!
But the farmers, when something happens to one of 'em,
they help each other.

Becoming Farmers

We farmed there with Summerville from nineteen fifty-two, when we rented the farm, until nineteen sixty-five. That was the year that Mike died. We finally got to be farmers, what we wanted to do for a lotta years.

It was eighty acres on the other side of the river. It wasn't very good land *porque los rusos* right away got those farms. But at least we was gonna work for ourselves and not for other farmers.

We knew the Summervilles because Loren had a filling station that we went to over there on Twenty-Seventh Street. Mike used to go to see him and talk to him about renting the farm. Loren wanted us to pay for all the costs, but we didn't have the money.

Finally, they made an agreement for Loren to buy all the seed for the first year, and he would let us have the house on the farm to live in. We had to put all the machinery and all the tools. And then we had to do all the work – naturally. Then, when we got the

---

[1] 'Out There on the Big Ranch', the title of a popular Mexican song.

money for the crops, we had to pay him twenty-five percent of that for the rent. With whatever we had left, we had to pay him back for the seed.

We hardly had nothing for ourselves to live with. It was a good thing that Bobby was working at the S&T because he helped us a lot. The first year, we barely made it. But we made it. Afterward, it was better, except when Mike got sick.

At first, we lived in the two-story house that was there on the farm. The house wasn't too bad, but it was old, and I had a lotta work to keep it clean.

It had some sheds there for all of Mike's equipment, and it had an electric pump for the water. The pump was right by the house, and it had a little motor this big on the side. I remember that I just pushed the button, and it had a pipe that went up and down, up and down to pump water. You could fill a pail of water real quick. The ones that you pumped by hand didn't have that. That was the first time we had an electric pump.

The year we started, we had to buy a tractor and all the machines to work the fields – the plows, the discs, the planters – everything. His pickup, too. We bought everything used because new machines cost too much money. We used up almost all our savings.

Then, when the time came to harvest, Mike had to buy a beet loader and a truck to take everything to the dump.(i) He rented the thrashing machine for the beans. That was the first time we took out a loan from the bank. We never borrowed money like my dad. Everything had to be cash. It was hard, but that way we didn't get so much in debt for the winter.

I used to go out there with him so he didn't have to hire a man to do the work. Well, money was tight on account of all the expense. I learned to fill up the truck with beets and take it to the dump. I don't know how I did it, but there I go with him – he drove the loader and I followed 'im with the truck. At first, before I knew it, the beets were on the ground or behind the truck. No. Mike just put some marks on the loader to guide me, and I learned how to fill up my truck without spilling the beets.

Mike's Illnesses

Mike was always sick. If it wasn't his back, it was his kidneys that made his wrists and his ankles get all swollen up. His joints got all full of water because his kidneys didn't work too good.

But he didn't wanna go to the doctor, I think because in Mexico a lotta people wouldn't see a doctor for nothing. A *curandero* was better than a doctor. That's what *don Juan* believed, and Mike got used to that way, too. He didn't have any faith in the doctors.

Decía, "No, those guys just give you pills for everything and they tell you to come back in two weeks so they can give you more pills. What they want is more money."

One time, I took him to the hospital at midnight so they could give 'im a shot. I made 'im go. I don't know what he had, but he couldn't even sleep because he couldn't stand the pain in his arms.

If it wasn't that, his legs. If not, his back. He went to get operated on his back. He had to. When he was irrigating, he couldn't even pick up a sack of tubes. He could barely walk. I think that happened because of all the years he worked bent over – thinning, topping, and picking potatoes.

He had to hire a man to come and water the beets and thrash the beans. The boys were in California, but he told me not to tell 'em nothing about how he was.

Dice, "Don't say nothing to nobody that I'm sick." He didn't want them to know.

Dice, "Right now, the boys have their own battles." Bill with his mean woman, and *Eduardo* with his family. Besides, Bill had Delfina and Adrienne who were small, and Edward with his five kids, he couldn't keep up, either. This was in nineteen sixty-two.

I took Mike to Kearney to get operated because there wasn't doctors here that knew how to operate on the vertebraes. It's a wonder he didn't get paralyzed. He didn't. Afterward, he turned out real good, but he couldn't do anything until the next year.

When he got out of the hospital, the topping time was almost over with because it was very cold already. Eee! It was really cold. And if the hard cold came, the dirt would freeze, and they couldn't take out the beets until about February.

For a lot of 'em, it froze. They couldn't take the beets out until the weather got better and it started to thaw out when the dirt got a little more soft. They still topped 'em, but they lost a lotta tonnage and a lotta sugar.

We would'a lost even more because the way it was, we only got fifteen or sixteen ton per acre and about nine or ten percent sugar. On our farm, it didn't produce too good. We never got a big crop of sugar and tonnage. Other farmers even got twenty-four ton per acre and up to fifteen or sixteen sugar. I don't know how they count it, but for us it was pretty good if it was twelve percent sugar.

So we would'a lost a lot, a lot if it froze. Besides that, we had all the expenses of the hospital because Mike didn't have insurance for that. And then, comin' and going' to Kearney, I didn't have no time to look for somebody to drive the topper. By then, they topped and loaded all at the same time. Ohh! I don't know how we was gonna do it. *¡Ay, Dios de mi vida! Estaba desesperada. ¡Ayúdanos Virgen Santa!*

The Farmers Cooperate

And she did help us. Because Carole called me in the morning. She was Bob Summerville's wife who lived in a big pretty house close to our farm. Bob was the son of the owner. We lived in town because we bought this house a long time ago.

Carole called me and said, "Vera, you're comin' over for supper."

"Oh!" I told 'er, "What should I bring?"

"Nothing. Just bring the kids and you come on over" – for me to take Robert and Leonard. "You can take something for Mike afterward. We're gonna have supper for all the workers."

I told 'er, "What workers?"

She said, "The neighbors all chipped in and came with their trucks to top your beets."

Oh! I didn't know they was topping. All the farmers from around there got together on our farm because Mike just got outta the hospital. That's why they did it.

Sam Schleicher and Orel Prickett came. They had farms right next to ours. Other ones that came were Ron Stricker who lived close to Haig School, George Schlothauer, and of course, Bob Summerville who lived in that big house. One of 'em named Hunt brought a beet topper and a truck, but I don't remember his first name.

They brought about three toppers that was big machines that took out the beets and topped 'em all at the same time. I don't know how many trucks there was. It was a really cold day. Those drivers must'a been freezing! But they finished all the beets in one day! All of 'em. The dump was just across the road, so real quick they took all the trucks full of beets to dump 'em. They didn't charge us anything. Nothing at all. They did everything for free.

The next day, all the fields froze.

The wives of all of the farmers, they were all there at Carole Summerville and made the supper for the workers. No. She called me in the morning to tell me, "You're comin' over to have supper." They made a huge supper for all the toppers.

The farmers were all really good. No. We got along pretty good with all the farmers. They liked Mike a lot around there.

George Schlothauer had a farm right close to ours. They were really good, him and his wife Esther. The Hunts were very nice neighbors. Everyone. Senator Morrison that's a big-shot politician here, his daughter was real friendly with Mary Lou. She invited her to go stay with her.

Everybody was so good. They saw us different, now, 'cause we were farmers and not just beet workers. It wasn't like before.

You know, the farmers all work together. Everybody helps everybody right away. If something happens to one of 'em they all get together, and they start helping each other. They really helped. Mike did, too. A lotta times, he went with his tractor or with his truck to help one of the neighbors. He was with all of 'em, and everyone was equal.

In town, nobody helps each other. Nobody helps nobody. If somebody gets sick, well, that's their problem. But on the farm, it's different. That's why I really liked the farm. It was hard work, but I really enjoyed it. *Pero todo se acaba.*[2]

Bill and Mike irrigating potatoes.

[2] 'but everything ends'.

Comments on Language and Culture

i   A 'dump' for sugar beets was a location where trucks full of beets deposited their loads. The dump had a scale to weigh the trucks before and after 'dumping' or unloading so that the farmers would be credited with the proper tonnage. The beets were unloaded onto a large pile and were later re-loaded into special railroad cars for transport to the sugar factory.

Chapter Twenty

A SOBER MAN

When don Juan went to Kansas,
he went there to talk about me
because I stood up to him. "No," don Juan told 'em.
"She holds Mike real tight. She bosses him."

The Homebody

Mike lived almost just for the farm. He worked so hard to give us a good life. All of us worked hard, but he kept on after everybody left because he didn't have a choice. There he is at midnight changing the water on the beets or the corn. When he was irrigating, he stayed there putting the dams and the tubes(i) and watching that everything was watering good. Then he came and ate a taco, he rested a little bit, and there he goes to shut off the water. At least when he wasn't irrigating, he came home when it got dark and he didn't go out no more.

And outside of the house, he never went noplace by himself. There's no chance he would get together with friends on Ninth Street! He wouldn't even go in a pool hall because they sold beer there – much less, a bar. He didn't like to drink, and he didn't like to be with men that was drunk. If he went out, both of us had to go. I was the one that went out by myself – to visit a friend, to buy groceries, or whatever.

When we had the farm at Summerville, I used to go to North Platte and sometimes even to Lincoln.[1]

When Father Portray became a monsignor, he invited us to the celebration. *Dice Maique,* "I can't go. You go in my place."

I went with three more ladies. We went with Father Dowd, and we stayed in his mother's house. It was three days – one day to go, one day for the *fiesta,* and one day to come back. And then, sometimes we used to go sing in the choir someplace else.

With Mike's team, if they went to play baseball to another town, there I was with him. The kids, too. We took everybody, and that's why we all liked baseball so much.

Mike learned to play baseball in Kansas before we knew each other. Then, over here, him and some of those same players made the *Zorros* team. Because a lotta people from Kansas came to Nebraska, and some of 'em knew each other from over there.

Here in Scottsbluff, they used to play with other Mexican teams from Bayard, Minatare, Lyman. All of the towns around here had a Mexican team. Mike was a catcher. Sometimes teams of *güeros* or *negros* from other towns came to play the *Zorros.* It was fun.

Eddie and Bobby played baseball ever since they were little. Mike used to take 'em out in front of the house to play catch. He taught 'em how to catch and throw the ball real good. And we signed 'em up on a team every year. They got to be good players, and they always put 'em on the All Stars. Here they come, all dressed up in their All Star shirt.

I remember when we was all workin' out in the field, Mike always told 'em to take their baseball gloves and caps. And when it was time for them to go to their game, he told 'em, "Go on. It's time for you to leave." Oh, they liked that so much! They even forgot that they were tired. So there they go to get their gloves and

---

[1] North Platte is in the center of Nebraska, about three hours by car from Scottsbluff. Lincoln is the capital and is in the eastern part of the state, about seven hours from Scottsbluff. See *Map 1,* p. x.

go to the baseball field. The field wasn't too far from the farm, about a couple of miles. They went to their game so happy.

Eduardo's kids also played ball, and they also taught their kids. That's why I have four generations of baseball players.(ii)

Other than that, Mike never went out. Of course, he went to the church because he used to belong to the Confraternity of the Sacred Heart and they made their meetings there. Also, he was the president of the Credit Union for the church that helped the Mexican people to save. So he went by himself to do his business. But, for him to go out alone to have fun, uh-uh.

He never liked to buy anything at the store. Nothing. Sometimes he had to go to town to buy a part for his tractor. I told 'im, "Now that you're going, bring me a loaf of bread," or something like that.

"No. I'm not stopping at the store."

"Okay. Get outta here," *le decía.* Then I would go by myself to buy groceries. Sometimes I stayed two or three hours. When Mike told the kids, *"Ahi viene Mom,"* they all yelled and ran to see what Mom brought 'em from the store.

No, if I didn't go with 'im, Mike never went out, not even to buy a pair of pants or a shirt. Nothing.

That's why we both went to buy a suit for our twenty-fifth anniversary. He liked a gray one. It's light color with a little more gray. But he liked it.

I told him, "Well, if you like it, buy it."

He said, "How does it look?"

"It looks all right, but you have to fix the leg." It was short because Mike was tall and thin. He was about six-foot tall. But I took the hem out and I made it the way he liked it, with cuffs. He didn't like 'em straight.

He took a portrait with that suit, and I have the picture. Elvira made a great big copy and put it in a frame.

Drinking Wine

No. Mike was nothing but a homebody. The rest of his friends all went out to drink beer. But Mike didn't know how to drink. And he didn't like it, either. That's why, in all the time that I knew him, I only saw him drink about two times.

The first time was when we were in Kansas City. We went so Mike could finish his electricity certificate at Sweeney's.[2] We just got married not too long ago. *Elvira* was still little, and I was expecting *Eduardo*. We stayed with *Coni* over there.

Well, one night everybody was there – *Chente grande, Coni, Chito,* and some cousins of *Chente*. That was before they killed *Chito*.

The *Velásquez*, they liked to drink quite a bit. They used to go buy grapes and they made a lotta wine. They had barrels full of that junk in the cellar. They still had the Prohibition then.

So there they are, bringin' pitchers full of wine. They wanted to make Mike drink. At first, they gave him a little bit. "Come on, Mike, just a little bit so you can relax."

I was just watching them. They didn't bring me any because they knew I didn't like it. Then they brought another pitcher, and they served 'im another glass.

I told 'im, "Mike, don't drink too much." I knew that Mike wasn't a drinker and that he could get sick.

Les dije, "Don't give Mike any more. He doesn't know how to drink."

Dijo uno, "Well, he's gonna learn here."

They served him another one, this big. A big glass. "Come on, Mike. A little bit more."

And Mike didn't wanna tell 'em 'no' because he was with his relatives.

---

[2] Sweeny Automotive and Electrical School.

But I said, "I don't want for you to give Mike so much wine. No, no more. Because he gets sick. ¿Why do you wanna give 'im wine?"

I think the drinkers aren't happy until they make the other ones drink, too.

After a while, Mike starts to 'make radios'. At Sweeney, they taught some of 'em how to fix radios. But Mike, just because he was studying electricity, he thought he could even make a radio. But it's not the same thing. The wine was already getting in his head.

He said, "Okay, now I'm gonna make you a radio. I know how to make radios."

I just watched 'im. No. He already drank too much.

He said, "Just bring me all the wires, and I'll make you a radio." Drunk.

Then I said, "You don't give Mike any no more."

I turned to Mike and said, "You're not gonna drink any more."

But one of *Chente's* cousins brought the pitcher to serve 'im again.

I told him, "¡Take your pitcher! ¡Stuff it over there! ¡You're not giving him any more!"

The one that brought the pitcher turns and tells *Coni* and *Chente*, "¡Eee! That niece of yours sure bosses her husband."

Because when *don Juan* went to Kansas, he went there to talk about me because I stood up to him. *"No,"* don Juan told 'em. "She holds Mike real tight. She bosses him."

"No. I don't boss anybody," I told 'em. What did I care what they said? I just didn't want Mike to get sick.

But he kept on with, "Bring me the wires. I wanna make you a radio."

One of the others, insisting, served 'im another glass. He said, "We're gonna bring another pitcher right now."

I told 'im, "¡Take your glass! ¡You drink it! Mike's not gonna drink any more. Look how he is."

I told Mike, "We better go to bed." I stood up.

Mike stood up but he could hardly stand. He said, "I have to go outside."

I took 'im outside right away. As soon as we got outside, oh, how he threw up!

"See?" I told him. "Let's go to bed." We went upstairs to the bedroom, and we let the other ones stay there drinkin' their wine.

Drinking with Friends

Another time in Scottsbluff, the *peones* from Neil went to work in town in a potato cellar.(iii) After work, especially on Saturday, they all went to a bar that was just across the street. This was about a year after we moved to the *chante*.

They told Mike, "Come on, Mike. Let's go get a beer."

"No," he told 'em. "I need to get on home. Vera's cooking supper."

But they kept on, "Oh, come on. We're not gonna be too long."

The whole bunch was saying, "Come on, Mike, ta ta ta tá."

Mike just started working with 'em, and so he wouldn't be a party pooper, he went with 'em. He probably thought, 'I'll just go a little while, then I'll go home.'

At the bar, one of the men ordered beer for the other ones, and they brought one for Mike. Then, a different one ordered, and they brought one for Mike, too. So when it was his turn, he had to bring one for each one.

At home, I thought, 'I wonder why Mike's so late.' I covered the food on the stove so it wouldn't get cold, and I went to sit in the living room with the kids. After a while, I put 'em to bed, and I sat down to wait for Mike.

Okay, then, everybody went to their home, but Mike didn't come. It was late., ¿'Well where could he be?' I went and asked Carl – Carl Schmidt, one of the *peones*.

"I don't know."

I went and asked Charlie. "No."

I said, "What were you doing? Why isn't he home?" Nobody wanted to tell me.

I even went to Johnny even if he wasn't with 'em. I woke 'im up.

"Johnny," *le dije.* "It's twelve o'clock, and Mike hasn't come. I have the kids asleep, and they're alone, and I'm just so scared. I don't know where he's at, and nobody wants to tell me."

He just told me, "I don't know. Don't worry. He'll come."

"No," I said. "I'm gonna go look for 'im.

From the day I got married, *Chole me decía, "Maique* is always gonna be my son. But now he's yours. He's your husband. He's not mine no more. So, don't let 'im be a *bribón.* His obligation is to his family."

Dice, "If some time he goes out, and he doesn't come back, go find 'im." She told me right in front of him. "Go look for 'im, and you get 'im by the ear because he's supposed to be in his home."

I went to ask everybody. I went to Walter. He said, "He went out with Max. Both of 'em left together."

So, there I go to *don Másimo.* They was still awake. *Petra* and *Luz* were in the kitchen and *don Másimo* was sitting in the living room. *Le dije,* "¿Do you know where's Maique? Everybody's in their home except him."

"No. He came out with us," *dice,* "but I don't know where he is."

I kinda thought something about Max, just by the way he told me he didn't know. *Le dije,* "You have to know where he is. He came out with you."

"But he left, and I came home."

I knew he wasn't telling me the truth. *Petra* and *Luz* didn't say a single word. Nothing. I was standing there by the door of the kitchen, right close to their bedroom.

And then, I saw Mike's boots! Oh! I got so mad!

Le dije, "¡Damn you, Max!" *Le dije,* "Mike is in there. ¿¡Why didn't you tell me!?"

I went in there, and I start to pick Mike up.

Dice Max, "No. Don't pull 'im so hard."

"¡You be quiet! This is none of your business."

Le dije a Maique, "Come on." They got 'im completely drunk.

Le dije a don Másimo, "Help me get 'im in the car. ¿What did you lie to me for?"

"Well, he told me that he didn't want to go home."

So, I took 'im home, and I carried 'im in the house however I could. The kids was all awake. They were all still little. Elvira was about eight.

And when they saw 'im comin' in drunk, "Aahh! Dad made a mortal sin! He has to go to confession."

I just told 'em, "Go to bed. Go to bed. He's sick. He's not drunk. He's sick."

After that time, I never saw Mike drink anything. Once in a long while, like when Bobby died, he probably drank one shot of whiskey to calm his nerves. But to get drunk, no. Never, no more.

Getting *Elvira* Drunk

A long time after that, we went to Kansas City. *Vicente,* Jr. and *Conchita* were big already. *Chente* was married to Marie, an Indian there from Kansas. One time, she tried to get me drunk. No. In Kansas City they were big drinkers.

They invited us to a dance. Mike and I had not danced in a long time, so we all went to the dance. Everyone in their own car.

We were at the dance, and everyone was drinking and smoking. After a while, Marie told me, "Drink a little bit of wine."

I told her, "I don't drink. I never have, and I don't want any."

"Okay. You want a pop?"

"Sure."

"What kind?"

"Whatever kind you wanna bring."

I drank a little bit of it. I didn't like it, so I told her, "What kind of pop is it?" I don't know what she put in it, but she put something.

"Oh," she said. "You know, they taste a little different here. It's not the same as where you live. Here, they have big factories, and ta ta ta tá."

No. I don't know what she put in it, so I told 'er, "I don't like it."

She said, "I'll go get you a different kind."

Okay, she brought me another one, and I drank it. I didn't like that one, either. At all. I think she put whiskey in it.

Entonces, Chente me dice, "¿You wanna dance?"

"No, I don't feel like it. I don't feel good."

"Andale, vamos," dice.

So, I got up to go dance, and I could really see the floor moving. I lifted my foot, and I saw holes. My head was getting all blurry. '¿What's the matter with me?'

Chente was kinda like laughing. He already knew there was something wrong. *Me dice,* "¿You wanna sit down?"

"Yeah. I better."

Then I thought, '¡These people got me drunk!" I said, "Mike, we're going home."

He said, "Why?"

I said, "Let's go home right now. Look. I don't like it what they did to me."

Then *Chente's* wife said, "What did we do to you?"

I told her, "You brought something in that drink that you gave me, and you got me drunk, and I don't like it."

Then Mike said, "We better go. She doesn't feel good." No, I thought I was gonna throw up, and I didn't feel good.

I got mad at 'em. *Dije, "I don't like people to give me what I don't like."*

That's why I say, 'They know me in Kansas City'.

285

FOUR GENERATIONS OF BASEBALL PLAYERS

The First Generation

The *Zorros* baseball team before the game with Bayard for the 16th of September Celebration in 1930. Mike second from the right in the back row. Johnny Mack is on the far left in front.

Para mi hijo Eduardo:

Este es un recuerdo de cuando tu Dad jugaba de cogedor en el equipo de los Zorros.

Mike in his catcher's gear in front of the *chante*.

The Second Generation of Ball Players

Bobby and Eddie on their way to play ball.

Eddie, straight from the beet field to the ball field.

The Third Generation of Ballplayers

Several of Eduardo's sons and daughters also played ball, but they are not pictured here.

Fourth Generation of Ballplayers

TWO OF MIKE'S GREAT-GRANDSONS PLAYED COLLEGE BALL

Aaron Hernandez,
University of Kansas.

Antonio Hernández
Solano, California Community
College.

Drinking alcoholic beverages in Kansas City, 1963,. <u>Left to Right</u>:
Maique, Vincent Velásquez, Jr., Elvira, Marie, Vincent's wife.

Comments on Language and Culture

i   Fields were irrigated by means of a ditch that ran all along the
ends of the rows or in other strategically located positions in the field.
Curved aluminum tubes (now of plastic) were used to siphon the
water into the rows. Canvas dams were used to raise the water level
along particular stretches of the ditch to a height that would allow the
siphon action to operate.

ii   Though she would have loved it dearly, Elvira did not live to see
two of her great-grandchildren play baseball at the university level.
By coincidence, one of them, Aaron Hernandez, played with the
University of Kansas in Lawrence, not far from where *Maique* played
as a youth. The other, Antonio Hernandez, played with Solano
Community College in California.

iii   Potatoes were stored in cellars that maintained an even and
appropriate temperature to keep them fresh. In the winter, workers
examined them along a continuous belt, sorting them according to
their quality and transferring them into burlap bags for shipping to
market.

Chapter Twenty-One

MIKE'S DEATH

*Mike told me, "Now I've got the same thing
that happened to Nabor.
I'm going to leave you here by yourselves."
These were his last words to me.*

Birthday Surprises

Me and Mike had a good life together. But God took him away too soon. He was so young when he went. Let me see – from when he was born in nineteen-oh-eight to nineteen sixty-eight – he would'a been sixty years old in 'sixty-eight. He died in 'sixty-five, so he was fifty-seven.

Mike was a very serious man, but he also liked to play his little tricks. He was always out at the farm, and I would help him in any way I could. One day, he went out early to change the water on the beets. Afterward, he came to eat breakfast, and before he went out again, *dijo,* "You know, Ish Schmidt is going to be on TV. Why don't you look and see how much a tractor costs. I might buy it."

Ish had a program every day where he announced farm machines for sale. So Mike told me, "Pay attention. I might buy one."

Okay. So, yeah. I turned it on. There's Ish saying about the tractors and all the machines. And then, when he was just about to finish, he said, "And I have a little surprise for Mrs. Hernandez."

'What? What?' I said. Then I did pay attention.

He said, "We have a record for her birth'ay from Michael Hernandez." For my birth'ay! I thought he forgot because he didn't say anything. Not even "Happy Birth'ay" or nothing.

They played me a record. I don't even remember what song, I was so surprised.

Another time – it was another birth'ay – Mike went to work. In the afternoon the florist knocked on the door, and I went out. She said, "Mrs. Hernandez?"

I said, "Yes?"

Then she said, "Here's for you." It was red roses. '¿Well, who's sending me roses?'

"No," I told her. It can't be for me. I think it's the neighbor's. That's not mine."

"Well, here," she said. "Here's the card. You can read it."

From Mike! Boy, that was really something. He was always doing things.

For another birth'ay, he gave me some earrings and a necklace of Black Hills Gold for a present. One day that we was goin' to Mass, I just put on my earrings and didn't have time to put my necklace.

So there I go, putting it on in the car, and I couldn't, so I put it on my lap. That day, there was a lotta snow on the ground, and I forgot that I had it on my lap. I got outta the car and it fell in the snow, and I lost it. I never found it again. So, afterward, I gave the earrings to Mary Lou.

Another time, I gave her a watch, and she lost it in the snow, too. A year later, Father Whalen found it all smashed. It wasn't no good anymore.

So, all the time, Mike would always do something for me. Like the day he got his stroke. It was my birth'ay, too. Imagine? We were even going to go to a restaurant for my birth'ay.

He told me, "Let's go to the races. It's your birth'ay." He wanted us to go to Wyoming to see the motorcycle races because in Pine Bluffs, it's flat where they do the races up on top. It's a little ways from Cheyenne, about eighty miles away from

Scottsbluff. And he knew that I liked going out to see those kind of things.

We were up there watching the races when I saw he had a headache. I told 'im, "Maybe we better go."

I told 'im, "Let me drive. You've got a really bad headache."

Dijo, "No, I'll do it. I want to drive."

Always Sick

But when we got home, *me dice, "¡Ay, qué jaqueca¹ traigo!"*

Le dije, "That's because you're so stubborn you won't go to the doctor." For his high blood pressure. He didn't like to go to the doctor at all. He would rather go see a *curandero.*

Yo le decía, "Take care of your high blood pressure." I had been telling 'im for two weeks, "Go to the doctor," and "Go to the doctor."

"¡Qué doctor!" Dice, "All he does, he gives me pills, only enough for a little bit. ¿Why doesn't he give me a whole bottle?"

I told 'im, "Because he wants you to go and get a check-up and see how you are." He had been out of pills for two weeks, and he would come home with headaches. But he would get mad because the doctor told 'im to come back and to come back, and Mike didn't wanna be payin' and payin'.

I told 'im, "Go to the doctor." I didn't know nothin' about high blood pressure. I didn't know nothin' about 'water in the system'. There was times when he got real well. He even looked fat. But it's because he was full of water. They used to take him to the hospital to take out the water. So, there he goes.

He got ulcers, too. That was in the summer, and the doctor told 'im that, well, they thought they were going to operate on him in November. Because Mike told 'im that topping didn't finish until then.

Decía, "I don't want to get operated."

---

¹ 'splitting headache'

I told 'im, "But if you keep a diet, you might get over these ulcers. They won't be so bad."

So I used to give him his diet. He wasn't supposed to eat the beef, nothing. Not meat. Just from a sheep. Aagh! But I used to put it in vinegar for 'im. In vinegar and salt the day before. Then I washed it because that way I take off all that taste.

One day, I was making my supper, and I was making his, too. And that's when he said, *"Oye."* He was sitting right there at the table. *Dice, "Oye,* this is terrible."

"What"?

Dice, "That you have to make two suppers – mine and yours. *Dice,* "I want to thank you for it."

I told 'im, *"No." Le dije,* "It's my obligation. To give you what you need."

"No," he said. "But that's a lotta work." That's the way he was, *pobrecito.*

He was really a good husband to me. Oh, we used to fight, but it was better when we would make up.

I remember one time, I don't know what we was arguing about. I told 'im, "Get out of here! Go on to the farm! Get out!" I was really a grouchy one.

He put his hat on. "Okay. Okay," *dice.* "You get mad for anything."

"¡Get out! ¡Get out!"

He left, and I stayed here cleaning the kitchen.

No. After a while, here comes his pickup. I wasn't mad no more. I don't even know why I got mad. It was nothing.

I said, 'Here he comes. I'm not gonna talk to 'im. I'm gonna make him think I'm still mad.' I was pretty stubborn. I was by the sink washing the dishes. My back was facing the door.

He thought I didn't hear 'im, so he came in real quiet, and he comes up to me. He wet his finger with his tongue. Then, he touched my cheek and right away took his finger away.

He said "¡Chss! Are you still hot?"[2]

Right away, he hugged me. I couldn't be mad no more. How could I? That's the way he was. Both of us. We were tight.

About a year before he died, we made 'im a little party there in the park.

He said, "I've never had this before."

I told 'im, "This is for your birth'ay. We did it especially for you."

"What do you think, I'm gonna die soon? I think that's why you're making me this." One year later, he did. Because he always felt sick. All the time.

Another time, we were in the living room. We had two little sofas, and he was in one of 'em over there and I was in the other one over here.

He said, "I don't feel good. ¿It's all right for me to sit here next to you?"

"Go ahead."

He sat down and he leaned up against me. He said, "¿Am I getting you tired?"

I said, "No. Why?"

"Well," he just sighed. *Dice,* "If I am tiring you, it won't be for long."

I told 'im, "Come on. You're not dying."

That was in the winter when we were sitting there inside. *Dijo,* "I'm not going to be here much longer for you."

I told him, "Oh, shut up. You're not dying." The next summer is when he got the stroke.

He was always sayin' that he didn't feel good.

He used to come from the farm, *"¡Ay!" dice,* "I really got tired. What's the matter with me, I'm so tired. Gosh, we are getting older."

---

[2] Wetting the finger and touching the clothes iron, which was heated on the stove, was a certain way to tell if the iron was hot.

I said, "No, no. There's something wrong."

No. Mike died too soon. If he lived, we would be here together getting old. But I know he was gonna suffer more because he would get cancer on account of the ulcers that he had. And then with his high blood pressure and the pains he got in his arms and his legs. I know if he would'a lived, he would'a suffered a lot, a lot. And I would'a suffered with 'im.

The Stroke

That Sunday that we went to the races for my birth'ay, Mike was already tired. Because the day before, he was one of the pallbearers at the funeral of *Felipe Castañeda*. And then, in the afternoon *Estanislao* Guzman got married – Stanley. So, after the funeral, there we go to the wedding.

About four or five o'clock, Mike said, "I think we better go home, I'm just so tired."

The next day, he got up early because the Mass was at seven thirty, so we went to Mass and came home. Afterward, we were gonna go to Pine Bluffs.

When we got home from Mass, he start to put on his work clothes.

I said, "Where are you going?"

Dijo, "Voy a arrimarle tierra al frijol."[3](i)

"I thought we were going . . ."

Dice, "It doesn't start until two. I'll be back by noon. *Nomás le voy a arrimar tierra,* because I'll be over there in the races, and I'll be worried all the time that there will be a wind storm and it will blow the beans over."

It was time that they were just growing. It was the 27th of June, and the plants were big enough to put dirt close to them, but he didn't had the time.

---

[3] 'I'm going to dig the ditches for the bean rows', literally 'place the dirt next to the beans'.

Mike said, "Afterward, when we get back, don't cook supper. We'll go eat at a restaurant." For my birth'ay. That day. But before, he was gonna go out to do the beans.

"Oh," *le dije,* "You and that farm. I've been telling you to leave the farm alone. You don't feel good." *Le dije,* "I'm so tired of that farm. I been asking you to quit the farm 'cause all you do is farm and you're so tired all the time."

Dice, "¿And what do you want me to do?"

"Well, something else but not the farm. It's too hard."

Dice, "¿Where am I going to work?" Because he couldn't work no more as a mechanic in a garage. His diploma is just hangin' there on the wall. So, he couldn't find anyplace else to work.

Le dije, "Look." I said, "Quit that farm and you get something in the city. You can go in your tractor, mow the lawn here, mow the lawn there, get something easier, not a farm."

He was standing there by the door, and then he said, "You know what? You're really a grouch. Because I'm making all these sacrifices so you won't be out on the street."

Oh, that made me feel bad. So I didn't say nothing anymore.

I knew that he had to go do that, but I didn't like it because I always saw him so tired. So, he went to the farm to work one or two hours before we went to the races.

Then, after the races when we got back from Pine Bluffs, he already had a big headache.

Le dije, "Take a couple of aspirins and go lay down."

"No," he said. "I'll feel better if I go out."

We had a big garden in the back. From the garage to the street, all that was garden. The cucumber plants were already nice and big.

Dijo, "I'm going to transplant a few. I'll see if this headache goes away." He took some aspirins and he went out. Robert was following him, watering the cucumbers. Robert was gonna be six years old the next day. Leonard was inside. I think he was reading or playing with his model trains. He didn't like to be outside.

297

I went to the garage to get a hoe to clean the corn because we had a big piece of corn there that was growing real nice.

I picked up the hoe, and when I turned around, here comes Mike. He looked like he was drunk. '¿What happened to him?' Oh! I went running, and right there on the cement, his leg folded on 'im. He fell down.

Robert saw him and he came running. And there he is, tryin' to pick 'im up. Of course, he couldn't. His face got dark red from pulling so hard. We called Leonard right away and we got 'im into the house the three of us any way we could.

Robert said, "What happened to Daddy? What happened to Daddy?"

I told him, "Well, he's sick."

Then, we heard Betty driving in. Robert runs and tells 'er, "My daddy broke a leg."

She said, "Where?"

He said, "In the cement. He broke a leg. Come and see 'im. He's in the bed."

Right away, Betty runs inside.

Le dije, "He got a stroke."

Dijo, "*¡Vámonos al hospital!*"

Mike said, "No, no. Don't take me. Now I have the same thing that happened to *Nabor.*"

Nabor

He was remembering the time that *Nabor Guzmán* got a stroke, a friend of ours who had a farm north of Scottsbluff. Mike was over there at his farm that day helping him to fix a tractor. Mike knew how to fix tractors and stuff.

Then, at noon, *Nabor* brought Mike home. *Le dije a Nabor,* "Stay and eat dinner."

"*No,*" *dijo.* "I have my boarder with me." That was his grandson. He was about seven.

Le dije, "Pos los dos." Finally, he stayed to eat, and we're talkin' and talkin'. We start talkin' about sickness, and goin' to the doctor, and this and that.

Dijo Nabor, "From the time I can remember, I never saw a doctor. Never. I'm going to die, and I'll never see a doctor."

Okay. They ate, and the three of 'em went back to *Nabor. Le dije a Maique, "¿*What time are you comin' home?"

"Oh, about three or four."

Well no. He didn't come and he didn't come. '¿What happened?' I was gettin' worried. *Dije, 'I hope something didn't happen to 'em.'*

No. After a while, he got back. He came in real quiet.

Le dije, "Oh, you got back late. ¿What happened?"

He just stood there, looking down. *Y dice, "Se murió Nabor."*

*Le dije, "¿*What? ¿¡What do you mean he died!?"

He just said, *"Eiy."*

*Le dije, "¿*Wasn't he just here eating at noon? He was sayin' that he had never seen a doctor and he would die before he would see a doctor." Well, he still didn't see one. By the time the doctor got there, he was gone.

Mike told me they was fixing the tractor and they were putting on a big tire – one of those big tractor tires – and it fell on *Nabor.* Then he got up, and they started to put it on again, but he said, *"¡Ay, qué jaqueca traigo!"*

Dijo, "I'm going downstairs." They lived in one of those houses that half was like a basement and the other half upstairs. "I'm gonna go downstairs and take an aspirin. I don't know why my head started to hurt so much."

María, his wife, says that he came in and leaned on the heater, and he said, "Give me some aspirins. I don't know what happened to me. This pain is really bad."

María had a picture of Our Lady there on a little table, and *Nabor* went to pray to the Virgin.

In a little while, one of the girls comes out, "Dad fell down here on the steps."

299

He tried to go up the steps and he fell down. There goes everybody inside and they put 'im on the couch any way they could.

They called the doctor right away, and they called the priest. By the time they got there, he was already dead. When the tire fell on 'im, one of the veins in his head broke. He died right away with that stroke. That was really, really sad.

His Last Words

That's why, when Mike got his stroke, *me dijo,* "¿You know what? I got the same thing that happened to Nabor. I'm going to leave you here by yourselves."

These were his last words to me. He didn't talk to me – never – in the hospital. He talked to everybody, but he didn't talk to me. He held me and all that, and he would look at me, but he wouldn't tell me nothing. I don't know why, he just couldn't. The kids got here from California, and he talked to them, but not to me. They was here for his birth'ay that was on July 5th, and they even sang "Happy Birth'ay" in the hospital.

Even in Denver when we took 'im there, he still talked real good to Terry and Mary Lou, but never with me. He just wanted me to be sitting there close to him. He held my hand, and his eyes filled up with tears. That's all.

Cesáreo wrote him a letter, and Mike read it real good there in Denver. Because Mike and *Cesáreo* always wrote to each other. I wanted to hear it, and he let me read it.

But no more. His last words to me were right here at home when he told me he didn't want to leave us by ourselves.

"Don't worry about us,worry about yourself," I told 'im.

He stayed here two weeks in the hospital, and in Denver he stayed until August. After a few days, they put 'im a tube, and he couldn't talk at all no more. A little bit after, he would go to sleep and he didn't move. At the last, he didn't wake up at all.

The priest and the doctors came and they wanted me to take everything off.

I told 'em, "Uh-uh. You don't take nothing from him." I told 'em, "Because he's still alive. He's not dead."

They said, "Well, he's almost gone." They told me, "He's going to be a vegetable if he is going to be alive."

I told 'em, "I don't care, and you're not gonna break his head, either." They wanted to see what he had inside his head. Afterward, they went ahead and did an autopsy to see how he died. It was a real thin vein that broke when he got the stroke.

But I didn't take anything off. I told 'em, "I know he's still alive, and I know why."

'Cause I talked to him loud in his ear, "If you can hear me, squeeze my hand." He could barely do it, but he squeezed it. Until he died. Then, no more.

Race to the Hospital

The day Mike died, I didn't wanna go all the way to Alta where she lived in Golden. I wanted to stay all night with him in the hospital. That was on a Friday. Friday, the 13th of August that I'll never forget because when he died it was after midnight, and it was already the 14th.

Les dije, "Yo no me voy."

But Mary Lou and Terry told me, "Mom, you're not staying alone."

There wasn't nobody else to stay. Elvira was in Scottsbluff with Robert and Leonard. And Bill and Edward had already gone back to California to wait for what was gonna happen.

Terry went home first, and she told Mary Lou, "When you're ready to go, take 'er with you." For her to go with me in my car so I wouldn't stay all night.

Okay. After a while, Mary Lou said, "Come on Mom. You leave me off at Terry, and then you go to Alta and rest."

I didn't wanted to go and I didn't wanted to go. But then I said 'Okay'. I had to take her to Terry. But I left Mike real sick.

Mike's Death

I left Mary Lou with Terry and I went to Alta after eleven. I used to go every day all the way over there to Golden because that's where I was staying. She lived about fifteen miles away from the hospital.

I got there to Alta and they were sitting outside on the steps, her and Junie.

I said, '¿Why are they waiting outside for me at this hour?' It was already twelve at night. 'Oh, my gosh! I bet Mike is worse.'

They called Terry from the hospital that he was dying. Right away, Terry called to Alta, and she said, "Come. Dad is very sick right now." She said, "He won't make it for tomorrow.

Right away, I turned around and we went flying to the hospital. Alta told me, "I'll drive."

I told 'er, "No, I'm going to drive. I'm going to drive."

I went sixty miles an hour, speeding. On purpose. I wanted a policeman to catch me, but he didn't catch me. *Altagracia* and Junie were with me. They were really scared. And it was so far from Golden to St. Mary's!

Except that one man yelled at us, "Lady, you're running all the red lights!"

I told 'im, "It's an emergency. I don't care." I did it. I just looked to see if a car was comin', I'd take off.

I got to the hospital, but he was gone. Yeah. Just like that. If I had waited a half an hour more, I would'a been there. But I wasn't there for any of 'em – to be with them at the 'hour of their death'. From Bobby they made me go from the hospital because he was already really sick. *Pobrecito.*

That's how Mike died. Alone.

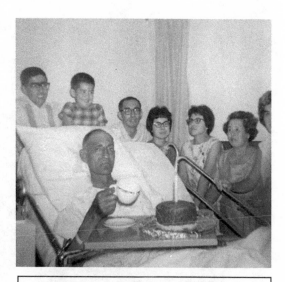

Mike in the hospital after his stroke,
surrounded by his family.

<u>Left to Right</u>: Leonard, Robert, Eduardo,
Mary Lou, Elvira, Jr., Elvira, Terry.

Elvira and Mike enjoying
a day in the country on
top of Scott's Bluff.

Behind them is the city
of Scottsbluff.

Photo taken in 1957.

The headstone that Elvira had placed for the joint burials of Mike and, eventually, hers.

Comments on Language and Culture

i   This involves 'ditching', i.e. removing dirt from in between the rows, placing it next to the young plants, supporting them and leaving a shallow channel, or ditch, for irrigation water to run. The ditching implement attached behind the tractor used special steel blades in the form of wings to move the dirt.

Chapter Twenty-Two

NO MORE FARM

I sold the oats. I sold the corn. I sold everything myself.
Oh! I looked at the farm, and I began to cry so loud.
'Nobody's gonna hear me out here.'

The Burial

Mike lasted seven weeks in the hospital before he went, and we buried him here in Scottsbluff. I bought two lots next to each other, one for him and the other one for me. They're gonna bury me right there with him, I don't know when. I pray to God it's soon.

Anyway, the boys came to the funeral from California. But coming in Nevada, their car broke down. A wheel, or I don't know what. There they are alone in the middle of the desert. They didn't know what to do.

They never used to see a policeman or anybody in that empty place. But this time, ten minutes later *de pura chiripada,*[1] there comes a policeman – a state patrolman. He stopped and asked 'em what happened. Then he called on his radio to get a towing truck from a little town that was not too far away. When they was waiting, they started talkin' to 'im.

He asked 'em, "Where you goin' to?"

---

[1] 'by pure luck'.

"We're on our way to Scottsbluff, Nebraska, for our dad's funeral."

"Scottsbluff!? That's where I'm from," the policeman said.

¡Fíjate! ¡Qué casualidad![2]

So, okay. The towing truck got there and he took 'em to where they could fix their car, and then they kept on comin'. They had to drive all night long.

We buried Mike on August 17, nineteen sixty-five. I buried him, I didn't cremate him. And they're not gonna cremate me, either. Oh, my gosh! Never! Burning them is like sending them to Hell. Even if the Catholic Church says it's all right, now.

Oh! I got so sad when they cremated my brother *Carlos!* Gee manee! They put 'im out in his coffin *en la mortoria* for the rosary. I went to see him, and I stayed there lookin' at 'im.

'Carlos', *le dije.* '*Hermano.* You're gone now, and they are going to cremate you.' Oh! I cried so much to see him whole, and the next day they was gonna burn him. It broke my heart a lot, a lot.

One of his sons came and hugged me. *Me dijo, "No llore, tía."*

Le dije, "I'm not crying because he died. I'm crying because of what they're gonna do to him. You're gonna bury him tomorrow, but not all of him. You're gonna take him to the cemetery in a little box like this. Just his ashes." I didn't go to the cemetery. I couldn't. I just went to the Mass, and that was it.

You can't forget all the sad things. Never! But you also remember the good things so you can enjoy talking and telling about 'em, and you can put all the bad things in the back. But you can never do that. Even if a person wanted to, they can't.

That's why I couldn't bring another husband over here. I think that would be terrible. I just couldn't.

Oh, my gosh. Someone asks me to go out to a lunch or something. He says, "Just friends." No, I can get a friend. Girl friend, or whatever. But I didn't want men for friends.

---

[2] 'Imagine! What a coincidence!'

One of 'em, every time he saw me, he was insisting for me to go out with him. Oh, I couldn't stand 'im! Aagh! I never went out with nobody.

Whenever I was working in the community action, I took people to the doctor. But when I took a man, *yo le decía,* "Look, I'm a widow and I'm alone, and I want you to respect me the way I respect you." That was it. So, they wouldn't tell me anything.

I just didn't want . . . .

Working the Farm

All the time I was in the hospital with Mike, a man that helped me so much on the farm was *Pancho Perros.* That's how everybody called him, but his name was *Francisco de Avila.*[3] I hired 'im to irrigate the crops and to look at the farm. He was somebody that we knew from Hunt's Acres.

They called 'im *'Pancho Perros'* because he had a lotta dogs. People came to his house, and there goes the bunch of dogs barking and barking. They wouldn't let anybody get off their car until *Pancho* came out. That's why they started calling 'im *'Pancho,* the one with the *perros',* and then just *'Pancho Perros'.*

That's the way the people were, always making fun of somebody. Like with Pat *Domínguez* that was *Pancho's* brother-in-law. Everybody called him *'El Chanate'* because he was so dark. See, *los chanates* are birds that's black, and Pat didn't like that. He told 'em not to call 'im that. He was one of the players on Mike's baseball team.

Pat's daughter was real dark, too, and not too good looking. But she had a flower shop there on Broadway. She was married to a *güero.* Oh, she thought she was somebody big. She didn't like to talk to the Mexican people. There she goes with her expensive

---

[3] Refer to Comment (ii), Chapter 5, p. 67, for an explanation of the derivation of 'Pancho' from 'Francisco'.

shoes and dresses. But the way we say it, *'Mona vestida, mona queda'*.[4]

One day, I got back from Denver to go pay *Pancho Perros* what I owed 'im, and to go see how the farm was. So, I paid 'im, and we started talking.

"Say," *le digo*. "And your mom, ¿How is she?" Because they operated her before I went to Denver. "¿Is she better now?"

"Oh, sí," dijo. "Ya está muy bien. Gracias."

Le dije, "She's kind of old now. ¿Do you have 'er in a nursing home?"

"¿What are you telling me? *¿¡Mi madre!? ¿¡Mi madre en la* nursing home*!? ¡Ni lo mande Dios!* My mother raised me. I'm alive in this world because of my mother. My mother isn't gonna move outta my house until she dies."

Me, too. Here's where I'm gonna die. I don't wanna go to no nursing home. Because I had gone to all of 'em. Every day, I was goin' to see somebody. They treat 'em real bad in there, and sometimes they even kill 'em. They stuck this one couple there – a couple that I knew from the church.

They told 'em, "Mom, Dad. They're selling the house because you owe taxes."

"We don't owe taxes."

"Well, you have to move, anyway." They had a really pretty home there on Tenth Avenue with a little garden in the back.

No, they kick 'em out. Anna told me – Anna Saldivar, the one that comes to help me. She used to take communion to them – she told me that every time that she went, she saw them crying because they was in the Center.

That's how they kicked Alta out – my sister. She didn't wanna leave her home. She really cried in the Center. She went crazy in there.

---

[4] Something like, 'If you dress up a dummy, it's still a dummy'.

But Jobita really liked to be in the nursing home where they took 'er. It's a nice one, not like the one over here where my friend *Rosa* is, real dark with those dirty curtains.

But Jobita, they killed 'er because they left her the thing with the buttons to make the chair go up and down. Jobita pushed the wrong one and she fell from the top all the way to the floor. That's why she died. They shouldn't'a left 'er alone with those buttons in 'er hand.

That's why *Pancho Perros* said that they would never put his mother in a nursing home. I ask God that my children will never put me in there when I get old.

Anyway, when Mike was dying in the hospital, I was over there with him – naturally. But another one that helped me a lot was George Schlothauer, one of the neighbors. He had a farm right close to ours.

George saw that the oats were good for harvest. He combined[5] it all. I didn't even ask 'im or nothing. He even took it to the mill, and he didn't charge me anything. Nothing. Not a penny.

We had about twenty acres of oats. A few days before he got his stroke, Mike told me, *dice,* "Come out and look at the oats, how beautiful they are."

I went out to the field with 'im to see them. Ooh! They was so big, starting to make grains so pretty.

Afterward, when I took Mike to Denver, I used to come and see how everything was on the farm. So, I went out to the fields. Oh! I saw everything growing so nice – and my husband dying in the hospital!! I didn't know what I was gonna do.

One time, I went in the pick-up and I sat there looking at all the fields. I couldn't stand my *sentimiento* and I started cryin' real loud. 'Anyway', I thought, 'here, nobody's gonna hear me.'

---

[5] 'harvest grain with a combine', a machine that 'combined' the operations of reaping and threshing the grain.

But, then, somebody hugged me from behind. It was George. He said, "Don't cry, Mrs. Hernandez."

So, I went back to Denver. One day, I was in the hospital with Mike, and I remembered. Oh, my gosh!

Dije, '¡Ay, the oats! They was so pretty. But it's time to cut 'em. ¿How am I gonna do it? No. I have to go cut 'em.'

I came back, and I went out to the farm as fast as I could to see. But somebody already cut 'em! Afterward, George came over and told me that he saw it was ready so he cut them.

When Mike died, after everything was over, I sold the oats,(i) and I asked George that how much I had to pay him for cuttin' 'em and takin' 'em to the mill.

He told me, "Nothing." Just like that – "Nothing." Nobody else helped me like he did.

All the time I was over there in Denver with Mike, Summerville was over here with Vera, pestering and pestering. She stayed at home taking care of the boys, and Summerville went almost every day to ask 'er when I was comin'.

He asked 'er, "When's your mother coming? She doesn't have to be over there."

So, one time that I came from Denver, I went and told Summerville, "You're not gonna make me come just when you want. I'm going to see whether Mike lives or dies, and I'm gonna stay over there."

"Well, we can take your farm away."

I told 'im, "You're not. It's a contract, and you can't take it away. Anyway, I have a man here that's taking care of the farm, so you stop bothering Vera. Everything is planted, and everything is done. All I need is the irrigation."

So then he said, "Okay, I'll buy the crops from you. I'll give you so much." I don't remember how much he offered.

I told 'im, "I'm not gonna sell 'em, either. Mike plant 'em and I'll finish 'em."

"How are you gonna finish 'em?"

"Just let me alone, and then I will!" But I would not sell it. I didn't want to. No. Summerville didn't talk to me no more. And he didn't go over to Vera any more, either.

Bringing in the Harvest

And I brought it in. I did it all by myself. But if I wasn't out on the farm with Mike every day, I wouldn't even know what to do. The only one that helped was George that harvested all the grain.

I harvested the beans and the corn, and I took 'em to the mill. And then, I sold 'em. Afterward, I topped the beets. I did it by myself, or else I contracted with somebody to help me. My sons couldn't help because they had to go back to their jobs in California. Over there, they had their families and they was barely makin' it themselves.

And over here, nobody offered. So many people in my family, but nobody came at least to give me some advice, to tell me what I had to do and how I was supposed to do it. They could'a gone to tell me, "Look, do it like this. Do it like that." Nobody did.

But what they did, every now and then, there they go to help Manuel. They even came from Denver to help him. What help did he need?

One time, I hired Paul. Because the beans had to dry out after they're cut. But from time to time, you had to turn 'em over with a pitchfork so they wouldn't get mold.

Le dije, "Oye, Pablo. Come and help me because I cut the beans and I have to turn 'em over. Oh, it's too much work to do that by myself." No. He came to help me for one day. Just us two, we turned over the beans.

So I stayed by myself with the farm. I didn't need Summerville. I went to the mill and did my business with them.

Summerville got real mad when I sold the beans. I used to go to the mill almost every day because the price was goin' up and goin' down. Then I saw that it went up. I said, 'I hope. I hope.' And I sold it. I can't remember if it was eight or nine dollars.

Afterward, Summerville went to the mill to see the price of the beans.

The man told 'im, "No. She sold hers."

Ooh, how he got mad!

The manager told 'im, "Why are you getting mad? They were not your beans. They were her beans. You don't have no business with her beans. You don't have to get mad."

He got mad because if the price went up more than what I got, he was gonna lose twenty-five percent of what it went up. But it didn't go up no more, so he didn't say nothin' to me.

Then I sold the oats, I sold the corn, I sold everything. I worked really hard when I was by myself with nobody to help me.

Some of the farmers told me, "Hire somebody to do this or that, and it'll be cheaper for you." So that's the way I made it. They're the ones that gave me advice. And when the beets were ready, I hired a farmer to top 'em for me.

Nobody else came to see how I was doing. Nobody.

And then, I finished! And I made more than what Summerville offered me for the crop.

Then, after I finished with everything, Summerville came over to tell me that he wanted to buy the truck. It was the truck that I filled up with beets. Mike would drive the loader, and I drove underneath with the truck and filled it up. That's all he came for, to see if he could get the truck.

I said, "I sold it." He didn't like it, but to heck with him.

Then he said, "You wanna take over the farm? You just hire a man to do the work, and you be the boss."

"Are you crazy? No, thank you. Get outta here." Take over the farm!? ¡Qué esperanzas!

No more farm for me!

Comments on Language and Culture

i   The mill stored the grain and the beans for the farmers, acting as an intermediary between them and the companies that bought the products. The farmer had to be up to date on the prices that these companies offered which varied from day to day according to the market.

Chapter Twenty-Three

GHOSTS AND APPARITIONS

My being scared comes from the stories
that they told us when I was little –
that dead people and ghosts would appear.
When somebody died, I believed that the dead person
was comin' to get me.

Sad Memories

When Mike died, my farm ended. Everything ended for me. I sold the crops, the truck, the machinery – everything. At least what I got from that helped me out a little because the doctor bills and the hospital bills were starting to come in.

I never stopped missing Mike. Never, until the day I die. Then I will, because I'll be ended, too. Only God knows when. I never thought I live this long after he died. Gosh, it's gonna be thirty-three years![1] *¡Ay!* I get so sad all alone.

I never stop thinking about him – what we did together and all the things he did for me. He was so good with me, and he worked so hard so he wouldn't leave us in the street. I thought a lot about his death and that I was never gonna see him, and I would just cry.

---

[1] Elvira made this statement in 1998. She died in 2012, forty-seven years after Mike.

'But, no!' I said. 'You have to get outta that. You gotta think of somethin' else.' So, I sit down to read the *Star Herald,* or sometimes to watch television, but hardly ever. If it isn't the news, I don't like the other programs.

So, I was left all alone with my two boys. Robert was just six and Leonard was fourteen, but they was in school all day long. And when they got home, right away they went outside or they went to visit friends close by. I just cooked for them and cleaned the house, and that was all.

I didn't even feel like goin' outside at all. We already had frost anyway, and all my flowers were turning brown.

Apparitions

At night, the boys used to go to bed downstairs in the basement. Mike fixed up that room real nice, with wallboard on the walls and everything. Then, he put in a carpet. They also had a desk for their school work.

I always stayed upstairs reading or crocheting or whatever. But then, I hear a noise over here or a noise over there. *¡Uuy!* I thought there was somebody or something there. I get up to see, but no. It wasn't nothing. I always been afraid.

I don't think about ghosts or anything, but all of a sudden I see something or I get a dream. One time, I was sitting here on the sofa, and I saw a shadow in the kitchen. It was somebody there by the table. All I saw was the shadow.

I said, "Who are you? Who are you?" It didn't answer. I asked it again, "Who are you?"

He said, "I just came for my baby."

"What baby?"

Right then, a little girl came crawling out of my bedroom. A little *güerita* with curly, curly hair.

I told 'im, "Is that your baby?"

He said, "Yes, that's my baby. I'm gonna take her home to Ocean City, California."

"Ocean City?"

"Yes. That's where Elvis Presley lives, too."

So I got up to open him the door.

He said "No, you don't have to. I'll go out." He went out with his baby through the door that I didn't even open it.

That's when I woke up. I must'a fallen asleep. Oh, what a dream! I didn't know that there was a name like that in California that they called 'Ocean City'. But there is, and I heard it in the dream. I even get chills.

Another time, I didn't see anything. But I heard it. I was at Edward's house in New Mexico when they first moved there. They had a long hallway to the other bedroom, and I was in mine.

It was time to go to bed, but I wasn't sleepy. They were in the kitchen. I was in my chair reading when I heard a baby crying over by the bathroom. It didn't say nothing, it just cried.

Dije, 'I wonder what that is. There's no children here.' So I got up to see. I peeked in the hall. It was kinda dark, so I didn't see anything. But the crying kept on, like a little girl.

No. I went running to the kitchen to call *Eduardo*. He went to see, but he didn't find nothing. *Le dije*, "But I heard a little girl. I could hear real good that she was cryin'."

Dice Eduardo – he was tryin' to scare me – "Don't think anything about it. They're ghosts. It must'a been the little girl that lived here before, and she's looking for her parents." Then I really did get scared.

But then he told me, "No, I think what you heard were some cats that were fighting. That's how they sound. Don't pay attention to them."

¡Ay! But what I heard for sure was a baby cryin' in the hall. I think I fell asleep and it was a nightmare.

I think I'm scared because of the stories that *Papá Lolo* and my mom and dad used to tell. They told us that dead people and ghosts would appear. Oh! I used to get so scared, I put on a blanket and covered my ears.

And then I remembered my *tía Adela* and the horrible way she died and how I got so scared when they killed *Chito* there in Kansas City. Oh, I was really afraid of ghosts and dead people!

When somebody died, I thought the dead person was gonna come after me. Like when we buried *Papá Lolo* a little while after they killed *Chito*. We lived with Baltes, right in front of the cemetery. Oh! I was so scared living so close. That was in April, nineteen thirty-four.

One day, I was tired and I laid down to rest a little bit. The door of the *chante* we lived in faced to the side of the cemetery. And then I saw *Papá Lolo's* grave open up, and his tombstone moved. And there I see *Papá Lolo* coming.

'¿Qué?' dije. 'This is not something good. Papá Lolo can't move. He's dead.'

But I see him, and there he comes walking real crooked. Oh! I really got scared! I start to yell, but I was just yelling to myself. No. When he was coming in the door of the *chante*, I woke up. I think I fell asleep, and it was a nightmare. That's how *Papá Lolo* came to visit me from his grave. *¡Ay! Que Dios le dé vida eterna.*

También, when Mike just died, I used to be very afraid. One day, I was laying down in my bed. I wasn't asleep yet when I heard the steps of somebody comin' in. I was turned to the side of the wall.

Here come the steps. I got so scared that I couldn't turn to see. '¡Ooh! ¿Who is it?' And then that person came and laid down close to me.

Dije, 'This is not a good thing. I have to turn to see who it is.' I saw that it was Mike there, and I jumped up. But he was already dead! '*¡Ay!*' I started to yell, but who did I yell to? Who could hear me?

Another time, I was real tired when I came home from work, and I went outside. It was on Friday. I promised to go to Mass on Saturday because Mike went every Saturday at six o'clock in the morning. He belonged to the *Cursillo.* Dije, 'In memory of him, I'm gonna do that Mass for a year.' I was gonna take that for a year every Saturday.

That time, I was really tired. I went out to the garden to relax, and I didn't go to bed until ten thirty at night. I woke up at five and looked at the clock. *'Ahh,' dije,* 'I can sleep a little bit longer.' I didn't have to leave until a quarter of six, so I turned over and went back to sleep.

Then I heard knocking on the door of the kitchen. Tá! Tá! Tá! *Dije,* 'There comes Mike. He wants me to take his breakfast. He came from the farm. I'm not getting up yet.'

Then, he comes in the bedroom, *y dice, "Elvira, Elvira." Dijo,* "Get up. It's late for you to go to Mass."

Dije, "I'm too tired. I'm not going to Mass."

He didn't pay attention. *Nomás dijo,* "After you come back from Mass, you take me my breakfast." I always took 'im his breakfast to the farm.

When he turned around to leave, *le dije,* "Hey, your pants pocket is torn. ¿Where's your billfold?" That was the billfold that I lost and wasn't able to find.

"Oh," *dijo,* "I left it there on the chest. It's right there by the bed."

That's when I woke up. It was a dream. It was almost six and I got up in a hurry. I was getting ready to go when I looked over to the chest, and the billfold was right there.

I said, '¿But how? I've been looking for it and looking for it, and that billfold wasn't there.'

I went to Mass thinking about that billfold. Because in my dream, Mike told me he left it there. When I got back from Mass, I went to see if the billfold was there. No. The billfold was there! I thought it was funny because I looked for it everywhere and couldn't find it. And then I saw it didn't have anything inside.

So I got the boys up, and I asked Leonard, "Leonard," I said. "Did you get your dad's wallet?"

He said, "Yeah, I was gonna ask you for it. Can I have it? I left it over there by your bed."

I thought, '¡Oh, good!'

319

"Sure, you can have it," I told 'im. But Leonard already took everything out from it and put it back on the chest. I think I must'a seen it before I went to bed, but I didn't notice it because I was thinking of something else. But it got in my head.

Yeah, that's what happened. It's funny the way things turn out. If I didn't ask Leonard. . . .

Losing her Fear

I was really afraid of the dark. I imagined that ghosts would come. But I was even more afraid of the live ones than the dead ones. *¡Qué esperanzas que* I would go out at night! Especially by myself.

When I got home in the night time, I was even afraid here. Not of a ghost but of someone that would hide in the bushes or the trees.

I had the garbage can outside next to the garage. A long time ago, I had to take it out to the street every week. I don't have to now because I'm old, and the trash men come in by the garage to take it for me.

Anyway, one night I forgot just 'cause I forgot. I went to bed to go to sleep when I remembered. '*¡Ay!* The garbage can. It's all the way full. I have to take it out.'

It was about midnight. Well, I had to get up and take it to the street. There I go. I felt like *¡chir, chir, chir!* I thought that somebody could grab me. But, there I go with the can. I took it to the street, and I came running back to the house. Ooh! Nobody grabbed me!

Another time, I was goin' through my papers here on the table, taking out my bills and other important papers, and throwing the other ones. The ones that were no good I took out to the garbage can. It was getting late, so I went to bed. I think it was almost twelve.

Then, it came to my head! *Dije,* '¿Where did I put my Social Security checks?' I couldn't remember where I put 'em. I was thinking and thinking and I couldn't sleep. So, finally, I got up to look for them. I didn't find 'em and I didn't find 'em.

Entons' dije, '¡Ah, caramba! I bet I threw 'em in the garbage with the other papers. ¡Oh, my gosh!'

I was gonna have to go out at midnight to look for them over there. There was three checks, so I had to! I didn't have no choice.

So, I got my flashlight, and I ran out in a hurry to bring in all the papers that I threw away. It was windy, and you could hear the sound in the trees. *¡Ay!* I felt that somebody was looking at me behind a tree ready to get me. I grabbed all the papers out of the can any way that I could. I held on to 'em so they wouldn't blow away, and I almost tripped running back to the house. I ran in with my heart pounding because I was so afraid.

But, yeah. The checks were in there. And nothing happened to me. That's when I started not bein' so afraid of the dark. But just a little bit.

Dije, 'I'm here alone with my boys. I have to quit bein' so afraid like I am. ¿How am I gonna do it?'

I start thinking. I had to find a way where I had to go out at night on purpose. I had to go out alone so that I would be afraid, but so that I had to face it. To see if I could quit it.

Then, it came to my head. At St. Mary's Hospital, they did the 'Twenty-Four Hour Adoration' where everybody that was Catholic would sign up for one hour. One hour every day to go to the chapel to pray to the Sacred Heart of Jesus. Each person had their hour for one week, and they would stay praying for one hour by themself until the other person came. We did it like that for the whole day and the whole night. With everybody, it was twenty-four hours, and that's why they call it the 'Twenty-Four Hour Adoration'. So, for one whole week they prayed to the Sacred Heart without stopping. Then the next week, it was another twenty-four people. I don't remember how many weeks they did it.

I had it one time before, but I used to go about three or four in the afternoon. Not every week, just once in a while.

Entons' dije, '¿You know what? I want to quit bein' afraid, so I'm gonna take it at midnight. I'm gonna be scared, but I'm going to go right at twelve o'clock.' I would leave the boys asleep anyway, and nothin' was gonna happen in one hour. But for sure I would lock all the doors before I go.

In the car, I wasn't scared, but when I got to the hospital and parked the car, everything was quiet. And I was by myself. I felt like somebody was gonna show themself. I ran to go inside the chapel. Father Whalen was in there. His hour was from eleven to twelve.

He asked me, "Vera, aren't you afraid here by yourself at this hour?"

I just told 'im, "No, Father." I told him a little white lie. "The Sacred Heart is here, and He helps me."

But it wasn't really a lie because He did help me. All alone at that hour there wasn't even a little noise. I paid attention to what I was praying, and the hour passed real quick until the other person came. When I went out to the car, I was still afraid, but it didn't seem so scary because I knew that Our Lord was inside over there, and outside over here.

Would you believe it? By the seventh day, I wasn't afraid no more. Not at all. I got to the hospital, and I didn't have to run to go inside. I healed myself just by praying to the Sacred Heart every night.

When I got home, here's where I was afraid. Not afraid of a ghost but that somebody would hide. I was afraid of the living. I flew inside because there was a lotta bushes and trees and things. I already cut those down.

Sometimes you have to be careful even in the day time. One day I went to Denver just to visit my sister Alta. They didn't put her in the Center yet. When I used to go, I stayed there with Terry. By that time, Leonard and Robert already went to live in California.

I always took Quint with me. My little dog, he was so cute. White, white and his tail was all curly. He died a long time ago.

Okay. We was goin' on the freeway on the other side of Cheyenne when I wanted to go to the bathroom. I found one of those rest stops, and I drove in. There was just one other car. That was funny. But I put Quint down, and I put his collar on when I saw a man come out of the toilet. He saw me, and instead of goin' to his car, he went to the other side of the building where the women's restroom was.

Le dije al Quint, "No, this isn't good. ¿Why did that man go over there?" I always talked to Quint even if he didn't answer me.

"No, I'm not goin' over there," *le dije al Quint. "Andele.* Get in the car. We're leavin' here."

As soon as I got in the car, I saw the man lookin' from the other side of the building. He saw me, and he hid. No. I started the car right away and I went. I didn't stop until I got to Terry. I told 'er what happened.

She said, "No. You gotta be real careful, 'specially where there's no people. Somebody is just waiting to steal your purse or to do something bad."

That's why I say that I'm more afraid of the living than of the dead. At home, I learned to lock my doors, even in the day. Sometimes, Bobbie or Rhonda came over – Bobby's daughters. When they rang the doorbell, I would open it.

"Grandma," *me decían.* "Why do you lock your door all the time? Nobody's gonna just come in."

"Oh, yes, they are! If I want 'em to come in, I can just open the door."

Watching the Park

Almost every night, I used to sit here in my chair to drink a cup of *atole.* I make it with oatmeal. I cook it until it's real soft, and then I strain it. Ooh! It comes out really smooth. Then, I put in a little bit of milk and heat it up. It's so good. A lotta people put sugar, but I don't, even if I put sugar in everything else.

When the boys went to bed, I got used to opening the curtain and turning out the lights. The City put a light on the electicity post that was on the entrance to the park. So, from outside, nobody could see me inside, but I could see outside. A lotta times I passed the time here in my chair lookin' at the people go by and cross the park over to Beltline.(i)

One time, I was sittin' here, and I heard some steps, but I couldn't see who it was. I stood up and got close to the window. I hid on one side, close to the curtain so they couldn't see me. It was a guy that came in my yard, on the lawn. I can see real good 'cause there's a lotta light outside.

Dije, 'That guy better not come to the door because I'll call the police right now.' I kept lookin', but he looked like he wanted to fall down.

Dije, 'He's drunk.' Yes. He came over here and then he crossed the street where the electricity post was. He laid down there, drunk. *Dije,* 'He can just stay there.'

Another time, a guy was walkin' around. I got up to see what was goin' on. That was a drunkard, too. I think he had a fight with his wife 'cause he was singin', "Wa, wa, wa, wa! Honey! Honey! Let me in, Honey!" His wife probably threw 'im out and locked the door. "Come on, Honey! Please let me in!"

That's why I say I always have the doors locked. One of those guys could come over and want to come in and rob me or something else.

I even feel something goin' on when I'm asleep. A lotta times, I get up at one o'clock or two o'clock – whatever time. One night, it was really late, some cars woke me up that was goin' into the park.

I got up to see, and I saw a whole bunch of boys there in the park. And then, another car came in, and a bunch of girls got out. It looked like the boys were beating up another one. Eeey! Right away I went to the phone to call the police.

I think there was one close by because the police car got there just like that. *¡Chun!* All the boys ran away. Boy! The policemens only could catch two of 'em, and they took ém away.

The next day, one of the policmens knocked on my door. He told me, "Ma'am, did you see what happened here last night?"

I told 'im, "Yes."

He said, "May I come in?"

"Yes. Come in and sit down." I opened the door, and he came in and sat down.

Then he asked me a lotta questions. How many cars were they? How many boys? How many girls? Who was fighting? And other things. We talked a long time.

He was real nice. He told me, "Ma'am, if you ever see anything like that again, or if you're scared, just call us. We'll be here right away."

I told him, "Yes, I will. Thank you."

He thanked me, and he left. The policemens in this town have always treated me very well. I don't hate 'em like a lotta people do because they have helped me a lot.

Police Encounters

It's like when we was living with *Chole* and *don Juan*. Mike and I almost never went out when we lived with them because we had *Elvira* and *Eduardo* little, and I didn't want to bother *Chole* to watch 'em. Only when there was a dance or something, but just once in a while. We rather take 'em with us.

One time there was some shows that we wanted to see in Gering, at the Grove Theater. I remember that so well. It was a double feature. One was *Dracula* with Bela Lugosi, and the other one was *Frankenstein* with Boris Karloff. We took Vera and Eddie even if they weren't gonna understand the shows. They was still real little. Elvira wasn't four years old yet.

Oh! But when Bela Lugosi came out in that big house that was dark and spooky, they got so scared! Both of 'em got under the seats. No. We picked 'em up and held 'em in our arms. Then they fell asleep, and it was okay.

We liked going to the Grove because we could sit where we wanted to. There wasn't as much discrimination as in Scottsbluff. Another time that we went, Bobby was already born. I think he was about two years old. There was a really nice show, so we took them with us.

The theater was on the corner and after that was an alley. The police station was on the other side of the alley. We stopped the car right there because the first parking was close to the alley, so we parked there.

We didn't take the kids inside because they were real sleepy. I made a bed for one of 'em on the front seat. Another one laid down in back, and I made her bed for Elvira on the floor.

So we went in the show. I just left the windows open a little bit. After a while, I went out to the car to see if they was all okay. I walked around the car, looking and looking. No. They was all quiet, so I went in the show again.

I think one of the policemens saw that I was lookin' in the car, and he followed me. I didn't see 'im, but he saw where I was sitting. After about fifteen minutes, the policeman came in to talk to me. He said, "Ma'am, one of your children is crying in the car."

I went out with him in a hurry. Mike stayed inside. Bobby was the one that was cryin', so I gave 'im his bottle, and he went back to sleep.

The policeman told me, "You can leave 'im asleep, and I'll watch 'im." The police station was right close by, so it didn't cost 'im anything to keep an eye on 'em. But I really appreciate it. I went in again, and none of the kids bothered any more.

That policeman was really nice about it. He didn't scold me. He didn't say nothing, just "I'll watch 'em for you."

If you do that now, they arrest you right away, worse if you're a Mexican. I say that from then at that time, the police in this town have been very good with me. At least they haven't taken me to jail yet.

Not too long ago, I was talkin' on the telephone with Terry. She was in Denver, and I was over here. I couldn't walk very well by myself anymore, and I had to use my walker. When we was talking, I tripped on the telephone cord, and the telephone flew all the way to the other room. I couldn't get up by myself, so I just sat there on the floor. I started to yell, "Help me! Help!" But who was gonna hear me? Nobody. Even less because I was in the kitchen.

I didn't know it, but the phone didn't shut off, and Terry heard me yelling. I couldn't hear her. She got scared and right away she called Edward. She called 'im from Denver to Albuquerque. Then Edward had to call somebody in Scottsbluff to get the telephone number for the police.

So, there I am sittin' on the floor. What else could I do? The telephone was way over there, and I couldn't reach it. It didn't do no good to yell. So, I just stayed there, waitin' until somebody came. But, who? And, when?

No. In a little while, a policeman came. I don't know why, but I left the back door unlocked. I didn't hear 'im come in because I didn't have my earphones on. I looked up and I saw 'im standing there in the door of the kitchen.

"Oh," I said. "Are you a policeman?"

"Yes, ma'am."

"Did I do something wrong?" He laughed because he thought that was funny.

He said, "No, I'm here to help you." I was surprised because I didn't know how he knew I needed help. No. He helped me get up and to go sit down on my chair. We talked for a while about how they called from Denver to Albuquerque and from over there to Scottsbluff. And he came right away. It didn't take 'im no time at all.

I don't know why, but the police have always been nice to me. They never gave me tickets. A lotta people think they're all bad. They're not, at least not to me. They treated me very, very well. Oh, they got mad at me sometimes, but I just told 'em why I did it, and then they calmed down.

Like the time this policeman turned me on his lights. So then, I was lookin' for a place to stop because there was a lotta traffic, so I couldn't stop right away. *Entonces,* he put on his siren real loud. So, finally we stopped, and he got down from his car and came over to me.

He said, "Why were you running away? You're supposed to stop."

I told 'im, "I wasn't running away. I was afraid of an accident. You didn't have to blow your siren so loud. I know where I was gonna stop." I was mad.

He said, "You don't have your sticker on your license." He said it like he was mad.

I had it in my purse, so I took it out. "Here! Is that what you want!? It looked like you was getting a killer or somebody. I'm an old woman, I'm not a criminal. You don't have to holler at me because I can holler, too!"

Then he changed. He said, "I'm sorry. Let me put your sticker on for you. But you're supposed to put 'em on right away." So, he took off and he didn't fine me.

Before the policeman stopped me, *Josecillo Castañeda* was driving behind us, *Timotea's* nephew.[2] He saw the policeman put the light on me.

Después, me dice, "¡Ha, ha! The policeman stopped you. ¿How much did it cost?"

"Nothing. He didn't give me a ticket. It was only the license sticker. He put it on for me."

"Liar. I don't believe he didn't give you a ticket. ¿And he put it on for you?"

"Yes." But *Josecillo* didn't believe me.

Then, one Saturday in the morning I was going late to six o'clock Mass. 'Cause I promised to go to Mass every Saturday in memory of Mike. That was the time I went back to sleep, and Mike appeared to wake me up.

I was in a hurry. It was dark, and there wasn't any cars. Well, I was going late, and I guess I was speeding. But I didn't see the policeman that was giving me his lights. I was looking in front to see if nobody was coming.

When I got to the light on Avenue B, he blew his siren. Loud. I got so scared, I jumped up. I thought I had run into somebody.

---

[2] *Timotea* was the wife of *José Castillo,* Elvira's uncle. See *Figure 3. The Family of Ysidoro Castillo (Papá Lolo) and María Ortiz,* p. 82.

The policeman came and he was laughing. He saw me jump. Right away he asked for my license. "Did I scare you?"

I told 'im, "You sure did."

"Where you goin' so fast?"

"I was a little late. I'm goin' to Mass."

He said, "You're going to church this early?"

"Yes, and I'm a little late."

He said, "Right now there's nobody, so go ahead and don't be late. But don't be speeding no more." He gave me my driving license back.

The same thing happened one time I was goin' to the beauty shop. My car was shaking because I had a crooked wheel. I turned there on Avenue B, and I saw a policeman behind me.

Dije, 'Here he comes. Here he comes. ¿What is he following me for, anyway?'

Entons' dije, '¡Caramba!' I had a year without a license. One year. 'Cause that's when I had my heart attack and I was in the hospital. In intensive care. Afterward, when I went to the court, they just put me a temporary one on top of the old one. But it was a long time that neither one was any good.

But he stopped me. I think it was on account of my crooked wheel.

I told 'im, "What did I do?"

He was a young policeman. I think he was new. He said, "You know what? You was ahead of me and I thought I better stop this old lady." That's what he said. "Because I thought she had taken one too many."

I said, "No, you don't know. I didn't take one. I took more than one." He laughed, and we started talking about where I was goin' and about this and the other. I told him I was gonna get my hair done, then I was gonna go fix my tire, and then to the courthouse to renew my license.

He said, "But you're going to the beauty shop first. You wanna look like a beauty girl." We stayed talkin', and after a while he said, "Say, can I see your driving license?"

Shu! And me, one year without a license. I gave it to 'im.

He said, "I see. There's a little problem here."

"Is there?"

"These are no good. They're over a year."

I explained that they put the new one on top of the old one, and that's why. I told 'im, "After my hair appointment, I'm going to the court to get a new one. Then I go fix my car. That way I can get everything done in one trip."

He turned to one side and he smiled. I think he said, 'This one is tryin' to fool me.' But then he said, "Oh, what time is your beauty appointment? I got you late! Okay. Go on." He gave me back my no-good license. But he didn't give me a ticket.

You see? Why was he so nice to me? I don't know.

Another time, there was a snow storm and there was a lot of ice and snow on the street. I was comin' back from town and I turned on West Overland on my way home. A policeman was comin' from the other way, and he turned behind me. I don't know why these policemens always found me and why they was always following me.

Well, okay. I saw the light on Avenue B, and it was green. I said, 'Oh, my gosh! I don't wanna stop. It's too slippery. I hope the green light stays.'

When I was getting close to the street, poom! The light turned to red. There was cars on both sides waiting for the light to turn. But I kept on goin'. So, after I crossed, I stopped 'cause I knew he was comin'.

Yeah, he stopped right in front of me. He got off, and there he comes. He looked real serious. He said, "You didn't stop on the red light."

I told 'im, "No, I didn't."

"Can you tell me why?"

I told 'im, "Yes. If you can listen to me, I'll tell you why. If I stop, I would'a slide. Then, I hit that car, and the other one would'a hit me. That be a big wreck. I rather you give me a ticket. I'll pay whatever for crossing the red light."

He just looked at me and he said, "I think you're right." That was it. He didn't give me a ticket.

They never gave me a ticket. Never. They stopped me, and I talked to them like they talked to me. I told 'em why I did this and why I did that, and they didn't fine me. I think they saw an old lady and they was sorry, or I don't know what.

It never happened to me like it did to my friend *Rosa – Rosa Gehlert*. She called me one day to tell me she had an accident with somebody in Morrill and she wrecked his car. The policeman came, and he got mad at her. He told her, real mad, "Can't you see a car? A person has to be careful what you're doing."

She didn't say anything. If that was me, I wouldn't'a let 'im talk to me like that.

I think they knew me. When I worked in the Community Action, I went around everywhere. They knew me – the farmers, the doctors, and in the churches. The policemens, too.

All these years that we have lived here and none of us ever had problems with the police or with anybody. That's why I thank the police of Scottsbluff. Everything is so different from when we first got here to Nebraska.

Elvira and her close friend Rosa Gehlert.

The wallet that Mike left on the chest when he came to visit Elvira after he had already died.

Papá Lolo, who told his grandchildren stories about ghosts. Elvira dreamed that she saw his headstone move out of the way when her grandfather went to visit her.

Drawing by Carlos Hernández Chávez based on the photo on p. 79.

Comments on Language and Culture

i   Across the street, directly in front of her house on West Overland, the city maintains an empty area approximately 150 yards long and 50 yards wide. It's not designated a park by the city, but Elvira calls it that because the lot has no buildings on it and it is planted in grass. On the far side of this 'park' is a wide boulevard named *Beltline* that is parallel to West Overland, the street on which she lives. A narrow, lighted roadway crosses the 'park', connecting West Overland and Beltline.

Refer to *Map of Scottsbluff and Vicinity* found on page 88, immediately before Chapter Seven, "A New Life".

Chapter Twenty-Four

ALONE WITH THE BOYS

My money ran out right away. So I had to go to work.
Leonard told me, "Mom, don't go to work.
When we get home, the house be too cold without you."

Good Sons

When we had the farm, Leonard helped in what way he could. He was still real young and he had to go to school, so he couldn't help us very much. After his dad died, though, he helped me a lot. I just told 'im to do something, and he did it right away. He watered the grass and cut it for me. And he cut the weeds in my flower beds. He left 'em so pretty.

A lotta times, him and me was in the yard together digging. Robert was out there, too, but he was little. But if we wanted Robert to bring us a shovel or something, he did it. Those boys were very good with me.

No. Leonard minded real good. He came home from school, and if I wasn't home, he didn't go out noplace. He stayed home. I told 'im, "No running around. If you do, we'll see."

A lot of 'em, the mother works and the children right away go out on the streets. But my boys was always here when I came home. They always asked me permission. "We just wanna go get ice cream," or to town to look around. I just told 'em, "Don't come late, and be careful." There they go, both of 'em.

Elvira Admits Herself to the Hospital

So, when I had to go to the hospital, I felt pretty comfortable leaving the boys with my sister Jobita. Ever since Mike died, I had a strong pain in my stomach.

Doctor Campbell kept telling me he didn't know and he didn't know. He thought it was shingles. One day, I woke up real early with a terrible pain. I called the doctor, but he just said, "Drink this pill. Drink that one. You be all right."

No. The next day, I still had a big, big pain. I called Jobita and told 'er I had to go to the hospital and for her to take care of the kids. I was gonna go to the hospital, even if the doctor didn't like it.

I told Jobita, "You can come in the afternoon and take them to your house. You make 'em their lunch and take 'em to school, and then after school you can go pick 'em up. However you wanna do it."

So, yeah. She took care of the boys for two weeks, and they didn't give her no trouble. They behaved real good with her, and I'm really thankful for that. Not even Robert gave her any problem. 'Cause ever since he was little, he was the one that gave the most trouble. He wasn't like that with Jobita.

So, right away, I went to the doctor. I was gonna tell 'im that he had to send me to the hospital. I already packed my little suitcase with everything I was gonna need. I was gonna make him.

I came in to the doctor, and he saw me. He just said, "You look pretty good."

"Maybe I look good, but I'm not good, and I want you to examine me right now. I want to know what I have."

He examined me, but he didn't say anything. He just told me to go home and get ready to go to the hospital. He said, "I'm going to send you to the hospital."

I said, "I'm going right now to the hospital."

"Right now?"

"Yes, I'm ready." And I picked up my suitcase.

"How did you know I was going to send you to the hospital?"

"I was gonna make you."

Yeah. Well, for almost two years I had that pain, and he was tryin' to cure me with the same thing that he was giving *Cuca* for the shingles! *¡Qué trazas!*[1] But this time, I said, 'I don't care. I'm going to the hospital to see what I have, even if I have to go by myself!'

Yeah, in the hospital they found out I had stones in my gall bladder, and they operated me right away. It's the same thing my mom died of because they couldn't find out and they couldn't find out.

That's why, after that operation, I threw Dr. Campbell and I went to Dr. Haney. I asked 'im if he could be my doctor. Because that other one couldn't find out what I had. I been with Dr. Haney ever since.

The Vale of Tears

After Mike died, I was gonna sell the house because I was almost out of money. It's a good thing I didn't. 'Cause I would'a had to get on welfare. I would'a run completely outta money in renting a house. Rent a house? What for?

But Elvira helped me a lot, too. She said, "Mom, why do you want to sell the house for?"

I said, "*¡Ay!* It's too hard for me." I had so many memories of him here.

He had fixed up this little house. He said, "Oh, we'll make it better." He said, "The way you want it, we'll make it."

We was gonna put in a double bathroom, and he would'a done a lot to this little house. He opened up those two rooms that are over there in the middle. They only had two little windows. Gee whiz! Oh, it looked so ugly! So dark. He opened those up and he made a big one out of 'em with that pretty counter. He did it all by

---

[1] 'What a terrible idea!'

himself, without bein' a carpenter! He was gonna do so many things. Well, it was God's will.

After he died, I had 'em put in those windows in the living room. They're 'Pella'. Two hundred dollars for the windows and fifty dollars to put 'em on.

One day, a guy came that was selling insurance and everything. He said, "We can fix your windows and everything."

I told 'im, "No, I don't need anything."

"Well, these are good windows."

I told 'im, "They're Pella windows."

He said, "They're pretty expensive."

I told 'im, "Well, they were expensive for me when I put 'em. I paid two hundred dollars to put the windows."

He said, "Two hundred!?" He said, "Right now, you won't put the three here for two thousand dollars."

Because the Pella windows are made of wood. It's good wood and everything. Besides, they have springs so you can take 'em off a window to wash it. Yeah, they just have a lock. In the winter, the spring rolls up, and in the summer you pull it down. And if you close the windows really tight, they don't get foggy, no matter how cold it gets. Not at all. Because they're double pane. This house isn't cold at all in the winter.

I put a new furnace, too. I don't know what brand it is, but it's the good kind I got – from Gering. 'Yeah,' I said. 'Before I run out of the money I have left over from the funeral and everything, I'm gonna put it so I can take out the heaters. It had a little heater here in the living room, and it had another one in the kitchen. Those didn't even warm up the house. I said, 'I'm gonna see if it doesn't cost me so much.'

I did all of that with the money I had after all the expenses. We had, oh, we had about fourteen thousand saved up from all the years that we worked. That was a lotta money to save in that time because we wanted to buy a farm. That way, everything we got out of it would be for us and not for Summerville. Besides, we could look for one with good dirt that would give us a lot more.

But Mike was two weeks here in the hospital and one month over there in Denver. I think they charged us fifteen thousand dollars. And then, with no insurance! They didn't give 'im no insurance on account of all the sickness that he had.

But I got a lawyer, and they made it twelve thousand. Besides that, with all the trips in the car and the expense of the funeral, everything cost me a lot.

So, I ran out of money right away. The only thing I had was my Social Security, but it was very little. They gave me $125 for each one. For all three of us that was $375 – to pay the groceries, gasoline for the car or if my car broke. All that and the utilities and everything. I just said, 'Ooh! How am I gonna make it?' Couldn't. So I had to go to work.

'No,' I said. 'I have to go to work. I don't have money for the kids.' I was paying for their school. Because they were in Catholic school, and I was paying a hundred dollars for each one for each semester. Imagine! A hundred dollars! Right now, how much would that be? I think it's a thousand dollars in Catholic school. For each one.

'No, no. I have to go to work. I have to find a job someplace. Someplace. Because I don't have enough.'

I start to look for work in 'sixty-six. Yeah. Because after Mike died, I stayed in the house almost a year without even lookin' for a job. I was so sad. I just stayed with the kids. But I didn't have enough any more for all my expenses.

I remember Leonard. He used to say, "Mom, don't go to work. When we come home, the house be too cold without you. It's not really cold, but cold with nobody."

I told 'im, "No. I have to go to work, *hijo*. Let's see what I can find."

So, there I go. I start to look. 'Oh,' I said. 'What can I work for? I don't want no house work.' I never did that anyway, and I didn't want house work.

So then I said, 'I'm gonna bug the schools – the kitchens. So, I went from school to school to school, but they only gave work full time. They wanted me to start to make bread at six o'clock in the morning. I said, "No, because I have to take my kids to school."

'Well, what am I gonna do?' A prayer that I said every day is *The Vale of Tears.* After the rosary, you say, *"Hail Holy Queen, Mother of mercy. Our life, our sweetness, and our hope. To thee do we cry poor banished children of Eve. To thee do we send up our sighs, mourning and weeping in this vale of tears. . .".*

Working in the Schools

And, you know? The Virgin really helped me. Because somebody told me about a little school on the other side of Gering that they needed somebody. But fifteen miles away, you know, it was a long ways. You had to go around by Gering, and then way over there in the country to a road that goes to the hills. It's on the other side of the Bluffs. Oh, about a mile behind the Bluffs, straight straight from where Jobita and Manuel used to live, except to the west. They was to the east. So, it was a long ways.

So, well, I went over there. But I told 'em that not earlier than nine-thirty. The principal said, "No. It's all right." She said they needed somebody to work in the kitchen, but they couldn't find nobody. I was the only one that went to ask, so I got it. They hired me.

It was really a good, nice, easy job. By eleven o'clock, the kitchen helpers was already eating lunch, and then the children got out for lunch. We finished the lunch early because we only had a hundred children, sometimes ninety-eight, sometimes ninety-five. Besides, we made lunch for all the teachers, too. By two o'clock, I was home already. At least I had a job. I worked five years in that school.

But the snow! It used to snow a lot then. A lot more than now. And then, the road was in the hills. Oh, goin' up was very bad.

No. I finally quit on account of the snowstorms. Three times I got stuck. One time, I was goin' up that little hill on the other side of Gering, and the snow on the road was really hard. Well, the car slid down. Poom! It went in the snow up to the doors.

I waited to see if somebody came to help me. But nobody passed by and nobody passed by. Finally, I took it out any way I could, with a shovel and everything. I took it out, and then I went.

Another time, too, I slid in the snow. But this time, oh! The car turned around all the way on the road, and it stopped straight straight for me to go again. So I went, but I got so scared!

Okay. Another time, the snow was terrible. Snowin' and snowin'. It was a snowstorm. We had to hurry in the kitchen.

"Hurry! Hurry! Finish the lunches!" The kids all ate, and poom! They left. We finished cleaning everything up, and then we left.

Oh! The cars of the workers was all covered with snow and getting stuck. We couldn't even get outta the parking lot. Imagine! Here come all the farmers with their tractors and chains to pull us out of the snow.

'No,' I said. 'I gotta quit.' That's why when school ended for the semester, I said, "Well, I quit." That was in nineteen seventy-one.

Then I said, 'Now, where am I going?' I said, 'The schools in the city want me there early, so I can't work in there.' But anyway, I put my application in the Scottsbluff Middle School, with the kitchen.

"Well," they said, "if we need someone, we'll let you know."

Well, all I could do was wait. *Entonces, dije,* '¿Now, what'll I do?' And then I saw in the newspaper that they needed a lady in one of the hotels to clean the rooms.

I told the woman, "Well, I can't come very early." 'Cause I had to take Robert to school. I didn't have to take Leonard because he had already graduated.

The hotel woman said, "That's all right. You show up tomorrow."

So, the next day, she came to tell me how to fix the beds and everything else. *¡Ay!* I sure didn't like cleaning the bathrooms! I never had worked as a maid.

Dije, 'Well, I cannot last here very long. I hope they call me. I hope some day they call me.' To the middle school.

Well, on the third day, that was the weekend, they called me to go to the school. Oh, boy! I was so happy! They wanted me to start right away, but I wanted to give 'em at least a week notice in the hotel. So, I told the supervisor of the cafeteria that I was just gonna work in the hotel until Friday, and then I could start over here. She said okay, that it was all right.

It was better for me here in the middle school because Robert was gonna start in seventh grade in September and we could go together. I took 'im to school on the way to work, and picked 'im up afterward.

Leonard Leaves Home

When he was nineteen, Leonard graduated from high school, so that was in nineteen seventy. I was still at Gering Valley School, and Robert was still in Catholic school.

It was five years since Mike died, and Leonard still missed him a lot. I was working, and Robert was in school, so I think Leonard felt all alone. That the house was too cold, without nobody. He wanted to find a different life.

So, right away after he graduated, he went to live with Terry. But it was worse for him with Terry because Richard treated 'im real bad on account of he was jealous that Terry helped Leonard a lot. She made him his meals, she washed his clothes, and a lotta little things. Richard didn't like that, and he scolded 'im because why didn't he go out to look for a job, and I don't know what else. I think they got into it.

Finally, Leonard found a little job, I don't know where. Terry saw they wasn't gonna get along and she helped 'im rent a little apartment close to where he worked, and he went to live by himself. *Pobrecito.* He was so young.

But he was just there for a little while. He thought it was better to go to California because he had his brothers over there. He thought he would live better than here, so he went to live with them.

No. They kick 'im, that's what they did. Because he was dirty or because he didn't do this or do that. He told me that it was too cold over there with them. They didn't like 'im and they thought he was lazy. They told 'im, "Go get a job so you can go live by yourself."

No. A few weeks afterward, he got a little job in San Francisco, and he made friends with a guy that worked there. Both of 'em went to find an apartment so they could live together. That's when he bought a motorcycle so he could go to work.

Afterward, I went to California to go visit him, and he told me all of this. He said, "Look. I haven't seen Mary Lou. She hasn't come over here to me not even one time."

Mary Lou never went, not even to give 'im a cup so he could start his new home. She didn't give 'im at least a plate. She had enough to give 'im. That was when she lived in that big house over there. He didn't have nothing – not even little things to hang, things to cook. He only had a little table and his bed. That was all. His friend loaned 'im a pan and other things to cook.

His brothers never went to see 'im. But Leonard did. He went to Mary Lou because she invited 'im to go eat. To Bill, I don't know because he was already getting a divorce.

He used to go to Edward to eat supper and to play pool with his children. They made a covered porch, and that's where they had their pool table. But Leonard didn't feel good there with them. Like he was in the way. *Yo creo que Leonor, Eduardo's* wife, didn't treat 'im too good. That's the way she was with everybody. That's why afterward Edward got a divorce from her.

So, when I went to visit, his friend asked 'im, "How long is your mom gonna stay?"

He said, "I think about a week."

"Oh. Then I'll go live with my mom. You come to stay in my room, and your mom can stay in yours." That boy was so good. He even loaned 'im his car so he could take me wherever he wanted to because I couldn't ride on the motorcycle.

One day, the boy went to the apartment to get some things he needed, and I cooked 'em a really good dinner. Mmm! The boy really liked it! I don't think he ever tasted Mexican food like ours.

Afterward, I found out that they stole Leonard's motorcycle, and he stayed without nothing. It's a good thing that his friend helped 'im when he needed a ride. That's why, when Leonard came on the bus to Scottsbluff to visit, I bought him a little car. It was a used car, but it was pretty nice.

No. He didn't keep it very long. One day before he went back to California, some guys he knew came to invite 'im to go out with them. One of 'em said he wanted to drive, *y lo requió.* He made it a total wreck. It's a good thing nobody got killed. They just got hurt a little bit, hardly nothing.

They was drinking beer, so the insurance didn't give 'im anything. Nothing. I went to the guy that was driving, and then with his mother, to help Leonard with what he lost on the car.

"No," they said. "We didn't have the fault. It's Leonard's car, so he's the one with the fault." They didn't wanna help him with nothing.

Leonard wanted to sue 'em, but I told 'im, "Just leave it go. Just forget it." It was gonna cost more for a lawyer than what the car was worth. That's why he went back to California without a car. But afterward, he bought a little pickup over there.

Robert Learns about his Mother

When I started working in the middle school, Robert start to go there, too. He was twelve years old. But he didn't like middle school for nothing. He was a troublemaker with the teachers.

But when he was here in the Catholic school, Robert did very well. One year, I think it was in second grade, he painted a really good picture of our hills – the Bluffs. It wasn't a painting. It was like a hand painting, all without brushes or anything. They put it in the Scottsbluff County Fair and he got first place. They gave 'im money for it. I have it downstairs, but I don't know if it's still in one piece.

He didn't like school, but he had a good head for art. Later, he made another painting – a smaller one – and they gave 'im first prize again. It was really nice. I don't know what happened to it. I think they gave 'im money for that one, too.

When he was in Catholic school, he knew all his friends since they was little. Besides, the school was a small one. But not the middle school. Over there, he didn't get along too good with the other kids. They all knew each other since the grade schools that they came from, like Roosevelt or Longfellow, and they didn't like the ones that came from other schools.

One day, Robert came home and told me, "Mom, I have to fight some boys. I don't wanna fight nobody, but they make me mad 'cause they wanna make me smoke and I don't want to." He said, "I'm not gonna fight in school. I'm gonna fight outta school."

When they got out for lunch, two or three of 'em was after him and sayin', "Come on. You gotta start smoking." Insisting for him to smoke.

I told 'im, "You don't have to fight." Robert was always big and strong, and I think he could'a beat 'em. But I didn't want 'im to start fighting, so I went to the principal. Boy! He really scolded 'em and he took 'em out of school for two weeks. That was it.

Another time, some boys was making little balls out of paper, and they was throwin' 'em when the teacher wasn't looking. One of the times, a little ball hit the teacher. She turned around and right away pointed at Robert. I think he had been bad with her before, so she thought it was him.

She told 'im, "Stop that throwing. You hit me."

"I did not!"

She said, "Yes, you did, Robert. Don't lie." And she went to grab 'im by the arm.

But Robert said, "Go ahead, touch me. I'll throw you out that window right now."

Oh, boy! That's the way he was. He wasn't gonna mind nobody. It was the time that he wanted to mind only himself.

Ever since he was little, Robert was stubborn. I think he got that from me because that's the way I was – I am. And the older he got, the more he got a hard head. The bigger he got, the more I didn't know what to do with 'im.

That's why every year when he got outta school, I started to send 'im to Mary Lou to pass the summer over there with her, so she could watch 'im.

The first time I sent 'im was the last year I worked in Gering. Robert was just eleven years old. By that time, Leonard already left home. That's why I didn't wanna leave Robert in the house by himself when I was at work.

That's the time that Michelle and Mary Ann came to visit me – Eduardo's daughters – and when they went back, I sent 'im with them to California on the aeroplane. We all went together to the airport in Denver.

On the way, he asked me why he was goin' to Mary Lou and not to Edward or Bill. I didn't know what to tell 'im, so I just said because she wanted 'im to visit. He was just goin' to visit. When school started, he was gonna come back.

We never told 'im he was adopted and that Mary Lou was his mother for real. I wanted Mike to tell 'im when he was little because he could explain it better. That's why I never told 'im. I think it was because I didn't want to explain how everything happened.

Okay. That time, Robert kept on asking, "Why am I going to Mary Lou?" I think he already noticed that there was somethin' goin' on. Something he didn't understand.

At the airport, when we got to the gate, he asked me again, insisting for me to tell 'im. He said, "Why are they taking me to Mary Lou?" That's when I saw that I had to tell him the truth.

¡Ay! Luego-luego he started crying, real loud. "You're not my mom!?"

I told 'im, "Yes, I am. I'm your real mom because we adopted you and we raised you. Mary Lou's your mom, too, because she had you."

The girls right away came and hugged 'im, and after a while he stopped cryin'. But then, he got real mad. "Why didn't you tell me!?"

I just told 'im that, when his dad died, I couldn't tell 'im by myself. But I was still his mom and I was always gonna be his mom. From now on, he was gonna have two moms.

He said, "No, you're my mom. Mary Lou is still gonna be 'Mary Lou' even if I know she had me when I was a baby." That was it because they had to get on the aeroplane.

When he came back from over there, he kept calling me 'Mom', and he still does now. He felt good with Mary Lou, too, and they get along really, really well. Now, his daughter Anne Marie calls Mary Lou 'Grandma', and that way there aren't any more secrets.

When he got out of eighth grade, Robert was gonna be fourteen, and he didn't wanna keep on goin' to school. More and more, he was gettin' mad and gettin' mad. He talked back to the teachers, and they was always sending 'im to the principal.

And then with me, Robert was really getting to be a handful. Sometimes, I didn't even know what to do with 'im. I told 'im if he wasn't gonna go to school, he had to go and live with Mary Lou.

Mary Lou lived by herself with Zachary because she was gettin' a divorce from her husband. I think Zachary was three years old. He was their adopted son. Robert was her son by blood but he was adopted by us. What a mess!

That's when Leonard came to visit me in his pickup that he bought. He came because I wanted 'im to come so he could take Robert back with 'im to Mary Lou. Then, he wanted to take back some little things he had here. He took his desk and some back slips that I made for his truck. I also gave 'im a box full of dishes and pans.

Robert and Leonard went back together in the pickup. It was on the twenty-third of May of nineteen seventy-three. I remember that so well because that's when I stayed here all by myself. Alone. The last one of my children went away.

They passed by Denver to Terry, and she gave them a lotta things, too. They had the truck full. Terry gave 'em a little bicycle and a toy tractor to take to Mary Lou for Zachary. But the steering wheel on the tractor was broken, and Terry ordered a new one from the factory.

When they got to California, they didn't go straight to Mary Lou. I think they got there at night, or I don't know what, but they went first to the apartment where Leonard lived in San Francisco. They parked the truck in the driveway, and they was gonna go to Mary Lou the next day. She lived on the other side of that big bridge – way over there. Leonard didn't have a garage to park, so they left it outside.

Well, in the morning, the truck was empty! They stole everything. Everything – the desk, the slip covers, the little tractor. Everything! He had so many things! Right there where he lived, the people were really stealers.

The boys didn't say nothing about that to Mary Lou. But about two weeks later, she got the steering wheel in the mail. The factory sent it straight to Mary Lou.

She said, 'Well, what's this?' She called Terry, and she told 'er it was for the tractor.

"What tractor?"

"The one I sent with Leonard for Zachary."

So, they had to investigate with Leonard, and he finally had to tell them what happened. Not too long afterward, they even stole his truck. Oh! Leonard always had such bad luck with his cars.

About three years afterward, Robert got a little job. I think it was in a filling station, so he rented a little apartment way up in the hills. He went to live by himself and to make his own life alone. He was seventeen. Imagine! Seventeen and living alone!

I went to see him. He had a little teeny place that had a stove that was broken on the legs. He had it on top of some bricks.

I sat down on the only chair he had. He sat down on a box he had there. I told 'im, "Gee manee, Robert! How terrible you live here!"

Then, I looked. There was something moving on the floor. It looked like a big animal. "Oh, my gosh," I said. *"¿¡Qué es eso?!"*

Dice, "Oh, nothing. It's a rotten potato."

"But, look! It's moving right there!"

He said, "That's the way they do here." I just stayed looking, and yeah! It was a potato, but it was all full of worms that moved. He just got it, and poom! He threw it outside. *¡Uuy¡* Horrible! Poor Robert. I don't know how he could live like that.

No. Afterward, he got better jobs. He went to Alaska for a few years, then he came back and got married to Carole, *una güera*. I don't remember her last name. They got divorced a long time ago. They had Anne Marie. She's a really pretty girl, and she's very good to me. Right now, she's in college. She wants to be a nurse.[2]

After Mike's death, Elvira was left alone with Robert and Leonard.

Photo taken in 1966.

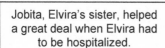

Jobita, Elvira's sister, helped a great deal when Elvira had to be hospitalized.

---

[2] Anne Marie graduated in 2016 and was immediately awarded a position at Stanford University Hospital in Palo Alto, California.

Chapter Twenty-Five

COMMUNITY ACTION

"¿What's that lady doing here?
She's a spy for the workers, that's what she is.
I'm gonna sue 'er."

Assisting the Migrants

When Robert and Leonard went to California in nineteen seventy-three, I was still working in the middle school. But I didn't feel like workin' there no more. I felt stuck in one place and just for certain times. I was alone now, and I was thinking of lookin' for another kind of work.

So then one of the workers of the school told me they needed somebody in the Community Action Center that could talk the two languages. They did a lotta work with the Mexican people, especially the migrants – illegals, I guess.

I didn't care if they was legals or illegals. They come here to make a living any way they can, crawling in the dirt like snakes to make at least a *peso*.

So, I went to see what kinda work it was. I talked with Shirley, who was the supervisor. They wanted somebody that could speak for the migrant workers. I had to go talk to them in their homes and on the farms. And then, if there was any problems, I had to talk to the farmers so they could fix it.

They also wanted me to start some classes so that the Mexican people could learn to become citizens. I was supposed to go look for persons that wanted to come to the classes and I had to work with the teacher so I could teach 'em.

I told Shirley, "Well, I don't know if I can or not, but I'll try and see how many I can find."

No. She hired me, so right away I started to talk to the people that I knew wasn't American citizens. I went all over the Panhandle[1] from farm to farm lookin' for people that wanted to attend citizenship classes and to see what kinda things they needed.

But, you oughta see the way I found 'em living. Not everybody, but most of 'em. I found terrible ways they was living. ¡Ay! We were poor when we came to Nebraska, but these families were a lot worse.

I think they came from Mexico only because they had to, and they passed without papers. You know, illegals. They had to move from one town to another one and even to other states wherever there was work. That's why the farmers could treat 'em like animals. I don't know what they did in the winter time. Go back to Mexico, I suppose. What else?

Not us. We came because of the Revolution, like my dad said, and not because we was starving. He was really smart and he never let nobody cheat us. In those times, there wasn't enough workers, so they had to treat us with respect, at least a little bit.

But not anymore. Work was getting harder and harder to find. A lotta workers were illegal, so they was always afraid that the Border Patrol was gonna catch 'em. So the farmers could do whatever they felt like it.

I went and I asked the families what they needed and how they was gettin' along on their farm. Some of 'em would tell me they was okay, but a lot of 'em told me they didn't like the awful houses they lived in and that the farmers took away a part of their pay.

---

[1] The western part of Nebraska is called a panhandle because of its shape.

I asked 'em if they told the farmer anything. They told me 'no' because they was afraid that if they complained, the farmer would get mad and tell 'em to leave.

They put some of 'em *en chantes tan feos* that I don't know how they could even live in 'em. *¡Caramba, cómo eran horribles!* They didn't even have springs on the doors and windows. Bunches of flies came inside, and the women couldn't hardly cook because there was so many flies.

I found one woman like that with a little gas stove they brought 'er. It was all broken with only two real little burners. How could she cook like that?

They had their little baby sleeping in back of their junky car. It didn't have no seats, and they had 'im on the floor of the car on top of a dirty blanket that was all torn.

The toilet didn't have a door on it, and you could see inside from the road. It had a roof that had big holes in it. What could they do if it was raining or hailing? Well, they had to cover up with a canvas or with a rag.

Right away, I went to the farmer. I talked with him and his wife. I asked 'em how they would like it sitting inside there or cooking in the kitchen all full of flies. I told 'em, "They don't even have springs on their windows or their door. Would you like that?"

The man just put his head down. He said, "No, I don't think so."

I also told 'em about the toilet and the stove and that they needed mattresses to sleep on.

So the next day, right away they put springs on the windows and the door. They brought 'em some old mattresses, and they fixed the toilet. At least it was a little bit better for them. That farmer was real nice. I just had to tell 'im what the family needed, and he did it.

But there wasn't too many like that. Some of 'em told me, "Well, if they don't like it, they can go someplace else."

Then I told 'em, "If I can find a place for them, I'll take 'em away from you."

One of 'em even told me, "I'm not gonna do nothing. That's the way they're used to living, anyway."

Oh! I got so mad! I told 'im, "They're used to living, but not that way. You're the one who put 'em that way."

So I went to the Agriculture Office,[2] and they helped me find another farm for them. I said, 'Those darn farmers! Let 'em stay without workers!'

A lot of 'em even stole from them.

One farmer was not paying four of his workers what he owed them. I took 'em to him to claim the money. He said he was gonna pay 'em when they finished the work. But you know what that dumb farmer did? When they finished the beets, before he paid 'em, he reported 'em that they were illegals.

Yes, they were illegals, but I just see that they're poor. They come here to earn the little bit that they pay 'em, and for them to steal from 'em!?

I went to the sheriff in Gering. He told me, "Well, I'm sure sorry. There's a lot of 'em that are goin' on like that, but the law can't do nothin'."

"Good gracious," I told 'im. "Look, those poor guys, they work hard. I wish you'd go out to the field so that you can see how hard it is."

"Oh," he said. "I can imagine that. I know it's so hard." He didn't do nothing.

They took 'em. And the farmer didn't pay the workers. Not one penny. It's really too bad that there are people like that who passed without papers and that didn't register – the ones they call 'illegals'. I feel so bad for 'em because they work so hard so their family can eat, and then for them to take 'em without paying.

Oh, those dang farmers! So many of 'em take advantage of the migrants. But not all of 'em. The ones we knew when we was

---

[2] The *Agricultural Labor Office*, an agency of the State of Nebraska that helped farmers find laborers and was charged with insuring fair working conditions.

farming weren't like that. They hired Mexican families, and they didn't ask if they had papers. The important thing was if they did good work.

That's the way Mike was. One day, the Border Patrol came. I don't know who reported them. Two guys came and they told Mike they wanted to talk to the workers.

He told 'em, "What for?"

They said, "They're illegals."

"What?"

They said, "They're illegals. Didn't you know?"

No, he didn't know. They was gonna take 'em away, but Mike said, "Wait. I gotta pay 'em."

But they told 'im that they couldn't earn anything because they were illegals. They didn't let 'im pay 'em.

Then Mike told 'em, "Okay. I'm not gonna pay 'em. I'm just gonna give 'em some money. I can give 'em what I want, and you can't say nothin'." He gave 'em the money, but they took 'em anyway.

I don't know why, but in that time, there was a lotta farmers that was cheaters. If they didn't call the Border Patrol, they still paid 'em whatever they felt like. The workers didn't know the prices, anyway. They had to work no matter what. That's what they came for.

They would tell 'em, "You thin one row, and I'll pay you a dollar." ¡Caramba! One dollar? They're not supposed to pay like that. You pay by the acre, not one dollar a row. Even by the acre, the pay was nothing. Not enough even to pay for food and gas. And for them to pay even less?! Gee whiz!

One of the farmers paid 'em half of what they worked because he told 'em there was so many rows per acre. I went out to the field with 'em, and I saw that the field was a lot bigger than what the farmer said. About double. I could figure that because I worked a lotta years on the farm, and I knew how many acres the fields were.

The farmer wanted to argue with me, but I brought the inspector from the Agriculture Office, and he measured the field. The farmer cut it almost to half! The inspector made 'im pay what he owed 'em.

I get into it. Even if I'm not worth nothing, I get into it. That's why when they put me with the migrant workers, I didn't let the farmers steal from 'em. If they stole, I reported 'em, and they had to pay. Oh, yeah. I got 'em. I would take the inspector.

Another one didn't wanna pay nothing to the family. Not even a penny. He said they did bad work.

Me dijo el hombre, "He made us do the cleaning three times, and we irrigated his beets, too. But he hasn't paid us anything. I don't know what he wants."

I went to the farmer and told 'im that if he didn't pay 'em, I was gonna bring the inspector so he could see. So, he paid 'em 'cause he didn't wanna have nothing to do with the inspector, but he didn't like it.

One farmer just paid the family part of their work. They ran out of money, and they didn't have enough even for food. Because the farmers never paid until after the work was all done. Sometimes it was two or three months before they paid 'em. So, they asked 'im to pay 'em at least something. He paid 'em just what they already worked.

The daughter was the one that knew a little bit of English. She was about sixteen years old. She told me, "He didn't wanna pay because I cashed the check so we could buy food."

Okay. When they finished all the work, they went to charge him what he still owed them. He told 'em 'no', that he already paid 'em. He said because the girl cashed the check, that was all their pay.

Right away I took her and her dad to the farmer. Her dad didn't know English, so he couldn't claim to the farmer.

¡Ay, Dios mío! When we put the claim, the farmer got so mad. He said, "She already cashed the check, so that's all she's gonna get!"

I told 'im, "Oh, is that so? They were starving. They had to cash the check, and you knew it! That little girl told you they was hungry and that's why they need the money."

I had to bring the inspectors. Three of 'em came with me. Oh! They argued so much. The farmer said he wasn't gonna pay no more.

They told 'im, "Look, we got the measurement here. You just paid half." They said, "If you don't pay, you're gonna pay for the court because you're gonna lose." They told 'im that it was gonna cost a lot more than what he owed. Because the Agriculture Office made a court with a lawyer where the farmer and the workers had to go.

Finally, the farmer told his son, "Go on. Go get me the checkbook. I gotta pay 'em."

I was standing outside by the car, just listening. The farmer turned around and saw me. He said, "What's that lady doing here? She's workin' for the migrants. I'm gonna sue 'er."

The inspector said, "On what grounds are you gonna sue 'er?"

"She's a spy for the workers, that's what she is."

Boy! He was so mad when he went inside that I think he wanted to get a gun – poom! poom! – he was so mad.

One farmer told the inspector right out that he was gonna shoot 'im. I went to talk to a family, and I saw two boys that hardly didn't have any hair on their head.

I asked 'em if that's how they shaved their heads.

La mamá me dijo, "No, it's falling out. That's how they been since we started working here."

Le dije, "Look. I'm gonna take 'em to the doctor right away."

"¿Con el doctor?"

Dije, "Sí. This could be serious." So I took 'em. The doctor told us that he thought it was on account of a spray they put on the field.

No. He gave 'em some medicine, and that's all.

357

So I went to the Agriculture Office to talk to the inspector. I told 'im I thought that the farmer put poison on the beets – for the weeds – and that they was all working there. The boys got poison, and that's why their hair was falling out.

He went with me right away to the farm. When we got there, the farmer's wife saw us and came out. Right away she went to call her husband. Oh, my gosh! When the inspector asked 'im about the poison he put on the field, the farmer got so mad!

He told us it was none of our business what he did and that it was a lie that he put poison on the field. Those boys didn't have nothin' wrong. They cut their own hair.

Then, both of 'em start to yell at us, the farmer and his wife. For us to get out of there, that we was on their property, and if he had a rifle, he would run us off. Then, the woman yelled, "Yeah! Get off our property or we'll shoot you both!"

The inspector told me that yeah, we was on their property and we had to leave. So, he told me to go tell the workers not to work there no more. In the morning, he was gonna come back with some deputies to change 'em to another farm if he could find another place for 'em.

I explained what he told me. But when they heard that some police was gonna come with 'im, they got scared. I guess because they was illegals. *Y luego les dije,* "Don't think they're comin' to take you away. I'm a Mexican like you are, and I'm here to help you in any way I can."

Me dijo el hombre, "That's fine, ma'am. We appreciate it." But his wife was real quiet. Nothing.

In the morning, the deputy, the inspector, and me came to the farm to move the family from there. No. They left already. Who knows where. I think they were illegals, and they were afraid of the police. They didn't trust us.

One day, Shirley, the supervisor at the office, told me, "You know? We're gonna have an open house for the ones that are very sick." It was gonna be in Gering, in the Agriculture Office, and there was gonna be about four or five doctors to see the people.

Right away, I went to tell all the families that on such a day and such a time there was gonna be a clinic for all the workers. Ooh! The first day they did it, there was a long line of people waiting to see the doctor. All the office was full! And there wasn't anybody else to go out to bring the people. I was the only one that spoke Spanish.

That was part of my work, to take the ones that needed it to the doctor. There was a lotta sickness with the migrants. Because they didn't have enough to go see a doctor. If they got sick in their stomach or they got cut or whatever, they just got worse without any medicine. Besides, who's gonna take 'em? It had to be somebody that could translate.

That's why they used to call me to the court. The inspectors and the lawyers were there. Sometimes even the sheriffs and, of course, the workers.

I got a little embarrassed because I had to interpret what they said in English and in Spanish. I didn't have any high school or nothing, and I didn't study the language. So, how could I be an interpreter?

But the inspectors and the policemens told me, "No. You're doing okay. You're doing right." They really appreciated it. Well, I just tried to do what I could.

One time they wanted to make a big meeting with all the farmers and all the workers. They was gonna bring some of the bigshots from Lincoln. They told me they wanted me to be the interpreter for that meeting.

¡Válgame Dios! I wasn't gonna be able to do that with all those bigshots from over there and from here. I told 'em, "I don't think I can interpret exactly what you're saying 'cause Spanish I don't know very much. I do. I talk. But I don't think I can interpret for this kind of meeting. I'm trying the best I can with the farmers and the migrants."

"No," they said. "You're doing wonderful."

But I told them 'no', and to see if they could get somebody better. So, they brought a girl from Lincoln. She spoke Spanish and English real good, and she was the interpreter.

Citizenship Classes

When all the migrants left after the work ended for the summer, I stayed working with the Community Action in other things. That's when I really started looking for Mexican people that wanted to become citizens.

I went to the homes of those that I knew wasn't citizens. And I went to the churches and talked to the people everywhere in the Panhandle. A lot of 'em told me, "Well, we don't know yet. Let us think about it."

Pero yo les decía, "Okay. But you are here now. ¿Are you goin' back to México?"

"No."

Les decía, "Look. This is your country now. It will be much better for you if you are American citizens because they can help you a lot more."

For the first group, I got a lot of 'em. Twenty-some, I think. More than they got in Mitchell and other places. So, I told Shirley, "Well, I think I have 'em."

She said, "Okay. Let's get 'em all together, for sure that they're coming. Then we'll get someone to help you with 'em. I'll get the teacher. You'll help her, and she'll be a helper to you."

That's fine. But on the third class, the teacher quit. She said, "I can't understand them. I cannot." So, she quit. Well, she studied Spanish in school, but she didn't understand the migrants. Maybe because they spoke Spanish from Mexico. I don't know.

Then, that gave me the job of doing it all by myself until I got somebody to help me. So, I talked with *Hilaria – Hilaria Esparza.*

Me dijo, "I haven't had too much school, but I'll help you."

"All right," *le dije.* "Me, neither. I didn't go to high school." *Le dije*, "I just had a little bit of school, too, so we're the same."

So, four people came from Lincoln to give us the list of what they had to know. They gave us a paper so we could know what we was supposed to teach.

They said, "As long as they know this." They had to know all the ones in charge here in Nebraska – the senators and

360

everybody else. And then they had to know the ones in charge in the United States. Those things and a few other things. But it wasn't too much, and the students learned it real good because we taught it to them first in Spanish and then in English whatever they could understand. Some of 'em had trouble sayin' the names in English. But they all tried hard. We taught the classes in the basement of the high school.

They came two times from Lincoln to examine if they could answer. I interpreted what they said. Because they told me, "We don't speak Spanish, but we understand a little bit. But you're here, so that's all we need."

The examiners thought it was funny when the students tried to say it in English. Because they turned the letters around and couldn't say it – *lo-lu-lo-lu*. But they tried hard. So, yeah. They all passed.

Ooh! When they went to graduate, the court was full of people. The ones for us was twenty-three. From another town, thirteen, and from another one, fifteen, or whatever. But it was full. And I was the one that had to take every one of 'em to become a citizen. To get their diploma.

There was a Mexican woman there that also goes to Guadalupe. *Una prietilla, greñuda,*[3] but she had the police star. Me and her got into it.

Dice, "¿What are you doing? ¿Are you telling lies here to make these people citizens?" Sayin' that I was counting them wrong. I think she thought I was bringin' illegals to become citizens. My goodness! Everybody that came was registered and had papers. Besides, what business was it of hers?

Le dije, "No, I'm not a liar like you." *Dije,* "You think that because you have a star I'm afraid of you? I'm not afraid. Take me to the court and we'll see what you say about me."

---

[3] 'a scrawny dark-skinned woman with disheveled hair'

A long time afterward when I already had to use my walker, she saw me in Mass one day. "Hi," she said, and she comes over in a hurry to help me.

I told 'er, "Thank you. I don't need no help to sit down." Especially from her.

So, I had a good job, you know. Not a good pay, but I was working. I worked with the migrants for five years. Afterward, it all ended. Because they invented a seed for the beets that only left one or two plants in twelve inches, and they didn't have to thin 'em no more. That work finished for the migrants and also my work with 'em.

But I kept on with the Community Action for a while teaching citizenship classes.

Chapter Twenty-Six

LEONARD'S DEATH

I had three heartaches en mi vida.
But the worse heartache was Leonard. I could'a died.
If it hadn't been for my faith,
I really think I would'a gone crazy.

Leonard Disappears

Leonard came to see me for Thanksgiving in nineteen seventy-three. He stayed until after New Year, until he got lost. I know he was suffering in California because he was very sad when he came. Real down. Sometimes he even would start to cry. I saw he didn't wanna go back anymore.

Over there, they stole everything he had when he took Robert. Then a few months later, they even stole his truck! *¡Ay!* So many things happened to Leonard with his cars and his trucks. Then, he was a lot in debt with his credit cards. I don't know how much he owed because he never told me, but what he told me was he didn't have enough to pay 'em. I think that's what he was living with.

Oh, I felt so sorry for him! I told him, "Look, *mijo,* you have your home here. This will always be your home." Tellin' him to come live over here if that was better for him. I know he could'a got a little job for himself. But he didn't say nothing. Just quiet.

One day after New Year, I told 'im, "*Hijo,* I'll be right back. I gotta take my uncle to the doctor 'cause his nose bleed doesn't wanna stop."

If I had thought, I would'a said, *"Vente, hijo, vámonos.* Come with me."

But I didn't because he told me, "I'm gonna put on the panel that you have here." He was gonna fix a panel on the wall of the basement.

When I came back, he wasn't here. I didn't see him no more. I still have that panel that he never fixed.

I said, 'He probably went to the store to buy some peanuts or something. He'll be right back.' He didn't have a car, so he had to go walking.

But he didn't come back and he didn't come back. 'Where could he be?' No, I even went out in my car to see if I could find 'im. It was snowing and it was really cold. *¡Ay, pobre!* That's when I really got worried. I stayed waiting for him all night long, lookin' out the window to see if I could see 'im coming. '¿What could'a happened to *mijo?'*

Right away in the morning, I went over to Betty to ask *Fernando* if they had seen 'im. No, nobody did. Then I called all my kids to see if he called one of 'em. Nothing. They told me to call the police and to report him missing.

Yes, I called the police. They asked me that how was he dressed. I told 'em that he took his heavy overcoat, his cap, and his gloves. They asked me to give 'em a picture of 'im, so I took it to them right away.

I don't know what day Leonard left, but it was a little bit before his birth'ay because he was born on the eleventh of January of nineteen fifty-one.

I remember him so much when he was a little baby. We still lived in the big house at Neil. We wasn't expecting him because I was more than forty-one years old. But God gave him to us anyway. All of us spoiled 'im a lot 'cause we didn't have any more babies in the house – Mary Lou was already nine years old.

We had a little white dog. A real cute little dog. It was a toy collie that was white, white with his tail that looked like a fan. He had a pointy face. He used to sleep on an easy chair that I had.

When the baby was born, I didn't have a baby basket no more, so I took the dog off the chair, I washed it and put a blanket on it so Leonard could sleep there. But that dog started crying', "Ee, ee, ee, ee!" He jumped up and grabbed the baby's blanket, tryin' to take it off.

I scolded 'im, "Get down from there! What's the matter with you?" 'Cause he kept tryin' to get up on the chair.

One day, I was giving the baby a bath in his little tub, and the dog was jumping up, "Ee, ee, ee!"

"Shut up," I told 'im. "You're getting me nervous." Well, he wouldn't even let me give the baby a bath because there he was jumpin' around the tub cryin' and cryin'. I think he was jealous because of the attention we gave to Leonard. Yeah, he was jealous.

So, I went and opened the door for 'im. "Get out," I told 'im.

We never saw 'im again. He abandoned us.

Mike and the kids all went out to look for him. Nothing. At that time, my brother *Carlos* lived over there with Siever, about a mile away. They told us the dog used to go there and they gave 'im to eat. He went over to *don Másimo*, too. He told us the dog was there all the time. But when we went to look for 'im, he would hide. Afterward, he didn't show up anyplace. I'm sure somebody picked 'im up and took 'im because he was so cute.

Anyway, when Leonard went, it made me think of that dog that ran away because Leonard took his place.

The days passed and they didn't find Leonard. *¡Ay, Dios santo!* I didn't know what to do. I was going crazy. I talked to Elvira in Vermont and I told 'er I was even gonna sell the house so I could go look for 'im. I didn't know where. I said, "I'll go to the end of the earth to find 'im."

But she made me calm down. She told me, "No, Mom. That won't do no good. You let the police find 'im."

Well, about three weeks later, Father Jim[1] came with a policeman came to tell me they found a boy up there on the Bluffs. They found him dead under the snow. I think the policeman didn't wanna come by himself.

I said, "Oh, no! That can't be my son! No, it can't! *¡No puede ser! ¡No puede estar muerto Leonard! ¡Dios mío en el cielo,* don't let 'im be Leonard!"

They said, "Can you come down and identify if he is or isn't?"

I told 'em, "No, but I'll call my children to come." I didn't wanna go see because they told me that the one they found was all decomposed because of the weather. How could I look at my son like that?!

They all came right away. Then Vera, Edward, and Bill went to the funeral home to see him. They told me, "Yes, it's Leonard."

Oh! I almost died! I really did want Mike to come for me. But he didn't.

The Miracle of Leonard

I had three big heartaches in my life, but the worse heartache was Leonard. I was expecting what happened to Bobby and to Mike, too, but I wasn't expecting Leonard. I could'a died. I wanted to. You know, if it hadn't been for my faith, I really think I would'a gone crazy.

There was a woman here that had a son. They was from Israel, but they weren't Jews. They was from another people. That woman's son got killed in a car. She used to go walking from here to the cemetery, and nobody could find 'er. They would find 'er sitting over there by the grave.

Her husband took her to their land over there and left 'er there. He was already older, in his late fifties, early sixties. Over there, he went with a young girl that was about twenty-eight or thirty years old, I think. He brought her over here and they had such a

---

[1] Father Jim Murphy, Our Lady of Guadalupe parish priest.

pretty family. They had six children. But his wife that he left over there went crazy.

That's what would'a happened to me if it wasn't for my faith in God.

I say that how they found Leonard was a miracle. Because the policemens told us that two boys came out of school to go walking to the Bluffs. They played hooky.

Elvira went to their house to talk to them. They live here close. They told Elvira about it.

They went to the Bluffs just to walk, and when they was goin' up, there was two roads. The low one is very narrow and they don't want anybody to go there. But those boys saw a little deer, and they went behind it on that narrow road. Then, the deer turned, and they lost it. There they go, looking and looking. Nothing.

They said, "Where did that little goat go?" They looked on one side and on the other side, and nothing. Then they looked down, and they saw the face of a person! There was a lotta snow, and the rest of 'im was covered. Just the head and the face weren't because the snow was melting. Oh! They got so scared, and they went running down the hills.

Right away, the police came to look, and they took 'im. They told Elvira that it was a wonderful thing that they found him on that day. If they let him one more day, all of him would have uncovered, and the animals would'a eaten 'im. ¡Ay! I don't even want to think about that.

That's why I say it was a real miracle. Why did those boys go out of school on that day? And why did they go to the Bluffs? And wasn't it a miracle that a deer appeared to them on that narrow road and that it disappeared right there where they looked down? That deer had to be my guardian angel. And if it snowed on that day or if the snow melted, who would'a found 'im? Who?

I don't know what happened to my son. The policemens said that because of where they found 'im, he fell from the road on top. They said he could'a slipped, but they thought he jumped by himself. He wanted to kill himself. "Why did he go up there?" they said.

¡Virgen santísima! I will never believe that. Leonard had the same faith in God that I have. Somebody took 'im and threw 'im down. I know that somebody came here to get 'im because he put on his overcoat and everything. Someone came to get 'im, and I still have somebody in my mind that did it.

The last time he came, he went with some friends, and they wrecked the car that I bought 'im. Just because of that I think and I think and I think. I think those guys thought Leonard came to press charges on 'em.

I'm sure that they came to get Leonard, because Leonard looked okay to me. I think they told 'im, "Let's go for a ride." And they took 'im. Then, they got 'im over there by force, and they pushed 'im down.

We buried Leonard on the eighth of February. That was the same day as Edward's birth'ay, but we had to do it. Even with all of that, we did a little party for Eddie with a birth'ay cake. I gave 'im a real nice sweater. My sister *Cuca* came, too. Then Mr. Hackman, the bus driver of the kids from a long time ago, came to give us his sympathy. All the kids were really surprised to see 'im after all those years.

Then, everyone left, and I stayed by myself. Alone.

So, that's what it was. But, well, life is life and we have to keep on goin'. I tried to keep on goin' the best I could, and I did.

Herman Hackman and his wife. Mr. Hackman was the bus driver who, for almost twenty years, not only took Elvira's children to school, he became a friend of the family. In this photo, Mr. and Mrs. Hackman stopped by Elvira's home to offer their condolences over Leonard's death.

Chapter Twenty-Seven

A SENIOR CENTER FOR WOMEN

*I told the ladies that we all had to get along,
because there was Germans and there was Mexicans.
There couldn't be any prejudice.
If you spoke in Spanish or in German, that's all right.
But nobody can talk about the other ones.*

Going back to Work

After Leonard died, I didn't wanna work no more. I felt like I wanted to die. I couldn't go to work. But Shirley, who was the supervisor, told me, "Vera, you have to go to work."

"I can't."

"Yes," she told me. "Not because of the job. We can get someone in your place. But you have to go to work. You talk with a lotta people. And that people will help you."

I couldn't. I just couldn't. No. After a month, I did. I went to work. I worked in the Community Action for about a year after Leonard died.

Not too many migrants came anymore because there wasn't no more *desahije*. Almost all the farmers planted the new seed that didn't come out so thick, so there wasn't as much need for thinning. They just needed workers for the cleaning and for irrigation, but that wasn't much.

I kept on lookin' for people to make 'em citizens. But a lotta the migrants didn't have papers, and that's why they weren't eligible to become citizens. I could hardly get enough people to make one class, so I wanted to leave the Community Action. I didn't know what I was gonna do.

Starting the Center

That's when Shirley told me, "Why don't you make a center for the older women?"

"A center? Can I do that?"

"Yeah. Why don't you try?"

So, the first thing I did was go to the priest to see if there was a place to put a little meeting room.

He told me, "There's that little room at the Guadalupe Center. It has a lotta stuff in it, but if you clean it out, you can use it."

So I got a few women together to go help me, and we cleaned that room out real good. We found a table and some chairs, and we put 'em there so we could work.

Then, I began to tell the senior ladies from the church to come. Because we was gonna do a lotta things so we could all go together on trips.

By that time, a lotta German people started coming to Our Lady. They were good people. I think because they suffered a lot over there in Russia where they came from. That's why I wanted to bring them to the center also. That's where we got to know each other because before, we just barely said hello in the church.

I talked to more and more women about the center, and a lot of 'em did come. I think about twelve or fifteen ladies came – *güeras* and Mexicans, but all of 'em was older, no younger than fifty-five or sixty years old. Some was even sixty-five years old. I was already sixty-five myself. I think I was the oldest one of all of 'em.

I told the ladies that we all had to get along because there was Germans and there was Mexicans. There couldn't be any prejudice. And if you talked in Spanish or in German, that's all right, but nobody could talk about the other persons. I was real strict with my seniors. That's how I called 'em, 'my seniors'.

We started first embroidering little things to sell – aprons and dishcloths and things like that. But every person had to bring her own cloth and her own yarn and everything to make what they was gonna make.

And when we finished, we put everything in a box or in a bag to take it home with us because we didn't have a key to the little room. There was a lotta people all the time in the Guadalupe Center, so that's why.

Then, I went to the priest to ask 'im if he would lend us a key to the room so we could leave everything to the next time. I told 'im, "We got quite a few ladies, and we need to keep our stuff there. That way we don't have to pack it all back home."

I'm pretty sure it was Father Jim, the same one that came with the policeman to tell me about Leonard. Here was his first church. He's retired now, and he went to live in South Dakota someplace because that's where he was from.

So he didn't know the Mexican people too good, and I think he was a little prejudiced. All the priests were, even the ones that spoke Spanish. Some more than others.

I remember Father Portray that Mike got so mad with. The Recreation Center had a baseball team and Father Portray was their coach.(i) One day, they were losing their game pretty bad, and the players got real depressed. When they went out to play, they walked real slow like they didn't feel like playin' anymore.

Father Portray looked at 'em real kinda mad, and he said, "That's so typical!"

¡Ay! Maique was like they burned 'im with a fire!

"What did you say, Father? That Mexicans are lazy?" He turned around and told me, "Let's get outta here."

Afterward, the priest came to our house to apologize. They was talkin' a lot outside, and finally Mike calmed down a little. Because Father Portray spoke Spanish very well, and he did a lot for the Mexican people. But that time, he showed us who he was. He kept comin' to the house like he always did, but Mike didn't like him too much anymore.

Dice, "¿Why does he have to come so often?"

Le dije, "We're the only ones. The Mexican people have a lotta respect for the priests, and that's why they don't invite 'em to their house."

That's how the people was before. Not anymore. Now, everybody speaks English and the priests also speak Spanish. So now they bring 'em into their houses. They feel more comfortable with the priests.

Anyway, when I asked Father Jim for the key to the room, he told me, "Well, I don't know. That, I have to think about it because I have some kids I wanna teach."

I told 'im, "But we cleaned the room, and you said we could have it."

"Yeah," he said. "But you can take your things home, and I can use it for teaching the children."

So I told the women that the priest wasn't gonna give us the room like he said.

One of 'em said, "What are we gonna do?"

I said, "We can stay here and take our boxes back home and bring 'em back. Or we're gonna look for another place. It's up to you, if you can find place."

Then, one of the German ladies said, "You know what? There's a house across from the church that's empty." The owners of that house died, and the children all went to other places. They didn't pay the taxes for a long time, and the City took it away from 'em.

Right away I went to Shirley and I told 'er what we wanted to do. She told Mary, her assistant, to go with me to find out. There we go to the City.

They said that be a very good idea. But first, they had to tell all the family that they had to pay the taxes that they owed for all those years. They told us that if they didn't want to pay, they would give us the house.

They didn't wanna pay, so they gave it to us. But they said we had to fix it and pay for the telephone and the lights. They gave us the house free. The City just charged us one dollar a year. One dollar!

Oh! All of us got to work fixing our house. We cleaned it and we put linoleum on the floor. We painted all the walls on the inside. One of the husbands of the seniors fixed the porch and some windows that was broken. The Senior Center turned out really pretty.

So then, we went out to see who could donate the appliances we needed. We went to the used furniture stores and to other churches. No. Right away we got a good refrigerator and a gas stove. One person gave us a sewing machine, and then another one. We got about six or seven sewing machines.

Jobita even got somebody to donate a piano. There she comes to play the piano, and all the rest of us started singing.

The Work in the Center

Okay, then. We all started working. We got together there on the days that each one was free. I was the one in charge, so I went almost every day to see who was there, what we had to do, what things we had to buy, and like that. I made a notebook to write down who came and what days they came.

We made everything to sell. Mexican bread and American bread, donuts, and even *enchiladas*. Everything. And *tortillas*. Eee! We made too many *tortillas*. Dozens and dozens every day. Because the Mexican families would rather buy tortillas than have to make 'em by hand. The *güeros* bought 'em, too, because they started to see how good the Mexican food is.

The Mexican women all knew how to make *tortillas*. Even the German ladies learned to make 'em. They liked it, and they got real good at it. I just had to show everybody the recipe how I wanted them so that they all came out the same.

Other women would sit down to sew aprons, towels, dishcloths, pillow covers, or whatever. Then they embroidered 'em or they stitched Mexican designs so they would look pretty. Some of 'em made real pretty blankets out of pieces of rags. They call

373

'em 'patch quilts'. That's what I had 'em doing – some of 'em sewing, other ones cooking.

At first, we went to the houses to tell people to come and buy. Then, the priest announced the Center in the church bulletin, in English and in Spanish. Shirley also helped us at the Community Action. She told everybody who came there about the Center, and she announced it in their newsletter.

No. Pretty soon a lotta people started to come to buy the things we had. Sometimes we couldn't even keep up, and they had to wait until we made what they wanted.

Especially the *tortillas*! We ran out of those right away. I think a lotta families ate more *tortillas* than what we ate workin' in the field!

We made quite a bit of money. I opened up a bank account to put the money and so all of us would know how much we had and what we spent it on.

Going on Trips

We used all that money to take trips. We all went on the bus, the ones that could go. We went two or three times to the faces in South Dakota.(ii) That's where we saw that great big Indian, sitting on his horse, that they are making on another mountain.

Other times, we made trips to Lincoln to see the capitol. Over there, they took us to see where the senators had their meetings, and they showed us the governor's office. We used to like walkin' around town in Lincoln, just looking and buying things for souvenirs.

On other trips, we would go to Cheyenne to see the Frontier Days or to North Platte to see the Buffalo Bill museum.(iii) I think that the trips that we enjoyed the most was when we went to Colorado to visit the Mother Cabrini shrine – St. Frances Cabrini, the first United States citizen that was made a saint by Pope Pius. That shrine is way up on top of the mountain close to Golden, Colorado. There in Golden is where Alta lived when Mike was dying.

There's so much to see at the shrine. It has a gift shop and a lotta paths to walk on and to see all the pretty sights. When we went, we always went walking in the Rosary Garden, and we prayed the rosary. It has so many beautiful bushes and flowers.

We also visited the Grotto where they have a chapel. Inside there, we prayed to Mother Cabrini to ask the Sacred Heart of Jesus to give us peace and love in our lives. The entrance is so beautiful! It has benches all around to sit on, and everything is full of flowers. A lotta people come there to leave their petitions to Mother Cabrini.

One time that we went, we climbed all the way to the top where there is a real tall statue of the Sacred Heart. White, white. To get up there, you have to climb four hundred steps. ¡Ah, caray! But we went slow, praying on the Stations of the Cross. Every station has a big cross that has the suffering of Christ painted there. And then, up higher, they put some big rocks next to the steps, each one of them a mystery of the rosary.

When you get up to the highest part of the steps, there's the Crown of Thorns that Mother Cabrini and some other nuns made. They picked up a lotta little white rocks from around there, and they put 'em in the shape of a heart. On the top of the heart, they arranged more rocks that signified the Crown of Thorns.

It's a beautiful climb up there. And when we got tired, every now and then there was benches for us to sit on. We just climbed up to the top only the first time we went. It's a really hard climb for older persons like us. They say there's a way to go up in a car, but we never went.

One time that we went, we were in Mass, and we were so surprised! There was two Masses at the same time, one of 'em on one side, and the other one on the other side. The other one was a 'dumb Mass'. They couldn't talk. The priest was saying Mass with his hands! Boy! He knew exactly how the Mass goes. And the people just looked at 'im and they moved their fingers at the same time. They answered him with their hands, right on time. They understood everything.

Oh, my gosh! We didn't even hear the Mass over here on this side. We were paying so much attention to the dumb Mass, and we couldn't stop looking. It wasn't 'dumb', like 'dumb'. It was for the ones that can't hear, and it was really beautiful.

All these were the most wonderful trips that we took. We traveled only in the summer because there was too much snow in the winter, and we didn't like to go then. Winter was sewing. Summer was going.

We had the Senior Center for eighteen years until we closed it in nineteen ninety-two. By that time, a lotta the women that started there got tired. They said, "I'm sorry, Vera, but we're too old to be doin' this."

Too old! I was the oldest of all of 'em. I was eighty three. But I was tired, too. Besides, I think two of 'em died, and other ones couldn't walk without their walker.

So, we closed the Center. We had a lotta sewing machines, and we gave 'em to the ones that wanted 'em. The other things, like the refrigerator and the stove, we left 'em in the house for if the City wanted to use them. We made a goodbye supper with the little bit of money we had left. It was sad, but we was all glad, too.

They gave me an award from Lincoln for putting in this center. I think I have three awards. The one from Lincoln was for being the first Mexican senior center. And they gave me two more.

The Day-Care Center for Children

Afterward, I stayed here at home for one year, and I felt terrible – terrible! Because I wanted to go back to work. I was here at home, but I didn't like the house by myself without work, so I went back.

I started lookin' for another place. Then somebody told me about a children's center where they took care of children for people that had to go to work. When they went to work, they dropped 'em off at the school.

It's right here close, on Avenue L. It's just about four blocks. I went. Ooh! Right away they took me because they needed somebody to be a 'foster grandparent' for the children, especially the ones that spoke in Spanish.

At first, when the weather was nice, I used to walk over there and back home. But afterwards, when I got old and I couldn't walk too good, I went in my car. I just worked three, four hours a day.

But I didn't wanna take the babies. They asked me, "You want the babies?"

I told 'em, "No. Not the babies." I didn't want the babies. I already had to take care of too many babies! Once. Now, I didn't have nobody.

That's why I chose the children from four to six. The ones four to six years old because the other ones that was seven had to be in school.

My work was only that I had to be with them. Sometimes, we was inside, and I read books to 'em or I played with 'em with the games they had there. I talked to them in Spanish or in English. Some of 'em didn't know English, so I talked Spanish with them. But they really picked up the other language with the other children.

They had their teacher to teach 'em. She told me, "Vera, why don't they understand us? They pay more attention to you."

I told 'er, "They don't speak your language, and I do. That's why."

They didn't pay attention to her. She talked to them in Spanish like in Spain. ¡Ta-ta-ta-tá! ¡Ta-ta-ta-tá! Well, they couldn't understand her! That's the way the ones from Spain talk – ¡Ta-ta-ta-tá! ¡Ta-ta-ta-tá! That's like when I went to Spain with Eduardo and Ysaura. Once in a while, we went out for a walk and talked to the people. But sometimes they was hard to understand because they talk too fast.

At the Center, when the weather was nice, we went outside. Out there, we ran around. We played ball. Everything.

Ooh! The migrants really liked me. "Gramma! Gramma! Gramma!" Yeah. Really nice children. ¡Cómo me querían! And I liked them, too. A lot.

One time, they got a kick outta me. Outside they had a plastic bucket or basket to put the children in and turn 'em around. Eee! They laughed so hard.

"Look! Teacher, teacher!"

"Yes."

So, one time, "Can you sit in there?"

I said, "Oh, yeah. I can sit." So, I sat in the bucket. And then, they started to turn me around! They laughed so hard. They were outside, and I was inside, "Stop it! Stop it!" I was round and round, and them laughing and laughing.

Finally, I got out. "You know what you're gonna get? You're gonna get a spankin' from me!" And there I go, running after them. They just turned around, "You can't catch us!"

You know, it was really a nice job. I really liked working with the children like that. Oh, sometimes one of the children would come crying because another one did this or that. I got 'em both, I hugged them, and I just told 'em they had to play good with each other.

So, there they go to keep on playin'. I worked with the children for five years, until I couldn't no more. My legs hurt me a lot to walk. And then, I think they wasn't gonna renew my driving license. Because I couldn't hardly see out of one eye. A few years ago, they operated on my cataracts, but I'm beginning to lose my vision, anyway.

Elvira Retires

I quit working there when I was eighty-nine, in nineteen ninety-eight. The next year, my children made me a big party for my ninety. So many people came! My sisters *Teresa* and *Consuelo* from Mexico and many of their children. And so many nieces and nephews! Some cousins from Chicago even came, the daughters of my aunt *María de Jesús* – *Gracia, Trinidad,* and *Jovita.* Three of their daughters came with them. A lotta people. I don't even remember who came and who didn't.

So, you see, son? This is my life that you have been tape recording. I don't know what you want it for. I worked hard all of my life, and I been through a lotta suffering. But, since your dad died, I have tried to serve the people, workin' in the schools, with the migrants, with the seniors, and with the children.

If it wasn't for this work that God gave me, I would'a gone crazy. I won't even talk about when Leonard died.

Like I tell Terry, "Help, so you can be helped." Terry lives always cryin'. She laughs, but inside she's always cryin'. First, Richard died, and then a year later, her daughter Beth.

I tell her, "Help those that really need something, and you'll see how you get better because you need something to give you peace."

I don't know what else I was gonna do with my life. That's why I didn't stop working until I couldn't do it no more. Then, I did. I even had to put away my *palote* because my hands didn't let me make no more *tortillas*. And I made so many *tortillas* in my life!

So, then, I just started to take care of my yard and my house. And I'm gonna stay here until I die. I just ask God for that to be soon.

I'm tired.

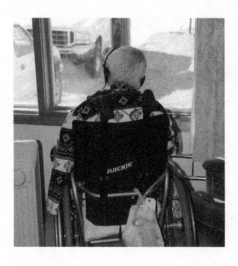

THE SENIOR CENTER

Elvira standing in front of the Senior Center with
her grandson Michael.

A group of women
from the Senior
Center on a trip to
the Mother Cabrini
shrine. Jobita
Ramirez is seated
on the left.

1980

Balance brought forward 27.56

April 25, Jobita gave this account of   62 doz
Tortillas made and sold
                                     90
                                 55.80

Marta and Joe did not paid   4.50
for 5 doz.   51.30
                             27.56
Expenditures   78.86
Weed-be-gone   2.90   —17 90
Paid Mr. Juarez   15 00   60.96
for month of April 17.90

May 2, Balance brought forward   #60.96
Tortillas made and sold 55 doz = 49.50
Delores Corbett   17 doz   110 46
Blanco   16 ”   — 2 42
Brijida   6 ”   108.04
Brakken   6 ”
Jissie   5 ”
Juarez   3 ”
Joe   2 ”
            55

May 6, bought dish detergent   1.59
3 small jelly rolls
                Tax .79
                    2 42
No meeting May 9, Mrs. Rodrigues'
funeral

A page from Elvira's account book for the Senior Center. The book provides details of the organization's income and expenses.

A Senior Center for Women

One of the many colorful kitchen cloths made by Elvira and other women at the center.

Some of the numerous buttons and badges that Elvira obtained during all the various excursions of the group.

Senior Center Thanked for all Their Work

Members of the Southeast Sr. Center in Scottsbuff are surprised as staff from the Gering office present them with a croquet set as a sign of appreciation for all the ladies have done. From left are Delores Morales, Brigida Ramirez, Jobita Ramirez, Madge Munoz, and Vera Hernandez. The ladies catered the lunch served at the workshop on April 2 in Scottsbluff. NPCAA Photo.

**TWO AMONG THE MANY AWARDS THAT ELVIRA RECEIVED
IN RECOGNITION OF HER COMMUNITY SERVICE.**

Recognition of Elvira for her service to the church,
her membership in the Carmelites society,
as well as for founding the Senior Center
and her service in the migrant program.

Recognition of Elvira as
an honored member of
the Nebraska Century
Society for one
hundred years of
contributions to the
history of the state of
Nebraska,

July 1, 2009.

A toast to celebrate Elvira's ninetieth birthday.

June 27, 1999.

Celebrating her 100th birthday with her very good friend Fr. Thomas Dowd.

June 27, 2009

Comments on Language and Culture

i   The Southeast Recreation Center (SERC) was established by Fr. Lawrence Portray, parish priest of Our Lady of Guadalupe church during the 1940's. He saw the need to create a place where the Mexican people could get together, especially the youth, for a variety of cultural, social, and sports activities. He arranged for the Scottsbluff School District to turn over for that purpose the old Washington Elementary School that was vacant but usable. He had it renovated, and they had dances, group meetings, cultural events, as well as sports and games for the young people. Many years later, the parish replaced SERC with a new building that is now the Guadalupe Center.

ii   This is the well-known Mount Rushmore, a bluff in the Black Hills of South Dakota that has the images of four U.S. presidents sculpted on it: George Washington, Thomas Jefferson, Theodore Roosevelt, and Abraham Lincoln.

On a nearby mountain is the monument to Crazy Horse, a famous warrior of the Oglala Sioux tribe. The monument is still in process of being sculpted by Korczak Ziolkowski, commissioned by the Lakota Sioux. Once finished, this will be the largest sculpture in the world.

iii   Cheyenne is the capital of Wyoming which is a little more than 100 miles southwest of Scottsbluff. Frontier Days in Cheyenne is an annual celebration of the pioneer settlers and cowboys of the region. North Platte, Nebraska, is less than two hundred miles to the east of Scottsbluff. Buffalo Bill (Bill Cody) was an explorer, Indian fighter, and bison hunter ("buffaloes") during the time of the "Wild West" in the U.S. He gained his famed nickname in a contest with another hunter, and he used that title to form a grand traveling exposition which he exhibited all over the U.S. and Europe. He founded his exposition in North Platte, Nebraska, the reason for the museum in that town.

Chapter Twenty-Eight

ONE MILLION TORTILLAS

When we got home from the rows of beets,
we came back home to the rows of testales.
Rows, rows, and more rows everywhere.

Note to the Reader:

In the homes of Mexicans in the U.S. in the early twentieth century, a central activity in the kitchen was making white-flour tortillas. These were used to 'sopear' or scoop up the food at meal times, eating a piece of tortilla with each 'spoonful' since people tended not to use knives and forks. Thus, each grown person would normally use several tortillas at each meal. Snacks and lunches also consisted of tacos (now known as 'burritos') made with white tortillas. All the tortillas were made at home, and since there was no refrigeration and there were so many that needed to be made, they were made fresh daily.

In the Fall of 1999, she sent us a package of tortillas by UPS along with a note informing us that this was her final batch of tortillas. She said that her wrists hurt her from so many she had rolled out over a lifetime and, besides, there was no reason to make any more for just one person.

I quickly put the package in our freezer, and on my next trip to Scottsbluff, I asked her, "Mom, how many tortillas have you made in your life?"

She said, "¡Ay! How do you count that? Only God knows.

"Well, let's count them," I said. I'll help you by asking you questions.

So, to document this, we went through all the tortilla-making stages of her life so she could calcultate how many tortillas she made per day during each period. She took careful account of the persons that lived in the household at any given time and how many tortillas each person would consume.

Below is her response in which she reviews her career as a tortillera *and gives her conservative estimate of the number of tortillas she made.*

How many *tortillas* have I made in my life? Only God knows.

I don't know how I can count that. But. OK. I started helping my mom make *tortillas* at about nine years old. She would get me up early because she wanted me to help her fold the *tacos* for the lunches.

We lived in Kansas City, and my dad worked at Cudahy's – they called it *la Caris.* My mom had boarders that also worked in the packing house. She had to make their breakfast *y sus taquitos para el lonche.* Then, when they got home from work, she had their supper ready. They paid my dad so they could help out, but I don't know how much. That's why they had 'em.

We had to get up really early to make their breakfast and their lunches. Mom would call me about four or four-thirty in the morning. She told me, "*Ay, Elvira.* Get up."

"*¡Ay, Dios, no!*" I just couldn't get up. But she got me by the hands, and there she is, doing *malacanchoncha* with me so I could wake up. She had to so I would wake up to help her – so she could help herself.

So, she would tell me, *"Andale, hija, come and make the tortillas."*

"OK." And I would make the *tortillas.*

I think she had about four *bordantes* plus my dad that were the workers. And then, the rest of us were six – the four biggest girls, my mom, and *Juan* who was little. He was a baby.

In the morning, she made the workers some scrambled eggs and beans for their coffee – maybe two or three *tortillas* each one – and a *taquito* to take. Then, I think she would give each man four *tacos* or so for their lunch. That's six *tortillas* each one. Then when they came home for supper at night, each one of 'em ate at least four. We didn't use forks, so I think each man ate about ten *tortillas* every day. On Sunday, she didn't make their lunches, but she made 'em all their meals anyway. So it was the same thing.

And the five of us who stayed at home would eat as many as we were hungry for. Put down two dozen for all of us. So, more or less, I think that we would make – let's see – two; two more, four; and two for supper, six – about six dozen per day, at least.

When we came to Scottsbluff from Kansas, I was ten years old. I turned eleven in June. Over here we still had boarders who worked in the beets – the same ones who followed my dad. So we still made about six dozen per day.

By nineteen twenty-three, when my dad gave up the boarders, it was just us. *Carlos* and *Juan* had already been born in Kansas, but *Carlos* was just a baby. *Juan* was – let's see, from nineteen eighteen to nineteen twenty-three – he was five years old. They didn't eat much. They would just eat some oatmeal or whatever.

But we did make a lotta *tortillas* because the older girls would get up and go out to the fields with the men. Oh, yes, we worked everywhere. There wasn't any law yet that said that little kids couldn't work. I started working at ten years old in nineteen twenty, and Jobita was eight, *descuatando* for my mom because she went out, too. Alta and *Cuca* also started working about that time.

And there's Mom, making tacos for our breakfast with the *tortillas* we made the night before. Then she'd take a bucket full of tacos to the field. She made enough for breakfast and lunch, and when I got home at night, then we'd make all the *tortillas* for supper and for the next day.

Mom would say, "OK, now you can help me make the tortillas."

"OK. I'll help you make 'em."

My mom would mix the dough. Then, we would make the *testales* in rows. We made about six in each row. Six *testales*, about the size of a biscuit. We would make about, oh, about eight rows of *testales*. Then, I made the *tortillas* so my mom wouldn't have to make so many in the morning. The next day, if she didn't have enough, she'd make a few.

So when we'd get home from the rows of beets, we had to go back to the rows of *testales*. Rows, rows, and more rows everywhere!

"Oh!" I said, "How many rows do we have left?"

"Oh, Mom, we only have two rows left."

"Oh, this is too many rows. We made too many *testales*."

So, I made a lotta *tortillas* until I got married, because we were a big family now. And that's how it was in nineteen twenty-three, 'twenty-four, 'twenty-five, 'twenty-six, 'twenty-seven, and 'twenty-eight, until I got married in nineteen twenty-nine. We already had *Joaquín, Teresa, Consuelo, Arturo, and Hermelinda. Juan* was already eleven and *Carlos* was nine, and they already started working in the fields. So, I think that in those years, we made at least a couple of dozen more than before. Every day of the year, because in the winter, we still had to eat.

When I got married, *Chole* made the *tortillas*. Nineteen twenty-nine, 'thirty, and 'thirty-one we lived there with them with the same kitchen. I lasted almost three years like that. I didn't make any until we got our own rooms and I put in my own kitchen. I didn't want to be together with them any more. I just didn't want to! They gave us two rooms. One I made into the kitchen, and one into a bedroom. The living room was for all of us, and the other kitchen was theirs. But I didn't make many *tortillas*. Maybe a dozen or so, just for the two of us. *Elvira* and *Eduardo* were still just babies.

In nineteen thirty-five, a lotta people were going back to Mexico because they wanted to kick out as many Mexicans as wanted to leave. They could take anything they wanted. My mom and dad had left. Then, *don Juan* said they were leaving, too. And he was insisting on us going with them.

I told 'im, "I'm not going."

Mike told 'im, "We don't have the money." We were saving. We had $100.

Don Juan said, "It won't cost so much. You'll take what you want from here, and we'll go."

Yo le dije, "I'm not going!" I didn't want to go with them. That was the main thing. I didn't want to go with THEM. Because we would have to live with them over there, and I was up to here! Oh, *don Juan* was so mad because we didn't want to go.

Then we moved over to the Baltes farm. The farmer came and told Mike that, if he'd help him, he'd give him work there. We already had *Elvira, Eduardo,* and *Roberto,* so I probably only made about two dozen *tortillas* per day.

When I started to make a lotta *tortillas* again was after we moved to the shack over at Neil. By then we had Terry, and the others were getting big, and I made more *tortillas.* At the least, I made three dozen or so every day. Yeah, because they ate a lotta *tortillas.* I made them a lotta tacos, and made 'em for breakfast and all. By then, *Elvira* was six years old, but I never taught her how to make *tortillas.* I made 'em by myself.

The boys still hadn't started to work because of the law. They would go with us when we were working in the potatoes to shake off the vines. But we would watch ourselves. *Yo les decía,* "Hurry up. Shake the vines and go sit over there in the yard where there's water." Because they were allowed to bring water or whatever, just so they didn't pick potatoes.

Not until Mike got hurt. Poor thing, that was hard. That's when the farmer said, "I'll let the two boys work."

We were working in the potatoes, and Mike was on the digger. It grabbed his pants and he fell underneath the machine. It tore the meat off his legs. It almost killed him. At that time, Eddie was eleven and Robert was ten – he just turned ten in nineteen forty-three. I had to take them out of school to top the beets. Poor guys, they worked so hard.

It was then that I began to make a lot more *tortillas* when Mike returned to work. And later, when Terry began to work with us, we were up to five workers. I would get up at four o'clock to make all the *tacos* for breakfast and the lunches. We ate a lot. We would get so hungry that every two or three hours we would sit down and have a *lonchecito* with *tacos* and coffee. Then, we also ate plenty at noon and for supper. They were all – all of us – were big eaters of *tortillas*. Now, not so much because of what they say about the cholesterol, or I don't know what.

We worked like that for many years, and in those years, I'm sure I would make no less than eight dozen per day. Not as many on Sunday, because we didn't work in the field.

Then, in 'fifty-two, Eddie got married and went to live in Lincoln. We still had Terry and Bill because Bobby got a job in town and then went to the army. But I still made a lotta *tortillas* anyway until Bill joined the army, too, and *Elvira* left.

So, I was left with Mary Lou, Leonard, Dad, and myself. Then, I made less and less *tortillas*. But I always made plenty. About three dozen per day. There was four of us. Each one ate about six *tortillas* plus a *taco* now and then and this and that. I always had *tortillas*. And nice and warm, too.

When Robert was born, Mary Lou went away and we were left with only Leonard and Robert. Then, after Dad died in 'sixty-five, well, I was left with just the two boys and I made very few *tortillas*. But I still made them. I made maybe two or three dozen a day.
The boys were great *tortilla* eaters, both of 'em. I was a big tortilla eater, too. I would make them at night when I got home from work. But I had their supper on the table.

And they wouldn't eat bread. They didn't like bread even though I put 'em bread for their school lunches. None of my kids wanted to take *tacos* for their lunch because the other kids would see that they ate *tortillas*. *Les daba vergüenza.*[1]

I used to be the same way. If a *güero* came to the house, I hid the *tortillas*. I don't know why. That was just our food. No. Now the *güeros* like Mexican food more than even the Mexicans do.

---

[1] 'They were ashamed'.

When Leonard went to California, Robert and I were left. Then Robert went, and I was left alone. Once in a while, I would make a dozen. He left to Mary Lou's in 'seventy-three. He was just going to be fourteen years old. Fourteen in June.

That's when I had the Senior Center, and I and my seniors would make a bunch of *tortillas* to sell for our trips. I would make three or four dozen every week, just me. And then I would make at least another dozen at home to eat myself.

I had the Senior Center until nineteen ninety-two. But I didn't like to be without nothing, so in about a year I went to work at the nursery school with the little children. I was there five years until I couldn't walk no more without my walker.

Then, I began to get strong pain in my hands. My fingers would even get numb, and it got real hard to make *tortillas*. How could I quit doing what I had done every day all my life? But I think I kept on making tortillas until about nineteen ninety-nine when I couldn't do it no more. I was tired. I was ninety years old.

Now, I buy them. They aren't as good as homemade because they don't put baking powder in them or they don't make 'em with lard, so they get hard real quick. But, what could I do? Once in a while, Terry brings me some, but not too often.

So, how many *tortillas* did I make in my life? *Sabrá Dios.*[2]

---

[2] See the table on the following pages for her actual count.

HOW MANY DID SHE MAKE? THIS IS HER COUNT

Time Period	Calculation of the Number of *Tortillas* per Year	Totals
1918-1922	Kansas City and Scottsbluff, with boarders, four adolescent girls: 6 doz. per day = 26,280 yr. x five yrs. = **131,400** **Subtotal**	131,400
1923-1928	Family only; Jacinta's family increasing to eleven children: 4 doz. increasing to 6 doz. per day (ave. 5 doz.) = 21,900 yr. x 6 yrs. = **131,400.** **Subtotal**	262,800
1929-1930	Married living with in-laws, Chole (mother-in-law) made all tortillas: **None added.** **Subtotal**	262,800
1931-1934	Living with in-laws, separate kitchen, 3 small children: 1 doz. per day = 4,380 yr. x 3 yrs. = **13,140.** **Subtotal**	275,940
1935	Work on the Baltes farm; growing family: 2 doz. per day x 1 yr. = **8,760.** **Subtotal**	284,700
1936-1942	Work on Neil Barbour farm; Elvira's family grows in size and age: 3 doz. per day = 13,140 yr. x 7 yrs. = **91,980** **Subtotal**	376,680
1943-1951	Five field workers; children growing in ages: 8 doz. per day = 35,040 yr. x 9 yrs. = **315,360.** **Subtotal**	692,040
1952-1959	Family begins to leave: declining from 8 doz. to 3 doz per day (ave. 5. doz.) = 21,900 yr. x 8 yrs. = **175,200** **Subtotal**	867,240

Time Period	Calculation of the Number of *Tortillas* per Year	Totals
1960-1965	One pre-teen, one child, two adults at home: 3 doz. per day = 13,140 yr. x 6 yrs. = **78,840** Subtotal	946,080
1966-1973	Widowed with one pre-teen and one teenager: 2 doz. per day = 8,760 yr. x 8 yrs. = **70,080**. Subtotal	1,016,160
1975-1992	At the Senior Center: 3 doz. per week x 40 weeks = 1,440 yr. x 17 yrs. = **24,480** Subtotal	1,040,640
1974-1999	Home alone: 1 doz. per week x 52 weeks = 624 yr. x 25 yrs. = **15,600**	
GRAND TOTAL		**1,056,240**

Elvira shows her granddaughter, Anne Marie Hernandez, how to make tortillas.

Left: Teaching her how to form the *testales*.
Right: Showing the proper manner to roll out a *tortilla* with a *palote*.

Commemorative plaque on Elvira's completion of more than one million tortillas. Made with one of the tortillas from her final batch.

Presented by her family on her 'Birth'ay'
June 27, 2000

EPILOGUE

Elvira died at the age of 102. For many years after she retired – with the help of a "Senior Companion" from the Office for the Aging of the State of Nebraska that chauffered her in her car – she continued visiting the ailing and old people who were in the hospital or nursing homes. The Senior Companion also drove her to Mass or shopping.

And, of course, until she was no longer able to walk even with her walker, she spent long hours working outside in her garden and tending her beloved flowers. This labor of love was the joy of her life which filled her both with vigor and with serenity. It was also a way to keep alive, on a daily basis, the memory of her and her husband *Maique's* most treasured times together.

Shortly after retiring from the Day Care Center, Elvira suffered a stroke and became partially paralyzed to the point that she could no longer walk. Her children demanded that she go live with one of them, but she refused. They finally convinced her to go stay with Terry in Denver "for a couple of weeks", never thinking that she would ever recover well enough to live alone.

At Terry's house, Elvira was at first unable to use a walker, yet stubbornly refused help in getting around. She got from one room to another by holding on to walls and furniture, with Terry standing close watch. Within a few days, she graduated to a walker. At first, she used it warily but determinedly and, by the end of her "couple of weeks", she was able to tool around Terry's house with no supervision and insisted on going home. She did, and for the next ten years, she lived alone depending only on the assistance of her Senior Companion and that of Elvira, Jr. who lived nearby and looked in on her frequently.

For Elvira's 100th birthday, her family planned a party to be held on her spacious back lawn. A few days before the event, she fell, injuring herself extremely seriously. She was immediately hospitalized, and it appeared to one and all that, this time, she would not survive.

However, the day before the party was to be held, she demanded to be taken home because she could not disappoint her guests, who had already begun to arrive in Scottsbluff from all over the country.

As it happened, her recovery was nothing short of astounding. On her 'birth'ay', she had two strong nephews carry her in her favorite chair to the backyard where she received her guests for most of the day. The following day, other family members brought a *menudo* breakfast for everybody. Elvira once more had herself taken outside where she spent the morning and half the afternoon. Then, on the third day, one of her favorite priests, Father Thomas Dowd, came to see her from Denver. Incredibly, she again insisted on going outside to visit with him and the several people who remained. Receiving them inside her small house would have meant capitulating to her condition.

From her death bed to a three-day party!

In her latter years, Elvira lost the use of her legs completely and much of her hearing and her sight She had to be cared for twenty-four hours a day, and her children took turns going to Scottsbluff to live with her for periods of time.

The Nebraska Office for the Aging provided the services of a local Mexican-American woman, Anna Saldivar, who went to her house daily to be a caring companion to her and to help in whatever Elvira needed. They came to love each other almost like mother and daughter, and our family is greatly indebted to Anna for the caring attention she gave to our mother.

During these years, Elvira slowly began to lose her memory and to become quite blunt, having also lost many of her social graces and reasoning ability. Anna remembers with sad fondness many incidents that showed this side of Elvira.

One New Year's Eve, Ysaura and Eduardo were in the kitchen listening to music and dancing. Anna saw them from the living room where she was 'mommy sitting' with Elvira. It was dark outside, but the curtains were still open. Anna motioned for them to bring the music and to dance for Elvira.

They went in, put on a *cumbia,* and began to dance. Elvira took one look at them and said, "Anna, close the windows! I don't want the people to see them. Me and my husband danced, yes, but we danced decent!" It didn't matter to her that we were right in front of her and could hear her.

Later, alone with Anna, she said, "*¿Ves cómo mueve la campana?[1]* They dance pretty good, don't they?"

Anna lived about a mile from Elvira's house, but she normally drove her car there. One day as Anna came in the door, Elvira said, "Anna, why don't you walk over here. It's not that far. Maybe you could lose some weight."

Anna said, "Are you saying I'm fat?"

"No. I'm just saying you could lose a little bit of weight." She was oblivious to the unintended insult.

Eduardo told Elvira, "Don't be mean to Anna. She's so good to you."

Elvira countered with, "Only because they're paying her." Sadly, in that moment she was totally unmindful of the closeness and the love that she and Anna had developed over the years.

Another time, Anna reminded Elvira that if she didn't take a certain medication, she wouldn't recover from an infection she had. Elvira looked Anna sternly in the eye and said – directly out of *Gone with the Wind* – "Frankly, my dear, I don't give a damn!"

---

[1] 'You see how she moves her behind?' Literally, 'See how she swings her bell?'.

This is the first time that Elvira was heard to utter any word stronger that "Dangit!" Encroaching dementia with its unrestrained nastiness began more and more to trump kindness and love. More frequently she began to dredge up expressions, mostly in Spanish, that one might expect out of the mouths of sailors. Neither her parents' family nor that of her in-laws were accustomed to using foul language. So, the most probable source of this particular store of repressed knowedge was on the playground at East Ward elementary school.

Elvira seemed to be quite aware not only that she was losing many of her mental faculties but especially that she had lost all of her precious personal independence – she could no longer stand or walk; she could not hold a spoon; and she had difficulty seeing and was extremely hard of hearing. She wanted very much to die. She prayed constantly to God to take her, and she wept frequently because of this.

One night, after all the lights were out, she was heard to pray in this manner, but in Spanish – scolding God: "¡Dios! I'm a Mexican and I speak Spanish. I know that you understand Spanish. ¿Why don't you listen to me? ¡Take me!"

She was genuinely anguished at God's unwillingness to grant her a final miracle.

Once in a while, she remembered that her mother spoke of "that little potion of rest" –"la agüita del sosiego". She said that people from olden times gave the elderly this drink, perhaps made of some indigenous herb, to help them die. Elvira's mentioning this memory of her mother's words only indicated her desperation to die because never in her life would her profound Catholic faith have allowed her to accede to such a remedy.

Over many years, Elvira had frequently expressed her strong opposition to being placed in a nursing home. She had often visited patients there and was dismayed by their poor level of care and their fervent desire to be taken back home. She recounted these experiences many times to her children, always commenting that she hoped she would never have to be taken to such a place.

Finally, on April 24, 2012, as she so fervently desired, Elvira died in her own home.

APPENDIX I
Code Switching by Elvira

In speaking with me and with other bilinguals, Elvira normally used a form of speech referred to as <u>code switching</u>. This usage involves the smooth, effortless, and momentary alternation between the main language of a given conversation and the bilingual's other language, even within a single sentence or phrase.

The reasons for code switching in general and for particular instances of code switching are very complex and not very well established by research. Nevertheless, it is clear that switching codes is often triggered by such things as the social and cultural meanings inherent in a portion of the conversation, the expressiveness of a particular word or phrase in one of the languages, or the communication of affective functions such as annoyance, greater intimacy, or emphasis. Also, quoting a third person is often, though not always, done in the language that the person used.

Particular instances of code switching are normally below a speaker's level of consciousness. The bilingual speaker subconsciously decides when, where, and with whom to use it and intuitively regulates the locations and the amount of switching in the stream of speech.

Nevertheless, most bilinguals are keenly aware that they engage in this way of speaking and sometimes comment on it, often disparagingly. It is popularly conceived of as an <u>unordered, corrupt mixture</u> of the two languages and as the result of ignorance and illiteracy. Derogatory terms like "Spanglish" are used to describe it.

Yet, research has shown that code switching is neither unordered nor a mixture. Switches take place only at defined places in the grammars of the two languages and the alternating segments of speech retain fully the pronunciation and structures of the language that those segments are spoken in.

It is clear that code switching has its own rules and norms of usage which do not allow mixing willy-nilly, as if put into a blender.

Additionally, educated bilingual speakers all over the world engage in code switching despite its being held in low esteem by almost everyone in their own speech communities, including these speakers themselves. So it cannot be a corrupt usage due to ignorance and illiteracy.

It is similar to stylistic variation within a single language used by its own speakers to cement bonds of group identity, to reveal particular emotions, and to express subtle cultural or linguistic connotations, among other communicative intentions.

Code switching is a creative device that has been demonstrated to have many of these same functions. It thus must be considered to enjoy equal validity and legitimacy.

Elvira used code switching in these ways both fluently and appropriately, regardless of the main language of a given conversation, so long as it was with another bilingual. In the original Spanish version of this book, she used it extensively. In the English translation – assuming that many readers will have but a limited knowledge of Spanish – I used this switching style sparingly in order to mirror, at least minimally, her usage in Spanish.

So, in this English version, code switching has been used mainly in places where the content of a Spanish word or expression has a special cultural or emotional nuance, or else where her turn of phrase in the original Spanish has no easy translation in her English. This is intended to reflect what her actual usage would be with the intended audience of English readers of this book and, thus, to enhance the authentic character of her English narration.

APPENDIX II
Select Glossary of Spanish Words
and Special English Terms

abuelo/a	grandpa/grandma
ahora sí	okay, now
ahora	now
astilla; astillosa	splinter, splintered
atole	a hot drink made of corn meal, oatmeal, or wheat meal; from Náhuatl *atol-li*
ayúdanos virgen santa	help us, holy virgin
bastante	enough
bendito sea Dios	blessed be God
bribón, bribona	trouble maker, cheater
bruja	witch
buenos días	good morning
cacas	cow pancakes; more generally 'turds'
caracho/a	dang, darn
carajo/a	dang, darn with a stronger connotation
caramba!	boy!, wow!
caray!	boy!, wow!
carro alegórico	float in a parade
casar	marry
center	Elvira's word for 'nursing home'
chante	shack, probably from Náhuatl *chantli* or *chanti*
chaquetero	turncoat; derived from English *jacket*
chaquira	shiny beading
chillona	crybaby
chiquito/a; chiquillo/a	little, little kid
chiripada	coincidence
chiva/o	goat
chueco/a	crooked
cleaning	weeding the grown beets
cocinera	cook
colchón	mattress
colonia	colony, the Mexican section of town
comal	flat metal plate on which *tortillas* are cooked, originally made of clay; from Náhuatl *comal-li*
comer	to eat

Glossary

comoquiera que sea	whatever, in any case
compadre, comadre	relationship of a godfather or godmother with the parents of the godchild
compuerta	weir or dam to regulate irrigation water
condolchito	a sweet fried pastry
corajudo/a	an angry personality
correyazo	spanking with a strap
criadero	breeding ground
cuna	crib
curandera/o	healer
desahije	thinning the beets (or other crop)
descanso	rest
descuatar	removing beet "doubles" to leave one plant, derived from Náhuatl *cuatl,* 'twin'
diche	adaptation of English *ditch*
Dios de mi vida	my goodness; (God of my life)
Dios lo tenga en su santo descanso	God keep one in his holy rest
Dios mío	my goodness; (my God)
Dios te ayude	may God help you
don, doña	Titles of deference for elders, used with the person's first name
donas	gifts to the bride by the bridegroom's parents; usually, her wedding attire
droga	debt
elotada	corn feast
elote	fresh corn; from Náhuatl *elotl*
empacadora	packing house, slaughterhouse
endrogarse	get into debt
enganchar	recruit; related forms are *enganche,* 'recruitment', *engancharon,* 'they recruited'
entonces; enton's	then
escándalo	a big ruckus
escandaloso	one who makes a big ruckus, a crybaby
escusado	outhouse
espinilla	shin
esprín	adaptation of both English *spring* and *screen*
fajillazo	spanking with a belt
feo	ugly
ferrocarril	railroad

fieldman	sugar company official in charge of irrigation water; same as *revisador*.
fíjate	imagine
fregado; frega'o	darn, dang thing or person
frijol	bean, the bean crop
frío	cold
ganó y se fue	he took off
garita	guard house
gaznate	throat, adam's apple
gracias a Dios	thank God
granos	small bumps on the skin, often with pus; sometimes due to stress
greñuda	having unkempt hair
güero/a, güerito/a	Anglo-american, white person, light-skinned person
guirao, pron. [gid-OW]	*Jacobo's* pronunciation of 'get out'
guiso	a sauteed dish, as in a stew
hervidor	an oval tub for boiling water; (a boiler)
híjole!	wow!
'hora, 'horita	right now, contraction and diminutive of ahora
hubiera	(there) would be
huesos	bones
hule	linoleum, rubber; from Náhuatl *ul-li*
Jesús te ayude	may Jesus help you
jocoque	a dish made of fermented cream or milk, from Náhuatl *xococ*
lámina	sheet, usually of metal
lavadero	washboard
llaga	open sore, abscess
llore y llore	crying and crying
lona	canvas
luego-luego	right there, right away
madrina	maid of honor, bridesmaid; more generally, godmother
malacanchoncha	children's game where they spin each other around; from Náhuatl *malacachoa*
malcriado	rude, misbehaved
manito/a	a person from New Mexico or Colorado, or their speech; diminutive of *mano,* a shortened form of *hermano,* 'brother'

Glossary

maquinón	mackinaw; heavy overcoat
masa	dough
mata	plant
mayordomo	supervisor
mija	affectionate blending of 'mi hija', *my daughter*
misa	Mass
mocho	broken, cut off
monigote	figure, shape
mortoria	funeral parlor; also, the hearse
muchacho	boy
mujer	woman
ni lo mande Dios	God forbid;, ("May God not command it.")
ni qué esperanzas	no way! ("Not even hope!")
novia	bride, fiancée, girlfriend
noviazgo	courtship
novio	groom, fiancé, boyfriend
olla	cooking pot
¿'ónde está?	contraction of where is she/he/it?
packing house	slaughterhouse, meat packing plant
padrino	best man, groomsman; more generally, godfather
palotear	rolling out *tortillas* with a *palote* or rolling pin
panteón	cemetery
pato	duck; metaphorically, a teakettle
payaseras	clownish acts
pedida	asking for her hand
pela'o	bum, tramp, no-good person
pendejo	fool
peón	hourly farmhand
peor me digan	especially ('worse, they tell me')
pepino	cucumber
petaquita	a little trunk or suitcase; dimin. of *petaca* from Náhuatl *petla-cal-li*
pieza	a song, a record; more generally, a piece
pila	cistern, stone water tank
piloncillo	brown sugar, usually hard in the form of a small cone
piojos	lice

el piojo	louse, sarcastic word for 'the Mexican theater'
pirul	pepper tree
plancha	clothes iron
pobre; pobrecito	poor, poor thing
poncho	blanket-like outer garment with a hole in the middle for the head; made of wool
por Dios	for God's sake
por qué	why
porque	because
pozol	hominy; soup made with hominy, red chile, and pork
preguntar	ask
presentación	engagement party
prieto, prieta (prietilla)	dark skinned
provisiones	merchandise; provisions
¡qué casualidad!	what a fluke! (what a happening!)
que descanse en paz	may he rest in peace
que Dios lo perdone	may God forgive him
que Dios lo tenga en su santo descanso	may God keep him in His holy rest
¡qué esperanzas!	impossible, no way! (what hopes!) Also, '¡Ni qué esperanzas!'
¡qué va!	really; my goodness! (what goes?)
quehacer	chores, housework
Quianses	Kansas; Kansas City
quítate	get away
recogedor	dust pan
renegada	crabby, grouchy; mean
revisador	sugar company official in charge of irrigation and of assigning acreage for planting sugar beets, a recruiter, same as fieldman
robón	thief
running boards	built-in steps on the outside of car or truck doors
sabe qué?	you know what?
sabroso	tasty, delicious
santo	saint, saint's day or birthday
satírica	joking, fun-loving
sea por Dios	It's God's will

Glossary

sección, section	a 'section' of the railroad with side tracks used to park trains and as an equipment yard
si Dios es servido	if God is served
siempre	always
silla	chair
sinvergüenza	a cheat, a no-good person
sorprender	surprise
spring	used for either a 'spring' (e.g. for closing a door) or for 'screen'
suegro, suegra	father-in-law, mother-in-law
suspirar	to sigh
tablones	bolts of cloth
tanto	so much
tapeo	sugar beet harvesting; from English *top*
taruga, tarugo	dummy
TB	euphemistic abbreviation for *tuberculosis*
tejabán	lean to; used here meaning 'shack'
testal	a small amount of dough formed in a flat round shape in preparation for rolling out a tortilla; from Náhuatl *teshtli*
tía	aunt
tío	uncle
todo, toda	all, everything
toma	here, take this
topping	sugar-beet harvest
traque	railroad, rail; adapted from English *track*
válgame (Dios)	God help us, My goodness
ve con Dios	Go with God
viejo	old; old man
ya	already, now
zaguán	foyer, a common architectural feature of traditional Mexican houses
zapatos	shoes
zarco	light blue eyes

c/s
ed-edited-it